WELCOME TO SHIRLEY

## a memoir from an atomic town

## KELLY MCMASTERS

PUBLICAFFAIRS
NEW YORK

Book Design by Timm Bryson

Library of Congress Cataloging-in-Publication Data
McMasters, Kelly.
Welcome to Shirley : a memoir from an atomic town / Kelly McMasters.
p. cm.
ISBN 978-1-58648-486-6 (hardcover)
1. McMasters, Kelly—Childhood and youth. 2. Shirley (Suffolk County, N.Y.)—
Biography. 3. Shirley (Suffolk County, N.Y.)—Social life and customs—20th
century. 4. Shirley (Suffolk County, N.Y.)—Social conditions—20th century. 5.
Working class—New York (State)—Shirley (Suffolk County)—Biography. 6.
Groundwater—Pollution—New York (State)—Shirley (Suffolk County)—
History—20th century. 7. Radioactive wastes—Social aspects—New York
(State)—Shirley (Suffolk County)—History—20th century. 8. Brookhaven
National Laboratory—History—20th century. 9. Shirley (Suffolk County, N.Y.)—
Environmental conditions. I. Title.
F129.S6623M38 2008
974.7'25—dc22
[B]
2007038193

First Edition
10 9 8 7 6 5 4 3 2 1

*For my parents*

I too Paumanok
I too have bubbled up, floated the measureless float,
and been wash'd on your shores,
I too am but a trail of drift and debris,
I too leave little wrecks upon you, you fish-shaped island.
—*Walt Whitman, "Fish-Shape Paumanok"*


Don't cut your losses; You're gonna need them.
—*Ill Lit, "Los Angeles"*

# CONTENTS

PART THREE

# THROUGH THE PINES

# AUTHOR'S NOTE

This afternoon, while walking in a nearby forest, I stopped in front of a sugar maple standing about sixty feet tall. The tree was split in two, twins growing out of a single base. The trunks twisted together, their rounded crowns of crimson and plum merged into a single canopy. Back in my home office, I looked up the reason behind this malformed tree and read that the embrace, so poetic and lovely when staring up into its branches, was a sign of struggle against stilted growth and lack of sunlight. The limbs had curled around one another out of survival.

I did not intend to write a book about survival. What began as a collection of place-based essays became a complicated knot of class issues, shame, marginalization, and what my editor calls the strange American habit of improvisation.

Often, when I told neighbors, friends, or family that I was writing about the town, they reacted with surprise. "Shirley?" they responded. "But there is nothing special about it," or "It is such a shit-hole," or "Lots of places have it even worse." The words were different, but the message the same: *Shirley isn't worthy.* I wrote mainly to suggest that it is.

This is a work of nonfiction. There are no conflated events or composite characters in this book. House numbers and the names of those who may have violated the law have been changed. Along with my own memory, hours of written and tape-recorded interviews were supplemented with other research, including newspaper articles, scientific studies, reports resulting from Freedom of Information Act requests, and hundreds of pages of documents culled from the (not so) public reading room at the Brookhaven National Laboratory. My imagined scenes of Walter T. Shirley were informed by history books and archives.

This is not my attempt to speak for the town as a whole or any other individuals in town. Instead, it is my attempt to tell a story about legacy, and how the decisions we make based on survival today—what we put into the earth, what we put into our bodies, what we put into our hearts—follow us into our families and our homes. This is the story of one girl growing up in one town, a town that is, unfortunately, not unusual in its deficiencies or dangers, and a neighborhood of people, very fortunately, not unique in their beauty.

—K.M.
*Rock Lake, PA*
*October 13, 2007*

My fifth birthday party in front of the rented Shirley house. From the left: Andrea is in pigtails; Margaret wears the fruit shirt; Melissa; I am in the center; Tina has her arm slung around my shoulder; Jenny is holding Louie; and Jonathan is on the end.

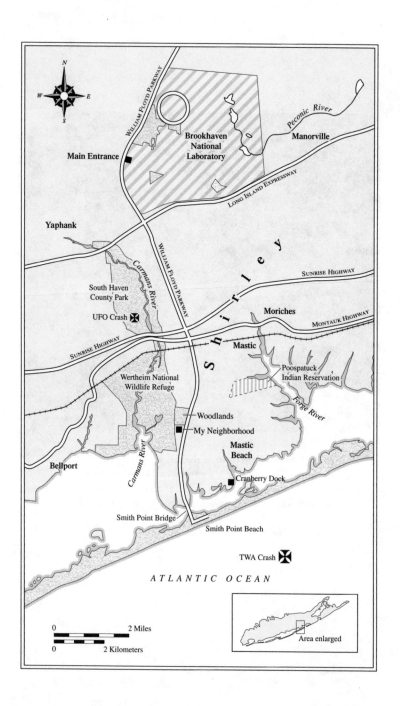

N

W    E

S

WILLIAM FLOYD PARKWAY

Brookhaven
National
Laboratory

Peconic River

Manorville

Main Entrance ■

LONG ISLAND EXPRESSWAY

Yaphank

WILLIAM FLOYD PARKWAY

Carmans River

S h i r l e y

SUNRISE HIGHWAY

South Haven
County Park

Moriches

MONTAUK HIGHWAY

UFO Crash ✠

SUNRISE HIGHWAY

Mastic

Poospatuck
Indian Reservation

Wertheim National
Wildlife Refuge

Forge River

Woodlands

■ My Neighborhood

Mastic
Beach

Bellport

Carmans River

■ Cranberry Dock

Smith Point Bridge

Smith Point Beach

TWA Crash ✠

ATLANTIC OCEAN

0    2 Miles

0    2 Kilometers

Area enlarged

# INTRODUCTION

I stared into our reflection in the bar window and saw three girls laughing. Fixing my eyes on the street beyond our trio's image, I watched fat snowflakes spiral heavily down from the night sky, piling along Crosby Street's cobblestones. The stones, round and smooth, were cut off from one another by the snow pooling in the surrounding cracks. Soon, the snow would swallow them whole and the stones would disappear, islands drowned by the tide.

Tomorrow the news would call this storm the Blizzard of 2005, but for now the three of us—safe and warm behind the glass—just watched the spooling drifts catch in the light from the street lamp and ordered more drinks, oblivious to the tempest that would close down the subways, derail commuter trains, and bring the city crashing to its knees in the morning. Later, wobbly from wine, we would trudge through the quickly accumulating snow, seeing each other off safely into the night, as we have for the past twenty-five years that we've been best friends.

I knew Margaret's and Andrea's faces as well as I knew my own. Or at least I thought I did. Against the shadows thrown by the candle on our small table, I could see the soft imprints of crow's-feet and smile lines beginning, hints of steely gray peeking out of parted hair. I'd known them since I was a girl of four, and in my mind we were still knock-kneed and bee-stung, running through sprinklers every summer. In reality, we were entering our thirties, not old but not altogether young anymore, and as I stared again at our reflections in the bar's window, I was surprised to see wrists no longer thin as spindles, bra straps cinching into flesh where there was once just bone.

We had ducked into this small tapas bar after a day of shopping for bridesmaid dresses. I was getting married in the spring, and Margaret and Andrea would be standing next to me when I exchanged vows, just as we three had stood beside Melissa two years earlier. Melissa was the fourth of our group and was in Arizona, pregnant with her first child, so she would have to sit this one out.

"Remember that time we blindfolded Margaret and threw her into the ball pit at McDonald's for her sixteenth birthday?" Andrea's blue-black hair and dark eyes caught the light of the candle, and her mouth held the same softness it did when she was a child. Margaret's name came out as *Mahh-grit* in Andrea's Long Island accent.

"And that time we cut school and sat in Andrea's base-ment drinking those jugs of wine?" Margaret's nostrils flared the way they always do when she's about to laugh, and her slender neck shone gold in the candlelight.

We had been in the bar for two hours, enough time for the alcohol to make us moony and nostalgic, but our talk always circles back to our childhood when we are together. As different as we'd become, it was the one thing we could all agree on: Our childhood was magical.

We grew up on Long Island, in the East End town of Shirley. Shirley—like its inseparable cousins, Mastic and Mastic Beach—has no bookstores. The restaurants are lim-ited to a handful of Chinese take-out spots, about twenty pizza joints, an assortment of fast food (McDonald's, Taco Bell, Burger King, Chubby Checkers, and Boston Market), and the Windmill diner, which was recently demolished. There are plenty of bars, and the large community library, high school, and firehouses serve as community meeting places. Strip mall after strip mall of delis, surf shops, thrift stores, tattoo parlors, and bait-and-tackle shops line the main strip of the parkway in town.

The four of us had grown up in adjoining houses in a neighborhood tucked into a green corner of pine forest near the Atlantic Ocean. Here, protected by our imagina-tions and our parents, garbage can lids became sleds, rivers became sparkling pools, honeysuckle and aloe our balm. And each time we got together as adults, the girls and I re-played the old yellowed reels in our heads, laughing and falling in love with one another all over again.

What we never talked about was how we were once a group of five, not just four. We didn't discuss the fact that none of us had spoken to Tina—who had been tied as tightly to us in childhood as the four of us still were—in more than ten years. We never talked about how the neighborhood fathers used to say they glowed in the dark. We never talked about the people we had lost, or our fears of what might be moving through our bodies, or our parents' bodies, until it was time to collect prayers.

Instead, we held onto each other, sometimes in silence, or in laughter, or in forgetting. We gave names to our tribe—the Shirley Girls, the Four Crazy Carnation Queens—and we made pacts and pinkie swears. We formed a shield against things that could hurt us, and together we tried to keep our small boat afloat. We are, and always will be, bound by our childhood, and buoyed by our neighborhood stories, the ones we repeat every time we're together, as well as the ones we will never tell.

One thing was certain; if ever we drifted too far, Shirley always called us back to her shores.

PART ONE

# THE TOWN OF FLOWERS

❖

*Praise the bridge that carried you over.*

—George Colman, *The Heir at Law*,
act 1, scene 1

could add another person to the already full roster for class that afternoon. They all knew him and all seemed to need a favor from him. I liked that my father was popular.

I would sit next to him, proud and smiling. His blue eyes sparked brightly against his shaggy dark hair and mustache, and he was good at making people laugh. He was scrawny then, his body a straight line from his armpits to his ankles beneath his quilted red jacket and flared navy blue ski pants.

When the snow melted, my mother and father and I would pack up our things and move to the next place—a golf course or summer resort where my father could give lessons and play tournaments for the club. For the first four years of my life, our small family followed this haphazard trajectory around the bunny hills and bunkers of the Catskill Mountains and New Jersey. It was always fun for me, racing through the new apartment or cabin, never knowing whether my room would have a single bed, bunk beds, or no bed at all. My father would teach ski school and make snow at night on the mountains, and at golf courses his lessons would turn into lunches or drinks or an invitation to play eighteen, so my mother and I were mostly on our own. We established a circuit in each town we lived in, moving between our newest home and the closest library, Laundromat, and supermarket. I knew not to ask for extras while riding in the little foldout shelf of the shopping cart, skinny legs dangling over an invariably cockeyed wheel. At home my mother and I read to one another, listened to the radio, put together jigsaw puzzles. I never imagined there could be anything wrong with my life. I never considered the possibility that my parents might not be as content or happy as I was, not until years later when they told me during late-night conversations how hard they had worked to make everything seem fine.

At Onteora, the last golf resort where my father worked before we moved to Shirley, he was only making $200 a week as the head pro and didn't have time for the extra construction jobs he sometimes took at other courses. So he started selling cans of soda and snacks to the members as they came off the golf course or tennis courts. I didn't understand until two decades later how hard it was for my father to keep smiling—both at Onteora and at home—while trying to sell those cans of soda. Just a few years before, he had been on the PGA tour, traveling across the country and playing golf for money, with sponsors paying his entrance fees and sending him boxes of free clubs and clothes. Yet there he was, scampering to deliver a cold can of soda into the waiting hands of a member, faced half the time with a simple dismissal—"Just bill it to my account"—instead of the handful of quarters he was hoping for and suddenly so desperately needed. He was thirty-five, and he knew he could only continue this way for a while longer before his wife—whose visits to her parents' home in New Jersey became progressively longer each time—lost her patience completely.

Just as I never noticed the tension between my parents in these years—mostly because, thinking back on it now, I hardly ever saw them in the same room—I was also too young to register the hierarchies within the country clubs and ski resorts. I was as oblivious to the complicated strata

that existed within the group of people who worked alongside my father as I was to the gulf between the members or
ski bunnies and my parents. It never seemed incongruous
to me that although the members wanted my father's attention out on the golf course, he took his meals in the
kitchen with the greenskeepers and other staff. I just assumed he preferred the greenskeepers, which, years later,
he said was often the case.

My mother later told me that she felt invisible at most of
the clubs. The wispy platinum blonde with a child on her
hip didn't improve the club members' golf swings or black-
diamond performances, so her presence was inconsequen-
tial. She stayed away from the courses and mountains as
best she could, preferring our ramshackle cottages and
drafty dives to the members' chilly indifference.

So it seemed perfect when my father started talking
about a job opening at a golf club on the East End of Long
Island in a place called the Hamptons. Long Island had
sandy beaches, like those of my mother's New Jersey childhood, and the job would pay more money than my father
was making at Onteora. I imagined the Hamptons as a collection of sand dunes, large terra-cotta bellies stretching
out along the ocean, one Hampton after another after another. I looked forward to our next move.

It was early afternoon, but it looked like night. The rain
hadn't stopped since my father had nosed our hulking station wagon toward Long Island. My mother and I could

barely see through the sheets of water as my father pulled into the parking lot of Cor-Ace, the realty company my mother had circled in the newspaper.

"I think it's best if you guys just stay here," my father told my mother and me in the car. "If anything looks promising, I'll wave and you can come in, okay?"

We agreed, watching as the rain flattened my father's soft dark curls before he could get his umbrella to open. The raindrops on the windshield traced rivulets down my mother's cheek as she sat in the front seat, hands folded together, squeezing.

"I hope they have something," my mother said, more to herself than to me. She sighed and stared at the agency door. My father's eyes were navy, but my mother's were usually a paler blue, like a faded cotton pillowcase. Today, they looked gray in the rain, and so did her long blonde hair. She blew some strands out of her face and sighed again. Then she reclasped her hands and turned to me in the backseat.

"Tomorrow the rain will stop and you can see the beach," she said, brightening. Her parents still lived on the Jersey shore, and we visited them every few months. I loved my grandparents' beach, and the playground with the cherry-red swing set, but hated the little plastic tags they made you wear on your bathing suit strap to prove you were allowed to be there. I asked if we would have to wear those tags here.

"No," my mother said. "I don't think so, Kell. I think this is a public beach, so anyone is allowed to come here. The beaches in New Jersey are private," she said, eyes unfocused.

I wondered if she was thinking about sitting on the beach right now, baking in the sun. My mother could tan golden, a warm summer brown that would stain her skin for months. Along with my father's brown hair and dark blue eyes, I had inherited his skin—pale Irish white that went red under the sun's rays. This hitch did not deter my enthusiasm for the beaches of the Hamptons.

My father had already come to Long Island on his own three times to look for a place for us to live. Hampton Hills, the golf club where he was going to work, didn't have any staff housing available, and he had quickly realized we would not be able to afford anything in the Hamptons. He had looked at some nearby towns he had heard about—Rocky Point and Miller Place—on the less-glamorous North Shore, but the places in our price range were either in terrible condition or only available in the low season, October through April. In the summer months, rents often rose prohibitively. After my father came back without good news the third time, my mother decided that she and I would accompany him on the next scouting trip.

So we had slogged from dumpy house to dumpy house, each one worse than the next, and worse than even the most bat-ridden, squirrel-infested, freezing cold apartment or cottage we had ever occupied in the Catskills. By Sunday afternoon, Cor-Ace was the last place on our list. A greenskeeper at Hampton Hills had told my father about a town called Shirley, which was only a twenty-minute drive to the club but was apparently one of the cheapest places to live on the island.

My mother and I sat in the car for an hour. We kept watch, tensing every time the door swung open, but it was always another realtor, running to their car with a newspaper over their hair or a plastic Baggie tied around their chin. Finally, my father appeared at the door and waved his arms over his head, beckoning us to come inside. My mother sighed, handed me an umbrella, and told me to make a run for it.

Joe, the realtor, had a wide black mustache that hid his upper lip and skin the color of the olives the clubhouse bartenders speared on tiny plastic harpoons. I could see two gold chains hanging around his neck beneath his shirt. I had never seen a man wearing necklaces before.

We sat in his dark wood-paneled office, made darker by a scrim of smoke emanating from an ashtray full of cigarette butts on his desk, and my mother answered questions that it was clear my father had already been asked. They were more personal than the questions other realtors had asked, and my mother's eyebrows raised at the religion and gardening-habit queries. Finally, Joe admitted that the house he had in mind for us was a special case: Not only was he the caretaker, but it was next door to his own home.

"I mean, you can understand a person being careful," he said to my mother, moving his hands rapidly in front of him while he spoke, as though he were conducting his own voice. "I mean, the neighborhood is really quiet and full of kids—I have two boys of my own—and all good families. So I have to be careful, you know, to bring in the right people." His black mustache was so thick that although I could hear the words coming out of his mouth, I wasn't certain whether his lips were actually moving. My parents assured him they understood. Joe gathered some papers, and we all ran out to his long black Cadillac sedan, where he promptly lit another cigarette.

Joe continued his pitch in the car, telling us about the great schools in the district and the Wertheim National Wildlife Refuge that flanked two sides of the house. My father sounded excited, but my mother was nervous. From her spot next to me in the backseat, she asked how much the rent was.

"Well," said Joe. "The owners would like $350 a month." He paused, letting the number hang in the air for a moment before quickly continuing. "But we can work on it, if you like it. We can definitely work on it!"

My parents exchanged glances. The price was right, and the house—if what Joe was saying was true—sounded better than any they had seen so far. In fact, it sounded too good to be true. Joe steered the car down the highway, talking about the ocean just down the road and how the house was on a corner lot, until, finally, we were parked in the driveway.

Even through the pouring rain, my parents could tell it was the best house we had seen that weekend. A single-story shingled brown box, the tidy house had homey yellow shutters on each of its windows. We followed Joe through the front door. The family living there had just bought the house across the street, and the rooms were full of cardboard boxes. A sunken living room opened up to the right of the door, and off a short hallway to the left were two bedrooms and a bathroom with gold-lamé wallpaper, which I found incredibly glamorous. There was a separate dining room, and a wide window above the kitchen sink looking out into the darkness.

Joe waved us through the back door. In the backyard, huddled under umbrellas in the darkness, we stared at a huge black tarp covering an inground pool. We weren't concerned when Joe said the landlady wouldn't allow tenants to open the pool or use it. Just the idea of having an inground pool in our backyard was luxury enough.

Riding back to the realty office in Joe's Cadillac, my father and Joe negotiated to the rock-bottom price of $250 a month. Joe told us facts about the town of Shirley: 20,000 people, a new marina being talked about, property values going up, close to the Hamptons. I didn't care about those things, but I did care about the name—Shirley. It reminded me of Shirley Temple and I loved it immediately.

A few days after we found our new house, my grandfather called us in the Catskills. He wanted to send a press release to some golf and ski resorts about my father's job at Hampton Hills, and he needed our new address. My grandfather had taken a job managing a ski mountain in the Catskills the year before. He had been let go from an advertising job in New York City, but even though he was now making a fraction of his old salary, he was determined to keep up appearances. A few weeks before our move to Shirley, a story that featured my father's parents had run in the *New York*

*Times*, on businesspeople trading in their upscale corporate lives for the quaint quiet of country life. My grandfather, who had been paid for his ability to spin the facts on Madison Avenue for more then twenty years, managed to spin his own story so that it sounded like leaving his job had been his choice, not the result of a pink slip and a string of rejections from other agencies. My father didn't normally send out a press release when he changed jobs, but my grandfather said this was different—this was the Hamptons.

When he found out we were going to be living in Shirley, my grandfather sighed heavily into the phone. He recited the press release back to my father, and when he got to the contact information, he read: "Gene and his family will live in the Moriches area, on the South Shore of Long Island." My father stopped him, saying that he wasn't going to be living in Moriches, which was the next town over from Shirley, east toward the Hamptons.

"Trust me," my grandfather said. "You don't want people knowing you live in that town."

My father was confused. "Dad, you're from Westport, Connecticut. What could you possibly know about Shirley?"

But my grandfather insisted. The press release went out announcing that my father now lived in Moriches.

Two weeks later, as we drove into Shirley and saw the town in bright daylight for the first time, my father understood. He remembers thinking that Shirley looked like a war zone. My parents exchanged looks across the wide front seat of our station wagon as we drove down the main parkway of the town. On the weekend we had first looked at our new house, the storms had cast a desolate gray patina over the town, one my parents had assumed would evaporate with the rain. But even with the sun shining, the strip malls that dotted the parkway were still depressingly dark, the majority of the stores vacant or vandalized. To a four-year-old, however, the boarded-up buildings and dirty mattresses on the side of the road didn't speak their message quite as strongly.

The family moving out of our new house was scheduled to leave by the first of the month. We had to be out of our upstate rental by the last of the month, which left us without a home for one night. We didn't have much furniture with us—aside from my orange beanbag chair and an old oak dining-room table, most of my parents' belongings were in storage and we had been living with makeshift furniture constructed from plastic milk crates, cement blocks, and pieces of plywood. All of our belongings could fit in the station wagon, and we strapped some boxes and four dining-room chairs to the roof. The plan was to drive to Long Island and spend the night at a motel in Shirley, then get up and move into our new house first thing in the morning.

The parkway, which shoots a straight arrow south through town, leads cars down the center of Shirley to the edge of the Atlantic Ocean. The Smith Point Motel is all the way at the southern tip of the town, just before the bay, and as we drove the houses that lined the parkway became sparser, giving way to scrub trees and pitch pines. A line of sand laced the edges of the blacktop. We saw a bridge ahead, but we turned off the parkway before we could swoop over it. My father had spotted the sign for our motel—black and white slanting script on bleached-out driftwood—and turned left into the parking lot.

I had stayed in a few motels, and I loved spotting their black eight-ball or cowboy-hat signs on the sides of highways. This motel was smaller than the chain-type places I had stayed in before. Only one level, the L-shaped building had an office close to the parkway. A dozen doors, each painted a different color, ringed the parking lot like the squares on my Monopoly board. The motel had once been painted white, but now the weathered shingles were flaking, like the old bits of shed antler my father and I would find during early morning walks on the golf courses.

As my parents unloaded a few of our suitcases into our room, I sniffed the brine of our new town. I had never lived near the ocean, and the seagulls, the sharp air, and the rock-'n'-roll sounds crowing out of the jukebox in the bar next door all confirmed my idea of the luxury that seemed to go with life in the Hamptons.

Inside, our motel room smelled like a summer house on the first day it's been opened for the season. The room had a turquoise door and two windows; one looked into the backyard of a house, the other into the parking lot and our station wagon. Our room had only one double bed, so the manager brought in a folding cot for me.

We went to bed early in preparation for the move the next day. After only a few hours, though, my mother shifted out of the fog of sleep. She sat up in bed, between my father on the other side of the bed and me on the cot, and listened. Something was moving in the room.

She knew the sound wasn't human, but she couldn't place it. The noise wasn't the recognizable scamper of squirrel feet, as in the attics of houses we'd lived in upstate, nor was it the shuffling of mice—my mother wasn't even sure if it was really a noise at all. More like a light rain, the *shush-shush* seemed to cover the whole room rather than coming from one corner or the other. She rubbed her eyes, trying to peer through the dark. Convinced there really was something there, she turned the light on. And screamed.

The stained brown carpet was pulsing with an army of termites. While we had slept, they had swarmed the room, covering the floor like a collection of writhing, ash-colored commas. The *shush-shush* my mother's ears had picked up was from the rustling of the thousands of tiny translucent wings. She shook my father awake. The termites had swirled up the legs of my wooden cot and were crawling all over—on the sheets, on my pajamas, on my hands and face.

I sat in the backseat of our station wagon in the parking lot while my mother unpacked the suitcases and bags we had brought into the motel room with us, shaking and swatting each toothbrush, book, and piece of clothing out under a yellow circle of light from a street lamp. The groggy manager offered us another room for the rest of the night. He and my father disappeared into the little office, smoking cigarettes and trying to broker a truce as my mother continued frantically shaking our belongings free of the small winged insects.

A few minutes later, my father came out of the manager's office and walked over to my mother, who was furiously beating a pair of pants. "Look, he's not going to give us our money back. Let's just take another room and get some sleep before tomorrow," my father said.

"No," my mother said, shaking her head violently. "No way am I going back into that building, and neither is Kelly. I wouldn't be able to sleep even a minute in there anyway."

My father nodded, tired, the skin beneath his eyes puffed thin and blue. We spent the rest of our first night in Shirley in our station wagon.

The next day, we crawled out of the car and stretched, and tried to get excited about our new home. We stopped at a 7-11 to use the bathroom and picked up some coffee for my parents and apple juice for me before driving back up the parkway and turning into our new neighborhood. At the end of and lining the backyards of Alcolade Drive West were the promised hundreds of acres of wildlife refuge. Our backyard, Joe's backyard next to us, and all the backyards on our side of the block opened onto the leafy wilderness, although most were separated from the trees by a fence. Ours was chain link, about seven feet tall.

Alcolade formed a T with Smith Road, which ran past our block just the length of our new house. Smith dead-ended right next to our lawn, with a low metal barrier decorated with black-markered initials and scribblings. The wildlife refuge also lined Smith Road, so the houses at the end of Alcolade were tucked into a lush pocket of forest. We turned into our new driveway, pulling up in front of the chipped brown garage door. We didn't know people were watching until later.

Margaret, a five-year-old girl almost as scrawny as me but with a mouth usually smeared pink with her chewable fluoride treatments, was watching with her aunt and mother out of her uncle Joe's window next door. She remembers staring in awe at the wobbly pile of boxes and furniture tied precariously to the roof of our station wagon. Melissa, two years older than me, with round brown eyes and blonde hair usually tied up in pigtails, cried as she watched us unpack from behind her new curtains across the street. She had just moved out of our house the day before with her parents and older brother, and even though moving to a new house meant she could have her own room, she still thought of the small yellow-and-brown house as hers.

No one came to visit us that first afternoon. My parents and I moved boxes here and there around the house, unpacking dishes and books. I sat in my room, staring at the fat bumblebees buzzing outside my window around one of the giant rhododendron bushes that lined the front of the house. I went into the bathroom and traced the shimmering gold lines of the wallpaper. I sat outside and stared at the big black tarp covering our inground pool. I decided I liked the Hamptons.

A moving van was on its way from the Catskills, carrying the furniture my parents had put in storage the last time my father had lost his job, so we upended boxes to make tables and chairs until it arrived. My mother recalls that a mattress company delivered beds that afternoon, but I prefer my father's memory: The three of us made the sunken living room into a slumber party, stretching out sleeping bags and quilts and pillows across the floor for all of us to sleep on for the first night in our new home. The May evening was warm and crisp, and the smells of cut grass and ocean drifted through the open windows with the promise of summer. We unfurled ourselves beneath the blankets, my mother on one side of me and my father on the other, whispering about what the next day might bring.

My parents had met on a blind date. My mother was working as a secretary at an insurance company in Westchester County, and her boss thought she should meet one of his clients, a golf pro he was insuring.

"He's young, just a little older than you, I think. And handsome. He really seemed on the up and up—I think you'd like him. And he's single. . . ." My mother's boss let the last bit of information linger. He was one of those self-satisfied married people who pitied anyone who wasn't paired off, and he couldn't understand why my mother was on her own. She had explained to him, more than once, that she was recently divorced and not exactly eager to jump into another marriage, or even a serious relationship.

"Nonsense," he would say. He didn't realize how determined she was, however. She came to work, her hair-sprayed platinum bob wavering above frosted eye shadow and lips, wearing mini-dresses, go-go boots, and the other requisite garb of the late 1960s. She smiled. She laughed at jokes the other employees made over morning coffee. She was in her mid-twenties, and her boss couldn't imagine the loneliness she had felt in her first marriage, the one that she had entered into when she was twenty years old, walking out the door five years later with only the clothes on her back.

She liked her single life. She drove a bright yellow VW bug with a peace-sign decal on the hood. She had just moved into a new apartment—the first she ever lived in by herself. For the past few years, she had shared a place with Linda. Their bosses had introduced them, thinking the two young women in the small office building might want to have lunch together and keep each other company. They quickly became best friends; Linda had also been married and divorced, and her silky black hair and the smile that crinkled her deep brown eyes allowed the two of them to pass as sisters, light and dark. Together they picked out window treatments, shared breakfasts of coffee and smokes, loaned each other money to fix their old cars. They were one another's family. But then their companies had transferred them—Linda to Staten Island and my mother to Westchester. So my mother found herself completely on her own.

My mother's boss had already given her work number to the golf pro. My father worked on the weekends, though, so they agreed to go out to dinner on a Monday night.

He picked her up in front of her office. He was driving a sporty yellow Karmann Ghia, and he opened the door for her with a flourish. She thought her date was handsome, but she tended to stay away from flashy guys, and my father's car and the giant silver watch on his wrist were working against him.

My father was in love before she even stepped into his car. He thought my mother was gorgeous, and he liked how at ease she seemed, so confident and regal. He had recently been divorced from his first wife, who often stamped across the greens in her spike heels if he was late coming home from work, even if he was in the middle of a lesson. The marriage had lasted only six months, just a bit longer than they had dated before the wedding. She had been a Playboy Playmate, which had impressed his friends, but in the end that couldn't compensate for her tantrums.

My mother and father were both new to the area, and as they drove around Westchester County, my father talked. And talked. And talked. He always talks too much when he's nervous, and my mother made him very nervous. With each additional restaurant that had a Closed sign in the window, he grew even chattier. He hadn't tried to make a reservation, so he didn't know that most restaurants in the area were closed on Monday nights. Thunder crashed overhead, and rain drenched the windshield. They drove up and down the small Main Streets of the area, peering through the swipes of the Karmann Ghia's windshield wipers and hoping for a restaurant with lights on. Finally, after half a dozen failures, my mother suggested he take her home.

"No, no," my father said, pleading. "The next one will be open, I just know it."

My mother was not so sure. "It's fine, don't feel bad. We'll just do it some other time," she lied, having no such intention.

But my father was lucky. He found a diner that was open, and they ran in through the rain. The new setting didn't seem to improve the date, however.

My father continued to talk about golf tournaments he had won, the companies that sponsored him, and all the free Izod clothes that were shipped to him. He listed all of the celebrities he had given lessons to, and the wives of the celebrities, too. He told my mother about his car, and his plans for the tour next year, and even how much his watch cost. My mother listened, nodding, feigning interest. She had been out with guys like this before. When the bill arrived at the end of the date, he made sure she saw the heft of his roll of cash. She rolled her eyes as he looked down to count out the bills.

The next morning, my father went to the bank before work. He handed over the thick wad of money that he'd let my mother glimpse at the end of their date, watching as the teller counted the bills, peeling them one by one off the brick of cash. He gave the teller the account number of the pro shop, like he did every day after work. He couldn't make his usual drop the night before because he had to pick up my mother, so he had just kept the money in his pocket. He thought about my mother while the teller counted. He replayed the night in his head: He had talked too much, and he should have made a reservation. He shook his head to himself, but her quiet, kind smile gave him hope. He could hardly wait until the afternoon to call her.

When my mother didn't call back, he called her again a few days later. And again a few days after that. Finally, he got her on the line. Before giving her a chance to speak, my father apologized.

"I know you don't want to go out with me again, and I am sorry our date went so badly. But I promise that everything will be different this time," my father said. "The restaurant will be open, the weather will be good, and I won't talk as much!"

On their second date, my father relaxed. As with the PGA tournaments he competed in, he was easily psyched out of his mental game. His swing was beautiful, though, when he was able to trust it. He stopped pretending he had a lot of money and connections, and just tried to make my mother laugh. He was simply himself. It took her a few more dates to fall in love with him, but six months later they moved in together. Three years after that, they went to a courthouse decorated with garland and tinsel two days before Christmas in 1975 and got married. I was born eight months and one week later.

And now our small family sat among moving boxes on the floor in a little brown-and-yellow house in Shirley in 1981. There was no furniture, very little money, and scarcely a friend for miles and miles. But I felt safe tucked between my parents, and all three of our stomachs fluttered with an anticipation that hadn't followed us into the dozen or so other homes where we had laid our heads together.

Waking up the next morning, the three of us set out to make the house ours. My mother wiped down the cupboards and appliances, scraping back the layers of grease left by previous renters. My father trimmed bushes and dead-headed flowers in the backyard. I walked along the edges of the rooms, following the turn of the walls as I memorized the layout of the house from the living room into the hallway into my new bedroom into my parents' bedroom into the bathroom into the kitchen and back into the living room. I counted my steps between the front door and back, and was relieved that there was no basement—one less place for monsters to hide.

# CHAPTER TWO

Across most of Shirley in 1981, houses lined the haphaz-ardly angled streets, packed together like points on a picket fence. Homes on my street were spaced about a car's-width apart, maybe two. The majority of them held families with two or three children, and possibly a grandparent as well. From our last place in the Catskills, I couldn't even see an-other house. Here, everyone seemed to know everything about everybody else.

A steady stream of women from the neighborhood shuf-fled up our driveway to knock on our front door in the first few weeks after we moved in. Each one brought food cov-ered in tinfoil and stories about our landlady, Mrs. Kutch. Most of the women had been living on the block for years, and many had grown up in town. They did not wear aprons or trade suggestions for getting stains out of lace curtains. Many of them wore blue eye shadow, had gold chains with little charms of gold horns hanging from their necks, and chain-smoked. They brought meat-filled lasagna and rice balls and told my mother where not to buy her cold cuts. They would pat my hair and ask me questions. "Where did you come from?" *Upstate.* "Where are your brothers and sisters?" *I don't have any.* "How old are you?" *I'll be five in a few months.*

Many of the women had daughters trailing shyly behind them as they came up our driveway, including the four girls close to my age within a few houses of my own. I slowly worked my way into the fabric of the neighborhood and became closest to Tina, the oldest at seven, who lived directly across the street. She was bossy and loud and funny, the leader of our group, with a head full of dark glossy curls. She liked to dance and sing; her older sister, Jenny, had just gotten a part in a Nestlé Crunch commercial, and Tina planned to become an actress like her sister. Jackie, their mother, always had homemade ice-pops in the freezer (frozen fruit juice with toothpicks in ice trays), and Jerry, Tina's father, was the unofficial Neighborhood Dad. Jerry worked as a maintenance man at the Brookhaven National Laboratory, a federal facility just up the highway, and unlike most of the fathers—who were in service jobs like my father, or in construction—he was home at a reasonable hour almost every night.

Melissa, the girl who used to live in my new house and now lived next to Tina on the other side of the street, was blonde, big-boned, and sensitive. She was the dreamer of our quintet, and her wide brown eyes would sometimes fix in one place until they clouded over and we could tell she was far away. This might happen during a quiet afternoon sitting on her front lawn, while we were rubbing the velvety petals of her magnolia tree on each other's cheeks, or she could break away into her private world in the middle of a heated kickball game at the end of the block.

Melissa's older brother, Jonathan, terrorized us every chance he got, pelting us with berries or pinching our arms. Their mother was loud and loving, quick with jokes. Their father, Ritchie, a steamfitter who would go away on jobs for weeks at a time, built intricate model trains—complete with real steam—in his basement, although not the kind that we were allowed to touch or play with. Ritchie and his friends also worked on cars. Big hulking shells of rusty trucks would sit on cement blocks in Melissa's driveway, and we would carefully pick our way around the legs stretched out underneath them. Melissa was always the Studebaker when we played SPUD, a combination of Freezetag and dodgeball, in the streets.

The third in our troupe was Andrea. She was the athlete of the group, fierce and strong as her long black hair. She lived on the other side of Joe, the realtor, and her house was always dark and quiet, like church. Frank Sinatra songs played softly on a loop, and her cupboards and refrigerator smelled like vitamins. Her mother kept a vegetable garden in the backyard and her father, Andrew, also worked at the Brookhaven National Laboratory. But while Jerry went to work in his pickup truck with a flatbed full of tools, wearing carpenter pants or jeans and a baseball cap and big boots, Andrew went to work in short-sleeve collared shirts and slacks, with matching belts and shoes. The briefcase he carried was pointy and severe, like his car. He fixed computers. He was meticulous about his lawn, and I quickly learned never to touch even a toe to his perfect green yard.

Joe's house was between my house and Andrea's, and there was usually somebody bustling in or out of Joe's with a bang of the screen door. That house was always loud, and sentences that were started in English were usually finished in Italian. Insults were doled out the same way, and I learned Italian curse words before I learned their English counterparts ("You *strunz!*"). Joe's two sons, Louie and Anthony, were younger than me, still in diapers. His niece Margaret was one year older, and even though her family lived on the other side of town, she came to play with our group all summer. Like me, Margaret's brown hair angled into a short pageboy cut. We would spin and spin on the street, pretending we were performing perfect Hamill camels. Margaret was the scrawny girl spying on us on moving day, and our similar builds and haircuts locked us into an immediate bond. My skin, dotted with more and more freckles as summer wore on, would never take on Margaret's warm brown tan, but we were sometimes mistaken for sisters. Margaret's outfits were always clean and ironed—even her play clothes.

Three houses within two blocks were full of Joe's extended family, and on Sundays I took to blending into the under-the-foot traffic, listening to the voices reaching louder and louder registers as people spoke over one another. Maria, Joe's wife, always made my pasta without sauce, since I didn't like tomatoes, and I would happily suck up the long strands of spaghetti one by one as loudly as possible. No one was listening to me slurping, anyway.

That summer in Shirley was the first time I was part of a group and a neighborhood. I loved the freedom of opening the door to someone else's house and being able to wander in and out, looking in their refrigerator or cupboards. Because I was an only child, some of the other mothers pitied me, using this as a reason to baby me more than the other kids. But after we moved to Shirley, I never again wished for brothers and sisters. Any time I wanted to be part of a larger family, I just walked out the front door and picked a direction.

There were some bigger differences between my family and the rest of the neighborhood. We weren't Catholic, we weren't Italian, and neither of my parents had grown up in the town, like the majority of our neighbors—and that made our absorption into the fabric of the neighborhood a touch trickier.

Most of Shirley's fathers worked at service jobs in the nearby Hamptons, but my father's job was a bit different. His uniform of a collared shirt and khakis made him seem fancy. The neighbors couldn't quite understand. "You play golf," they would ask, "for a living?" Playing golf in general seemed cushy enough, but getting paid to play golf? That was just over the top.

As for my mother, her quiet smile and unnerving silences came across as snobbery, as they had often enough since high school. She wasn't the only mother who didn't work, but this fact—a decision she and my father had painstakingly decided to stick to, at least until I was a bit older—didn't work in her favor. The combination of a man skimming by hitting a little white ball around the lawn and an attractive blonde woman who seemed to think just a bit too highly of herself meant the neighborhood regarded us with some suspicion at first.

It was Jerry's friendship that eventually cemented my parents' place within the group. All of the families on the block adored Jerry, and just as his daughter Tina was the natural leader of our group, the adults often turned to him about problems or decisions they faced. Both men often worked seven days a week—my father at the golf course and Jerry at the Brookhaven Laboratory and then in the Hamptons as a weather-stripper on the weekends—so they must have first met late in the day, after work but before the summer sun started to climb down its ladder. One of them was planting some flowers by their mailbox, and the other crossed the road and introduced himself.

They liked each other immediately. They talked about plants and flowers, a favorite hobby for both men. Jerry had dark brown eyes, and dark hair like my father, but his was straight instead of curly, and he kept it cropped short. Both men perpetually had what in my house was called a golfer's tan from working outside most seasons. While my father spent his days at Hampton Hills Country Club fixing members' slices at the outdoor driving range, Jerry cleaned up spills, buried carcasses of dead laboratory animals, and dumped chemicals into big diesel trucks and boxcars. He didn't enjoy his job, but unlike most of the other fathers, Jerry had a strong benefits package, since the Brookhaven Laboratory was owned by the Department of Energy and funded by the U.S. Department of Defense.

He liked his benefits, but during late-night games of gin rummy in our backyard, Jerry told my father he wanted to leave the Brookhaven Laboratory because he was nervous about the chemicals he handled. In 1979, just two years earlier, the nuclear reactor on Three Mile Island had suffered a partial core meltdown, and since then Jerry would never let his wife or kids touch him when he got home until after he had showered. If we were playing out in the street when his truck pulled into the driveway, he would hold us back by our foreheads, shouting that he'd been "green-slimed"—a term from a popular Nickelodeon television show at the time—at work and had to wash up.

So he was saving money from his weekend construction work, and he hoped to start his own weather-stripping business. Jerry just needed a little more time, and he would have enough money to quit his job. My father, whose jobs rarely came with health insurance or any other health or retirement benefits, could sympathize with Jerry's wish to work for himself, but he also understood the draw of security and stability—two things he could never quite manage to hold on to.

When my father reported to work at Hampton Hills for his job that summer, he was surprised to find not a single blade of grass on the course. It had been late winter when he interviewed, and the dead grass hadn't seemed out of place underneath the layer of frost. He was also surprised to hear that the club only had seven members.

He asked around and pieced together a story from the greens crew and kitchen staff. The year before, there was a fire at the pump house, destroying the course's irrigation system, greens- and fairway-mowers, and the fleet of golf carts. Most of the staff claimed the former pro manager was the one who started the blaze in the first place, and instead of reinvesting the insurance money into the club, he headed for the racetrack. A few months before my father interviewed for the job, the former pro was found in a motel room near a racetrack in Bridgeport, Connecticut. He was dead, and there was no money left. He had gambled, and lost, every last penny.

At first, my father tried to make things work, brainstorming for ideas on resurrecting Hampton Hills golf course and devising plans to get the membership numbers up. The club's owner, John Cody, had given him some money to replace the irrigation system and carts, and let him hire a local restaurant manager to take care of the clubhouse food service. Meanwhile, my father worked out a plan to attract more members, charging only $50 to join the club if they paid a monthly greens fee. He also offered a $1,500 annual membership, knowing that no golfers would take it since the course still had no grass.

Those first weeks, strange people appeared on the course whenever John Cody visited. Along with running the golf course, Cody was president of the International Brother-hood of Teamsters Local 282, which encompassed eastern New York. Cody grew up on the Lower East Side of Manhattan and started working as a trucker's helper at age fifteen, and he'd been in and out of prison since he was seventeen. By the time he became my father's employer, he was in charge of fleets of trucks driven by the local's members that delivered concrete and building supplies in an area ranging from Montauk to Manhattan.

Cody always arrived at the golf club with an entourage of cars, and a single black boxy sedan with two men often trailed behind. These two men never carried golf bags or clubs, and they weren't dressed for golf. Instead of inquiring about playing time, these men would take corner seats in the restaurant near the window, remaining there as long as Cody did, not speaking, not reading, just sipping their sodas behind dark sunglasses. A few times when Cody played the course, my father noticed helicopters buzzing overhead. There were small private airports in the Hamptons, but these helicopters hovered over Hampton Hills, following the same zigzag pattern that the course did.

My father claims he didn't know exactly what Cody might have been up to at the time, and I would like to believe him. He had a wife and child whom he had just uprooted and delivered to a new neighborhood, and this was the only job possibility that worked out. Regardless, my father got the feeling that the presence of these strange men and helicopters were not good signs, so he gradually started looking for other opportunities.

By midsummer, as my father was beginning to untangle himself from the intricate workings of the golf club, I was plaiting myself deeper into the rhythm of the neighborhood girls. Every morning, like clockwork, Margaret or Tina would knock on our door. If I was awake before everyone else, I always went to Tina's first, hoping her mother, Jackie, would offer me some orange juice—made from boiled water and frozen orange shards from a tin cylinder out of the freezer. If Margaret was around, I would sneak bowls of sugar cereal at Uncle Joe's.

Most mornings began with the girls and me meeting along the border of the wildlife refuge at the end of our street, plucking off spiny blooms from the thick honeysuckle bushes that lined the forest. We sat on the edge of the street, laps full of sticky flowers, and drained the syrup out of as many as we could until our stomachs started to ache. The refuge was cool even on the hottest summer days, and the pitch pines brushing up against one another sounded like the forest breathing. Melissa, Tina, Andrea, and Margaret each had an older sibling, and if they were willing to play with us that day, we would tromp deeper into the refuge, past the honeysuckle border and through the fire trails, hiding behind aging oaks or prickly wild rosebushes during games of Manhunt. If the brothers and sisters decided not to play with us, we would make up story lines and act out scenes, pretending to be the older kids, trying on their personalities and gestures like pulling on someone else's coat.

We'd eat lunch at one house or another, alternating depending on whose mother was at work or out food shopping. We spent hours screwing and unscrewing the braided metal mouths of rubber hoses, trying to match the most powerful water pressure with the least kinked hose and the sprinkler with the widest reach so we could jump through the spray. We played softball in the street with a plastic yellow bat and picked overripe strawberries from patches that dotted an overgrown lot on the other end of the block. We locked flat silver rollerskate plates and wheels to the bottom of our sneakers and zoomed up and down our weed-cracked driveways, taking orders and delivering imaginary piles of chocolate shakes and burgers to the people waiting in their imaginary cars. Tough bosses and fresh customers filled in most of the drama, but there was also the occasional kidnapping and holdup.

The smooth skin under our thighs was perpetually indented from sitting or lying out in the middle of the pebbly gravel street, and we were always sweaty and out of breath, on our way to the next adventure as our mothers tried to wipe our mouths or stick Band-Aids across scraped elbows or knees. It was probably just a normal summer for the other girls, but the camaraderie was new for me. I still had my imaginary friend, Michael, who had traveled with my family through the last few moves, but he now spent most of his time sick with the chickenpox at home or on vacation.

By mid-June, the girls started talking about the Fourth of July. From the stories the four of them told me, it was the favorite neighborhood holiday—the families had a tradition of blocking off the street with sawhorses and other barriers dragged out of their garages, clearing the way for a daylong block party.

That morning, husbands and wives scuttled card tables, picnic tables, and even folding TV trays down their driveways to the street. By 11:00 AM, the women brought out the first shift of food, steam curling through tinfoil. The adults dragged folding chairs up and down the block as they visited one another, lighting each other's cigarettes and topping off drinks from thermoses decorated with flower patterns. The whole block smelled of hot dogs.

But the best thing about the Fourth of July, and the part that I had heard about when the girls started talking it up a few weeks before the actual day, was that while the adults ate and chatted, the kids had free rein over all the backyards on the block for an entire afternoon. We spent hours going to the key backyards that had swing sets, lobbing our bodies as high as we could before jumping off, and then we headed to the special three that had inground pools.

Tina was the only kid in our group whose house had a pool; it measured four feet deep and about six feet across and was aboveground. Jerry had built a pool-height deck around it in the small space behind their house, and when any of the kids had to pee, we would hoist ourselves up onto the deck and let the urine run through the cracks of the wooden slats of the deck to the ground below, splashing our laps with the chlorinated pool water before jumping back in.

With four or five of us girls swimming around, though, Tina's pool felt very small. The pool behind my house was long and inground, and we dreamed of swimming lengthy circuits across it, but this was forbidden, of course, because the landlady still wouldn't let us remove the tarp.

At the other end of the block were three pools that we all coveted: the Mundys', the Coracis', and one at another house that was a rental and always changing hands. Those pools were all inground, complete with deep ends, and two even had slides and short diving boards. There was at least one parent stationed in the backyards for safety during the holiday, although they were usually sipping a piña colada. We sauntered up to the edge of each pool and dropped the towels that we had kept slung around our necks for most of the morning like miniature prize-fighters. Then we splashed our way in, throwing our arms behind our heads and kicking out our legs, feeling as though we had the very ocean in the middle of our little neighborhood.

Melissa, Andrea, Margaret, and I followed Tina from one end of the pool to the other, playing Marco Polo or tag. Our favorite game was Mermaids, and the wiggle movement had to start in the head and end in the feet, ripple after ripple. We imagined green iridescent tails, long tendrils of hair flowing behind us, underwater gardens of exotic flowers— never mind that we were squat or scrawny, bee-stung and mosquito-bitten, awkward with knotty hair. In the water, we became beautiful.

The Fourth of July also happened to be Jerry's birthday, and the entire neighborhood gathered at sundown for his birthday cake, singing to him as he pretended to be surprised, the girls and I still in our soggy, chlorinated bathing suits. The adults who had not already retired for a nap after too much sun and booze ate cake, and Maria brewed endless cups of coffee until the night turned navy blue.

As the scrubby tops of the pitch pines pierced the darkening blanket of sky overhead, the neighborhood congregated at our end of the block, standing between our house and Jerry's as the men prepared the fireworks with the wildlife refuge as a backdrop. Joe had relatives in Brooklyn and Queens who always came out the week before the holiday with car trunks full of M-80s and Sizzlers and Jumping Jacks. Only the men were allowed to set the fireworks off, pulling lighters from back pockets to light the wicks sticking out of coffee cans, pails of sand, and crevices in street signs. One after another the flares would be sent up into the night and explode with color so blinding I could still see it even when I shut my eyes in fear.

There was a charge in the air, with the men together, moving a bit sloppily after a day of drinking and the wives or mothers calling out warnings or names in cautious tones every few minutes. Some of the fireworks were duds and would do no more than fizzle or pop. Others would shoot horizontally instead of vertically, shearing a line into a crowd or disappearing into the depths of the refuge. I was particularly terrified of the Jumping Jacks that hopped and spun close to the ground, skidding across the gravel in uncontrollable bursts, and clung to my father when these were sparked.

For much of the evening, the girls and I danced around with our own sparklers, writing our names against the inky canvas of night. When those were gone, we simply watched wide-eyed, clapping with each colorful explosion or shrieking over the seismic booms of the M-80s until, full of cake and exhausted after swimming all day, we let our heads loll back against a cushion of grass. After the last firework was set off and the rickety tables had been dragged back up the driveways, our fathers scooped our limp bodies off the ground and slung us over their sulfur-scented shoulders, laying us on our beds on top of the covers and sheets, the muffled sounds of distant fireworks bursting into our dreams.

The next morning, all of the kids were shoved back outside early, armed with mops and brooms and leaf bags by our bleary-eyed mothers, still in bathrobes and clutching mugs of coffee. It was our job to clean up the trash—half-eaten hamburgers, greasy paper plates, and pounds of confetti-sized paper from the fireworks. The night before, along with the rest of the neighborhood kids, I had chased after the miniature plastic soldiers that rained down in paper parachutes after bursting into colorful swirls hundreds of feet above us in the air. As I pushed our big horsehair broom across the street, I could see the thin sheaths of parachutes and hard green bodies of the army men caught up in piles amid the crumpled napkins. I tried to untangle one, but his legs were smeared with mustard and there was a tear in his paper parachute. I laid him softly on the top of my pile and silently told him he had fought bravely.

After the Fourth of July, the rest of the summer days were still spent traipsing through the wildlife refuge or hopping through sprinklers. By early August, the girls and I were gathering on the uneven street in front of our houses almost every evening, where the sharp tang of barbecue mingled with the sweeter scents of chlorine from our hair and sweat from our bodies.

At that hour, televisions hadn't been turned on for the night yet, and neither had porch lights. We relaxed under the unfolding arms of the oaks and pines that reached toward each other from opposite sides of the street. We traded stories and jokes, listening to the sounds traveling freely between the small, tightly packed homes—the murmur of after-dinner conversation, the rhythmic beating of a box fan lazily circulating the cooling air, the soft clink of dishes being washed under an open window. After dinner on these summer nights, the girls and I would mill around in the middle of the block waiting for Jerry.

Once he joined us, we would fan out on the ground so our feet pointed into the middle of a circle. Lying down with our hands behind our heads to cushion us, we made a brightly colored pinwheel of shorts and tank tops against the gravel. Jerry, tanned brown and tidy in his neighborhood uniform of jeans and a T-shirt, smelled freshly scrubbed from his daily post-work shower. He would ask us about our day and laugh at our jokes until, just as the clouds turned from pink to violet, our chatter grew hushed and we all stared into the sky.

At first, the dark shapes looked like dry sheaths of leaves caught up in the wind, or sparrows darting drunk. Soon, the solitary forms would turn into threads of twenty, and then sheets of hundreds, as the bats flew out of their secret homes in the cool recesses of the wildlife refuge for the freedom of the night. Jerry shouted out numbers with us as we tried to count them, attempting to force order onto the flitting mass. Their ear-aching screams echoed against bedroom windows, mailboxes, bikes propped against cement stoops, and other ordinary things from our day-lit lives, seeping into them and claiming the objects. When we could no longer keep track of the bats we would shriek, overwhelmed, imagining that the creatures were swooping down on our circle, hard little bodies taking over our world.

Though the ritual felt much longer, the flight of the bats probably only lasted ten minutes. Slowly, as the night grew darker and the outlines of the packs of winged animals melted into the black of the sky, the street lamps would blink on, turning our bedroom windows, mailboxes, and bikes back into the objects we knew. Finished with the dishes, our mothers would lean out of windows and doors and begin calling us home, one by one.

That entire first summer in Shirley was magical. It was my first experience of what a real family home could be, with neighbors who knew you and pulled you in to be a part of them. By the end of the summer, my mother was sharing afternoon coffees with Tina's mother, and my father had become a regular face at Joe's basement poker games. The neighborhood learned that although they were no longer practicing, my parents had once both been Catholic, which was good enough. We'd never be Italian, but there were worse things than being Irish, apparently.

My father gave golf lessons to some of the other fathers in our front yard using whiffle balls, and he showed them some trick shots, like hitting the ball with the grip of the club or even the old yellow plastic baseball bat. The women became used to my mother's reserved nature and realized that her silences were usually out of contemplation, not judgment, and they learned that she was also an attentive listener. My parents planted flowers in the backyard and bought dressers from barn sales that my mother refinished in the garage. Our freezer filled up with meat and vegetables for future dinners, and my mother even bought magnets for the refrigerator. She set out her collection of cactus and aloe plants, which followed us from house to house— my mother loved flowers and plants, but these hardy specimens were some of the only plants able to survive the number of moves we had been through. Although there were still unopened boxes of books and records in the garage, we felt we had finally settled in.

The leaves on my favorite tree on the side of our house were shifting from pale green to gold, and I knew that with a new season usually came a move. But none of us wanted to leave our new home. My father's job was still not working out the way he had hoped, and after an argument at the clubhouse with Cody, he was fired. He was relieved, actually, but so far had found only one job lead since he started looking. After Cody fired him, my father spent his days pacing our small ranch house, making phone calls and not receiving any in return.

A few weeks before losing his job, he had learned through a friend about a Japanese golf company that was looking for a salesman to cover the New York area. He knew that trying to sell a product from a new company would require at least two years of slow sales as he built up a customer base, but he had little to lose. After three weeks of agonized pacing and only dead-end leads for other jobs, the phone finally rang: Mizuno, the Japanese company, offered him the position. My mother and father discussed it, and decided to put their life savings—about $6,000—into golf bags, clubs, socks, and gloves that my father would then stuff into his station wagon and try to sell to pro shops in the area. He would have to travel and would be away for days at a time, but we could stay in Shirley.

And so the summer ended with all three of us snug within our new neighborhood. We were still hanging by a string—my father's new job was as unpredictable as all of the others he had held over the past few years, but my parents were hopeful. The low rent made it possible for them to take this chance. Even though the town itself was run-down, our neighbors were solid and strong families, though some may have had rough edges. We all felt safe.

In early September, my parents threw me a party for my fifth birthday. The night before, my father came home with a papier-mâché donkey. I had never seen a piñata before. The donkey was orange and yellow and hot pink in places, with black hooves and nose, and was about the size of Margaret's dog, Prince. The night before my party, I helped my parents stuff the donkey's belly with Starburst, Jolly Ranchers, and Hershey's Kisses, looking forward to cracking the animal open and having the candy rain down on my head.

On the morning of my birthday, Jerry helped my father string the piñata up in the front yard between two oak trees. There was a slight chill to the air, and I wore a pink-and-white striped sleeveless dress with a white turtleneck underneath to keep me warm. My mother gave me a cardboard tiara to wear on my head, with the words "Happy Birthday" written across the top in silver and pink letters. All of the kids walked around with noisemakers hanging out of the corners of their mouths like cigarettes.

After some party games and cake in the backyard, everyone collected out front and made a circle around the piñata. I took off my shiny black Mary Jane shoes and frilly white socks, and my father handed me a plastic bat and tied a bandanna around my eyes. Blindfolded, I swung with all my might. I missed. I could hear my father shouting, "Higher!" or "To the left more!" and laughing as I continued to swing.

I was laughing, too. I kept missing, but I didn't care. I couldn't see a thing, but all around me were the voices and laughter of my family and friends. Tina ultimately cracked the belly of the donkey open that afternoon, and I cheered along with the rest of the kids, diving for the watermelon-flavored Jolly Rancher suckers that we all favored. It was my first real birthday party, and the lawn beneath my feet was cool and firm in the front yard of my little brown-and-yellow home.

# CHAPTER THREE

My new town's name had nothing to do with the curly-haired child actress it made me imagine. I didn't know yet that the blueprint of my house that I liked to trace with my feet was reproduced on almost every block in our new town, or that most of the houses had sprung from the earth within a single decade, sprouting up where scrub brush and fields had covered the ground for hundreds of years. It would be years before I heard about the man it all started with, a Brooklyn boy named Walter Turnbull Shirley. Walter T., as he was known, was dead twenty years by the time we moved to town.

Walter T. built the town of Shirley in the 1950s, as well as Mastic and Mastic Beach, the villages that flank his namesake. Locals see the three towns as a single entity and usually refer to them as Shirley and the Mastics, like a singing group.

Soon after we moved to our new house, I learned that the towns are also often referred to as Drastic Mastic, Mistake Beach, and Shirlée.

When Walter T. first saw the patch of South Shore that was to become his town, he was nineteen, a scrawny kid learning how to shoot guns and dig foxholes at an army induction camp in the middle of rural Long Island in 1917. Like most of the young men in his Brooklyn neighborhood, he had signed up to fight in the Great War and was put on a train and shipped out to Camp Upton. The camp was located in an area called Yaphank, halfway between the Atlantic Ocean and the Long Island Sound, an isolated and sandy spot surrounded by forests and farms.

At the time, most of the eastern end of Long Island was a tumble of potato fields, dirt roads, and fishing villages. East Hampton's stately mansions were surrounded by rows of lettuce and corn instead of the wineries and swanky restaurants that dominate the landscape today. When he first came to the island, Walter T. never traveled far enough east to see the manicured lawns and circle drives of the Maidstone Country Club or the surrounding estates. His train stopped a few dozen miles west of the Hamptons, leaving him in the middle of a barren landscape dusty with sand. But for the boy from Brooklyn, Camp Upton—and the trees, birds, ocean, and wildlife around it—was opulent enough.

"I didn't see a tree until I was nine years old," Walter T. once told a reporter. "And then I thought it was a Flatbush water main frozen green!" Walter T. grew up in an Italian neighborhood near Bay Ridge, Brooklyn, where his father worked as a trolley conductor. Unlike the open expanses around Upton, most streets in his neighborhood were strung together with narrow brick row-houses, one carbon-copied box after another. Most of Walter T.'s early childhood was spent on cracked city sidewalks, playing in public pools and weed-choked dirt lots. At an early age, Walter T. became enamored with the stage and hung around the playhouses in Brooklyn whenever he could, learning how to work the piano by watching shows and practicing whenever the big dusty keys were free. He was a thin boy, but his barrel chest helped him carry his notes long and deep, and by the time he was fourteen, Walter T. had quit school and was working full time at McSweeney's vaudeville house in Bay Ridge. He brought home $5 a week for song plugging, a form of music advertising—Walter T. would sing a song for audiences be-tween acts, getting people to chirp along in hopes that they would purchase the sheet music.

At these dark, smoke-filled vaudeville houses, Walter T. met famous performers and musicians, and their shiny gold beads, smooth voices, and swish lifestyle made his quiet Bay Ridge block seem small-time. He wanted to be up on the stage, performing. He was easily intoxicated by any whiff of celebrity, so badly wanting to be the one adored, watching the stars as they came in from the Manhattan houses and

Orpheum circuit. When he was a teenager, Walter T. met songwriter and performer Irving Berlin at one of the play-houses, and the fellow Brooklyn boy hired Walter T. to plug his songs all around the city. Walter T. hammered out Berlin's melodies on house pianos, learning how to grab and hold an audience's attention, swaying them to take his pitch and buy the music he was selling. He coaxed a friend from the neighborhood, J. Fred Coots, to quit his bank job and zoom around the city with him, playing the piano so Walter T. could focus on vocals. After a year of plugging Berlin's songs, one melody gave them more trouble than all the rest. Walter T. couldn't sell the sheet music no matter how energetic his and Coots's performances were. He told Berlin that the song, called "Smile and Show Your Dim-ples," needed a new title and tempo, that the audiences couldn't connect to it the way it was. He stressed that it wasn't for lack of trying on Fred's and his part but was a flaw in the music that was making it unsellable. Berlin fired them. Walter T. and Coots returned to McSweeney's in Brooklyn, where they stayed until Walter T. decided to en-list and hopped the train to Long Island.

Walter T. felt strangely at home in this foreign landscape. The nineteen-year-old was amazed that the beaches and forests that surrounded Camp Upton were only a train ride away from his little block in Brooklyn. It was the first time there was room in his heart and ambition for something other than the glamour of vaudeville. Just as his moments on stage, or even near the stage, made the colors and realities of his home life seem even more monotonous and dull, I imagine the flat greens and blues of the countryside on Long Island—no droning brick row-houses or gray clouds of smog or trucks honking—made him feel that he could breathe for the first time.

*After stepping off the train and filling out his paperwork, Walter T. is handed a horn and told that he will be a bugler. Scared to let the instrument—the first he ever owned—out of his sight, Walter T. takes the bright yellow horn with him on his first trip to the beach with the other soldiers. He and a group of boys bounce along over the rickety wooden slats of a bridge in the back of a truck, the backs of their necks beating red under the sun. Walter T. has never been to the ocean before, doesn't know what to do there. So he brings his bugle, even though the other guys make fun of him.*

*At the soft curves of the dunes, Walter T. takes his boots off and carries them in one hand by their laces, socks tucked into the toes. When he sees the water he stops, standing still just for a minute. The smell is different, not the heavy stink of the docks he was used to in Brooklyn. And the color is different, too—the water back home was a murky black, a gray-green on the calmest day. The ocean in front of him is a deep, bottomless blue, the frothy caps of the waves moving toward him like nets thrown from invisible boats.*

*The white of the sand hurts his eyes, and so does the salt, and as the other men peel off their clothes, Walter T. just stands at the edge of the water, surprised at how cold it is, how it makes his ankles ache. He watches as the men splash into the ocean, arms and legs disappearing under the water until they are just a bunch of heads bobbing. Sea gulls cry out, alarmed at the intrusion. One of the guys rides the waves on his back, arms folded on his stomach like an otter. Another calls out, "Hey, Shirley! Play us a song!"*

*He is not yet twenty, and has none of the jowls or back flab or meatiness that he will take on in his adulthood. He strips down to his undershirt and presses the bugle to his lips. He sucks in a deep gulp of salty air from either side of the mouthpiece, soft boy-skin rolling over the rungs of his ribs as he inhales and blows. The wind whips the notes out of the horn and back toward the big sandy hills. The guys can't hear him. He tries playing louder, running to different spots on the beach, going into the water up to his knees. No luck. So he wraps his yellow bugle up in his shirt and leaves it with his pile of clothes on the beach before jumping into the big blue ocean.*

Later, after he founded his namesake town and became a millionaire, Walter T. loved to tell his war stories to reporters during interviews. According to Walter T., only months after he arrived at Camp Upton, Private Shirley found himself in France in the middle of one of the most famous battles of World War I as part of the Lost Battalion. In this battle, five units mostly made up of boys from Camp Upton were sealed off, a small pocket of red, white, and blue behind enemy lines. For three days, the men suffered heavy casualties as both the enemy and their own fighters aimed their fire and lobbed bombs at their spot in the Argonne Forest. The battalion, to which many soldiers from New York City belonged, was presumed lost until Major Whittelsey could get a scrawled note to the forces on the other side of the forest. The message was attached to the leg of a carrier pigeon, saying simply:

*We are along the road parallel to 276.4.*
*Our own artillery is dropping a barrage directly on us.*
*For heaven's sake, stop it.*

Back in New York, Walter T. told reporters about his gold medal for the risks he took during the battle of the Lost Battalion. This battle was one of the most famous in the war—the pigeon, whose breast was pierced by a bullet that also chewed through one of the bird's wings, was named Cher Ami by the men of the Lost Battalion, and his small broken body stands in the Smithsonian Institute in Washington, D.C., to this day. To be a part of it was to be a celebrity, something Walter T. greatly desired. There was much confusion during the days of the battle, and it was well known that the task of confirming exactly who had been in the Charlevaux Ravine in the Argonne Forest during those three days would take months, if not years. Robert J. Laplander, a historian and Lost Battalion expert, has found evidence of numerous people in the 1920s and 1930s alleging to have been part of this historic battle. "Many less than scrupulous people made the claim in order to get attention, capitalize on the fame some way, or to cover up the fact that they didn't really do anything during the war and felt bad about it," he wrote to me after searching his list of men who were involved—the most comprehensive available—and finding no mention of Walter T. Shirley. "Even Al Capone was known to have made the claim that he got his famous scar as a member of the Lost Battalion—which he most certainly did not."

Walter T. may have fought in Europe. He may even have been near the Lost Battalion battle, but he almost certainly was not directly involved, as he suggests in many interviews. It was just an added bit of song plugging, spicing up the story in the hope that someone would buy it.

After the war, Walter T. returned to his parents' house in Brooklyn and went back to work in the vaudeville houses. Vaudeville, however, had taken its own hits since the war, with many playhouses showing the silent movies that were overtaking variety acts. When Walter T. told his war stories, he often spoke of Camp Upton and the ocean and trees out on Long Island and also of performing. He had met up again with Irving Berlin, who had also trained at Camp Upton but did not go to Europe to fight. The two reconnected when Walter T. performed in some of Berlin's revues at the tiny military Oprey House. While at Upton, Berlin wrote a play called *Yip Yip Yaphank,* showcasing a song with the now-famous refrain, "Oh, how I hate to get up in the morning!"

The years continued to unravel behind Walter T., and although he still spent most of his time song plugging and doing odd jobs at playhouses like McSweeney's, it soon became obvious that he would never become the famous performer he had always dreamed of being. He just didn't have a good enough voice or act. He couldn't write his own music; he only knew how to play other people's songs. His partner, Coots, on the other hand, was already hooked on the scene and determined to continue. Coots had started writing his own songs and selling his own music, and just as Walter T. had cajoled Coots into song plugging, Coots tried to get Walter T. to stick it out a bit longer. But Walter T. was twenty-six, and he was tired. He needed a change.

And so, in 1923, Walter T. quit. He left Coots and got some work at a bond brokerage house. He still played piano at parties, and he started amassing a huge collection of movie posters and signed celebrity photos. But now he focused his attention on money. As the war years disappeared further into memory, the housing market heated up, and Walter T. turned his eyes to real estate. His old Camp Upton pal William O'Dwyer, who was working as a cop during the day and going to law school at night, had invested in some homesites in Rockville Center on Long Island. The homesites were about forty minutes away from the city— nowhere near Upton, which was still another hour east of Rockville, but Long Island just the same. O'Dwyer offered Walter T. a job selling off the plots, and he jumped at the opportunity. This move was a lucky one for Walter T.— when the stock market crashed in 1929, just a few years after he got out of the bond brokerage, real estate was a relatively safe place to be. He married a petite blonde named Rose in 1930, and by 1932, he had a namesake son, Walter T. Shirley Jr. Unlike many families in their Brooklyn neighborhood, the 1930s were good to the Shirleys.

Through his real estate dealings in Long Island, Walter T. heard about William K. Vanderbilt Jr., who was building an expressway on Long Island—the first major roadway to be built on the island since 1908. Designed mainly to pursue his love of motorcar racing, the roadway was originally planned as a sixty-mile stretch between Queens and Riverhead, but land acquisition was more difficult than Vanderbilt had anticipated and the project dead-ended at forty-five miles in Ronkonkoma, a few miles past Rockville Center. After World War I, the Vanderbilt Expressway had too much competition from superhighways, such as New York State Parks Commissioner Robert Moses's Northern State Parkway, to continue as a toll road. By the early 1930s, when Walter T. got his first look at the road, the strip was primarily used as a shortcut by New York City socialites driving to their country estates.

In 1937, with the threat of war looming again, Walter T. used his connections with his old Upton buddy O'Dwyer, who had advanced greatly by then and was now a New York court judge in Kings County, to get an appointment with Vanderbilt. He had been eyeing some property in Lake Ronkonkoma, where Vanderbilt's road had been forced to end, and wanted to make an offer. During the meeting, Vanderbilt told Walter T. that he had about $100,000 invested in Lake Ronkonkoma, a figure that Walter T. knew was way beyond his wallet. "I saw a solid gold horseshoe on his desk and asked him about it," Walter T. later told a reporter. "It turned out to be a memento from the great heavyweight boxer Fitzsimmons and before you knew it, we were comparing notes on all the great fights of the century." Their meeting, in Walter T.'s recollection, continued for an hour as they talked about boxing matches, until Vanderbilt finally brought the conversation back to real estate, asking: "Well, Wally, how much can you really afford?" Walter T. boasted to the press, "His cashier almost fainted when Willie K. [William K. Vanderbilt] told him Mr. Shirley will be paying us $8,000 for the Ronkonkoma property."

Walter T. walked away with 250 acres. By June 1939, advertisements were running in the *New York Times,* promoting "4-Room Bungalows with inside toilets" going for a price of $995 for both a bungalow and the land it sat on, payable with a down payment of $150 with a five-year term loan. As World War II played out on other continents, families moved from the city out to the country, buying into the dream that Walter T. had created, calling the pint-sized lots of land "acres" and pitching the sales to small-salaried people who wanted a summer home. "I always wanted a home in the country," Walter T. explained in one of his sales pamphlets, "and figured other city folks did, too."

Nicknamed the "Acreage King," Walter T. continued to buy up land bit by bit until he acquired 8,000 acres, and as Lake Ronkonkoma took off, he again recalled the ocean air and pitch pines of the East End that surrounded Camp Upton. Construction was forbidden during World War II, but with his new earnings, Shirley bought 1,200 acres just south of Camp Upton anyway. His friend O'Dwyer was supportive of Walter T.'s purchase, although most people thought he was making a huge mistake because the area was so remote. There were no towns or amenities nearby, just potato fields and Camp Upton, which, after years of being abandoned, was active again, the sounds of target practice exploding across the area. Walter T. just ignored talk of Nazi submarines patrolling the Long Island Sound and Atlantic Ocean, and of the island being the ideal spot for a land invasion. He was patient. As soon as the war ended, Walter T. bought 700 more acres and wound up his sales pitch.

By 1950, Walter T. owned 10,000 acres in the area and was employing the same tactics he had in Ronkonkoma—offering low-cost, small plots and second-home summer dwellings to blue-collar city folks who shared his dream of a slice of green all their own. He named the new development Mastic Acres, the core of what would later become Shirley, and he sold one-quarter-acre plots with diminutive ranch houses and bungalows to middle-income families for $149 each, a deep discount compared to his Ronkonkoma prices. Walter T. even offered a plan that allowed people to buy with only $30 down and dollar-a-week payments. He gave himself a $200,000 marketing budget, which entailed billboards and full-page advertisements in New York City papers.

The marketing paid off: More than 5,000 tiny houses shot up in the area during those first few years. Walter T. used his own builders to construct the houses, mimicking the Levitts' low-cost strategy of designing houses atop concrete slab foundations rather than digging out basements. The houses could be constructed in under a week. With this plan, he hoped to clear $1 million within the first four years of development.

Walter T. had never drawn up any formal plans for the shape of the town—he just started in one place and kept building out, and while in some sections streets were built in grids like Manhattan, other parts rambled and curled inward like seashells. Although he had sold most plots as summer homes, each year more and more families were moving out of their city homes and into their bungalows year-round, adding potbelly stoves for heat. There were never—and still aren't—any sewer systems. In many seasons, families were not able to flush their toilets. If there had been a heavy rain or if the tide was in and the surrounding land was saturated, there was nowhere for the toilet water to go, and so it just stayed in the bowl.

The town kept growing. By 1952, Mastic Acres had its own drive-in movie theater, supermarket, and Howard Johnson restaurant, all at opposite ends of the town, like three points of a triangle. The residents petitioned for a post office, and in exchange for donating land to house the service, Shirley requested that his name grace the outside of the building. With this, the town of Shirley was born. Walter T. was finally famous.

In celebration of the renaming, Walter T. drew up new marketing materials reflecting his just-christened namesake. New full-page ads highlighted some of his celebrity friends—most of whom had never set foot in the area, of course—such as columnist Dorothy Kilgallen ("Women agree that Shirley, LI is ideal for the whole family"), *Daily Mirror* sports editor Dan Parker ("Shirley, LI is a year round Sportsman's Dream"), and Walter T.'s personal friend, Ed Sullivan ("Shirley, LI is America's Vacation paradise"), coaxing Manhattanites with promises of oceans and forests and, more than anything, flowers. Walter T.'s main advertising slogan was "The Town of Flowers," and he promised a flower box with every house. He also ceremoniously presented the first flowers to every new homeowner once they moved in.

The majority of deals were struck in Walter T.'s midtown Manhattan sales office rather than on-site in Shirley. House choices were featured in promotional pamphlets; an early foldout guide to the houses available showed only four options. The Catalina, for example, was a ranch with three bedrooms and a California picture window in the twenty-one-foot-wide living room, whereas the Shirley Rancher boasted a "Wife Saving" kitchen that included a luxurious sink and drainboard with chromium settings. The more modest Brookhaven Standard (like our little yellow-and-brown ranch) was a "rambling, country-styled home with a bow windowed living room, beautiful kitchen, two bedrooms, and a glamorous bath," although the only thing even nominally glamorous about our tiny bathroom was the wallpaper. In large red print along the bottom of the foldout pamphlet was the claim of easy monthly payments that would add up to less than city or country rent. In smaller black letters below, the text reads, "In many instances the deed to your plot will be accepted as downpayment."

The cover of one sales pamphlet featured a mermaid with long yellow hair, a green tail, and the kind of face a child would carve into a pumpkin, a triangle for a nose and arrows for eyes. Her entire body is suspended high above the ocean in an arc, and she is jumping over clusters of flowers, growing algae-like on the water's surface. Beneath her body in small, tight print are the words: "Shirley, where the country meets the sea." Of course, Shirley did not actually butt up against the ocean, but rather the Moriches Bay. And though the bay was brimming with clams, crabs, and flounder, it did not change the fact that the ocean was on the other side of a wide sandbar, with no access from the town. From Walter T.'s marketing campaign, prospective homeowners would have imagined walking out their back door and right into the blue Atlantic. And in the early 1950s, he was trying hard to make this promise come true.

In 1946, Walter T.'s good friend O'Dwyer, who had originally pulled Walter into real estate, won the election for mayor of New York City. O'Dwyer had risen from court judge to Kings County district attorney and had prosecuted one of the country's largest organized crime syndicates, called Murder, Inc. This made him a national celebrity, and Walter T. was able to add another name to his long list of famous friends.

In 1941, shortly after his famous court case, O'Dwyer threw his hat in for the mayoral race but lost to Fiorello La-Guardia. He then retreated to his army days, reenlisting and reaching the rank of brigadier general before World War II was over. In 1945, he was again nominated by Tammany Hall Democrats and won the mayoral election in a landslide. During his first term, O'Dwyer appointed Robert

Moses to a post he created especially for him, called the co-ordinator of the Office of City Construction. O'Dwyer also strove to locate the United Nations permanently in the city, and he raised the subway fare from five cents to ten. He was reelected in 1949 but resigned when the new Kings County district attorney, Miles McDonald, uncovered a huge po-lice-corruption scandal that ran all the way to O'Dwyer himself. More than 500 police officers were forced to retire or resign, or be fired.

O'Dwyer had named Walter T. to a post as commerce commissioner of New York at the end of his term, and Walter T. kept it under the new acting mayor, Vincent Impellitteri. Walter T. and the new mayor worked well together, and Im-pellitteri hired Walter T. to run his own campaign for mayor in 1950. Impellitteri won, and Walter T. kept his position as commerce commissioner, promoting New York City as a place to do business. After the election, Impellitteri also named Walter T. the "Goodwill Ambassador for New York City," which required Walter T. and Rose to take multiple trips to Europe each year, dining with heads of state and being received, if not quite as celebrities, at least something close.

By the mid-1950s, Shirley's year-round population had climbed to 400, and more and more people were lining up in the midtown office, down payments in hand. Walter T. had prophesied that his town would be known as the At-lantic City of Long Island and spoke of grand hotels, five-star restaurants, and opulent seaside resorts. As people who often bought plots sight unseen discovered, the ocean beaches that were such a strong selling point in Walter T.'s pitch were on the other side of a wide bay, not on the edge of the town, as indicated by the illustrations in the pamphlets. Walter T. stationed a motorboat (named *Shirley*, of course) at the water's edge to ferry oceangoers between the town and the other side of the sandbar, but he knew that for the wide-scale construction on the sandbar he was imagining, he would need a bridge. He would also need to buy the sandbar, which was currently the property of Suffolk County, part of the Fire Island Seashore. The first few times he had approached the county officials about purchasing the land, they had rejected him. But now that he had a few years of New York politics under his belt, Walter T. had a feeling that if he built them a bridge, they might change their mind.

Many rickety wooden structures had been built between the mainland and the sandbar in the past, similar to the ones the boys from Camp Upton would have had to bounce over in their truck when Walter T. first saw the ocean, but all had been swept away by hurricanes or February ice flows of the Great South Bay, or had simply rotted through. In 1955, Walter T. broke ground for a 1,206-foot steel-deck bascule drawbridge. More than 12,000 people showed up for the groundbreaking. There was little Walter T. liked better than a good party, and I imagine he must have felt elated as he uncorked a bottle of champagne in celebration.

*As Walter T. pierced the sandy earth with the tip of his shovel, a smile of uncomplicated happiness broke across his tan face. He watched Rose step gingerly around the spots on the beach damp with champagne, trying to keep her pumps from becoming a sandy mess. Rose and Walter T. never actually lived* in Shirley—they always drove back and forth from their Upper East Side apartment in their Lincoln Continental—and he knew she didn't have a change of shoes with her that day.

Walter T. continued to smile into the bursting flashbulbs, his eyes— starry and spotted from the camera flashes and bright sun reflecting off the water—searching the crowd for his son. He should be up here next to me, Walter T. thought. Now that he and Rose spent most of their time traveling, they spent less and less time out east. Wally Jr. had really taken command of the Shirley site, managing the foremen and construction companies working around the clock, building block after block of houses. Shirley even had its own newspaper, Shirley News, which ran features on local families ("The Coracis are the first in town to build a bomb shelter!"), events ("The winning fish were weighed at Keenan's Fishing Station at the end of Beaver Drive"), and contests for best-looking yard. Walter T. still came out to deliver the window boxes of flowers to new families, but mostly he took care of the paperwork from midtown.

He looked down at his feet, the bottom of his pant legs dark with damp from the wet sand and sea mist. He stared across the water and tried to imagine the high arc of a bridge there. He thought of the way the Fifty-ninth Street Bridge near his office in Manhattan sparkled at night, and hoped his bridge would be just as grand. He decided that when the bridge was completed, he and Rose would be the first ones to drive across it. By then the sandbar would also be his, and his Atlantic City of Long Island would be close to completion.

Staring into the crowd and the houses beyond, Walter T. felt proud that the dream that began when he was a scrawny nineteen-year-old boy, stunned to awed silence by the tall pitch pines and seashore, would be the dream that secured him his first true million. He had made it, and even *though it wasn't a stage, all the people standing at the base of the bridge on the beach that day were there to see him, Walter T. Shirley.*

By the time my family arrived, Walter T. Shirley's namesake hadn't been known as The Town of Flowers for decades. Most people had completely given up on the grand visions the founder had once had. Construction on Walter T.'s Smith Point Bridge had been completed in 1959. But the sandbar and beaches were owned by Suffolk County, and although Walter T. bargained his best, the county refused to give him rights to build on the land. He was hoping the bridge would be accepted as a type of offering, or bribe. Despite his connections from the work he did for the mayor's office, the county thanked him for his generous contribution but refused his requests to break ground on the sandbar. Meanwhile, during the four years that the bridge was under construction, sales in Shirley continued to grow. A June 1960 census calculated that Shirley was the fastest-growing community in Suffolk County, with the year-round population nearly doubling in ten years.

Like Levittown, the first of four mass-produced communities built by Abraham Levitt and his sons in the late 1940s and 1950s, Shirley's houses were built in a highly efficient, assembly-line fashion. Material costs were kept low, and the machinelike proficiency of the workers and uniformity of structures allowed Walter T. to churn out dwellings as if they were cars.

Walter T., however, did not share the Levitts' commitment to the idea of community and never bothered with the village centers that ultimately made Levittown so appealing. A salesman at heart, Walter T. never gave much thought to infrastructure at all. His initial plan was to build a beach bungalow town, a place that would go into hibernation come Labor Day, and so he had never considered that his town's population would one day need amenities and municipal basics, like schools or community centers or a business district. As the town was built out, the streets curved and angled in anarchic spurts and chaotic clusters, resulting more from the blocks of time it took for that particular construction than from any strategy or preplanned sequence. There is no Main Street in Shirley. Neighborhoods simply unfold along the sides of the William Floyd Parkway. There is no town center.

When Walter T. died of a heart attack in 1963, he must have known that his namesake would never match up to the nearby Hamptons, or even Levittown, as he had once hoped. In 1966, construction was completed on the Long Island Expressway, and it became clear to the inhabitants of Shirley that Walter T.'s promise of a thirty-minute commute to the city on the expressway was more than an exaggeration, dousing hopes of city jobs and paychecks. The two main employment prospects—the city and the hotels and restaurants on the Smith Point strip—were now impossibilities for the hopeful new residents of Shirley.

Long Island was a major beneficiary of government farm aid, and many new Shirley residents signed up for the Federal Housing Administration loan program. In 1950, more than fifty mortgages were approved by FHA in a two-week time period in Shirley alone. In the 1970s, however, eligibility requirements were relaxed for these low-cost FHA mortgages and they became available to marginally qualified buyers. Across the nation, the loan program began to implode as the federal government was forced to pay hundreds of millions of dollars for defaulted mortgages. The FHA suddenly owned tens of thousands of abandoned homes that it couldn't get off its hands fast enough.

Absentee landlords took advantage of the cheap deals, and more and more of Shirley slid into neglect. Schools were cobbled together, and in response to student overflow, expansions were made out of flimsy mobile units held off the ground by concrete blocks. Trees were torn down along the parkway to make room for strip malls so the townspeople could have places for food and sundries beyond the local Handy Pantry and bait-and-tackle shops. A makeshift business district formed along Neighborhood Road, including two pizza shops, a gas station, a tobacco and candy shop, and a bar. By the mid-1970s, the bungalow community had descended into a desolate blue-collar last alternative.

The families that began coming to Shirley were usually broke or unemployed, people who wanted a safe place to raise their children but couldn't afford to buy in other parts of Long Island—families like mine.

# CHAPTER FOUR

When looking at Long Island on a map, I've always seen an alligator. Most people refer to the island as being shaped like a fish—in school I learned that the Native Americans had in fact named the place Paumanok, or fish-shaped island—but the eastern end of the 118-mile strip gets muddled in that description. What kind of fish really has a tail that forks so dramatically that it could stand in for the thin slip of Montauk? To me, Long Island looks like an alligator facing away from the continent, his tail curled up alongside his body. He is yawning out into the Atlantic Ocean, Gardiner's Island dancing like a shrimp above his elongated lower jaw, mouth about to snap shut on its prey. Shirley is located at the spot where the upper and lower jawbones connect, just beneath his chin.

As the weeks turned into months and we became increasingly entrenched in our new home, I became more and more fascinated with Long Island. Because my father was at the

golf course most days, my parents bought a second car—
Jerry's brother's scrappy green Concord—so my mother
could run errands without relying on her husband's erratic
schedule. She took me on short drives, and I was soon able to
distinguish routes and roads, and where we were on different
road maps. I would trace the branching highway lines running along the middle of the island, calculating the miles between our town and New York City, which felt as far away as,
say, Kentucky, or even London. At the time, I could not have
cared less, anyway; I was content to spend my time outlining
our craggy little area on the Hagstrom maps my father pored
over at night for his new job, searching for back roads and alternate routes to get to his clients faster. I quickly learned to
identify Shirley by the way it sticks out of the island's south
shoreline like a bucked tooth, as if the rest of the island is
shying away from the town.

I always liked coming back to Shirley if my mother's errands took us away from the town, and I still do. Driving
along the Long Island Expressway back home, the commercial strips and parking lots and street lamps dotting the sides
of the highway fall away. The gully dividing the lines of traffic grows from a mere strip of concrete to a wide swath of
field where deer lazily feed, ignoring the cars whizzing past.
The pines are tall and scraggly, like teenage boys growing
too fast for their clothes to keep up, awkward skinny limbs
sprouting out at odd angles. There are signs along the highway in this area that announce these trees as part of the Pine
Barrens, one of the largest protected pine forests on the East
Coast. In the midst of these Pine Barrens is Exit 68, where the

name "Shirley" is stenciled across the dark green of a highway sign in white day-glo lettering. A second, smaller sign notes that Exit 68 is also the turnoff for the Brookhaven National Laboratory. This sounded very official, and because the laboratory was hidden under a thick cover of trees and I never saw it, the compound felt as far away as Manhattan, even though it shared an exit with Shirley.

In the summertime, my mother would get off at Exit 68 with about half of the other cars on the Long Island Expressway. We would travel with the pack southward down the William Floyd Parkway until we hit the sunburn-orange Roy Rogers and squat white church with giant black letters spelling out "Jesus is Lord" across the back of its building. Here, the majority of cars made a left turn, following signs for the Sunrise Highway, the road that would take them the rest of the way to the Hamptons at the eastern end of Long Island. For most people, the spot was simply a bypass or shortcut, an easy place to switch from one highway to another. Our small square Concord, however, would continue straight with the few cars that were left, and my mother and I would drive on into the heart of Shirley.

One afternoon, when I was standing in the road with the neighborhood girls after elementary school, Jerry's truck turned into his driveway earlier than usual. He got out of his blue pickup and walked over to the group with a wide grin, holding something behind his back. When he got closer, he produced a simple black plastic canister, the kind that a roll of film comes in. After a quick lesson about kidneys and the way they function, he told us about how one of his stopped working correctly, and how a spiny little creature grew in his organ. He had just returned from the doctor's, where they had removed the creature, he said, and now he was keeping it as a pet.

He uncapped the canister and dared us to hold out our hands to handle the thing. I don't remember which of us held her hand out first. Andrea was the bravest of our group, and Jerry's daughter Tina must have already known what was in the canister; regardless, I am certain my own hand was not thrust out first. Jerry gingerly shook the contents out onto the up-stretched palm as though spilling out grains of sea salt, and we saw that the creature wasn't really alive, just a prickly stone the size of a peanut. We passed it around the circle, from hand to hand. The kidney stone looked like the dainty bones inside an ear.

Jerry was as giddy as a kid who has just lost a tooth. After he retrieved his prize, we watched him cross the street toward his driveway, his long straight-backed stride as familiar as our own fathers' walks. He probably checked his mailbox and then disappeared up his walkway along the side of his shaker-shingled ranch. The girls and I stared in his direction even after his slim form ducked beyond our line of sight, our palms still tingling from the sharp teeth of the stone.

The school year sped by—I collected candy in my plastic pumpkin and dodged shaving cream and eggs with the girls

on Halloween; on Christmas Eve we made our rounds car-
oling for the neighbors, Santa hats on our heads; New Years
was spent in Joe's basement at his annual party—high on
sweets and with permission to stay up late, we hammed it
up with little Louie and Anthony, choreographing dances
to songs while the grownups sipped their drinks and
munched on Maria's delicious food. It felt like we were skat-
ing on the iced-over puddles on our uneven street one
minute and sitting on the gravel near the street corner in
tank tops and shorts, talking up Fourth of July again the
next.

My father's new job had picked up; he had made contacts
at so many of the golf courses and pro shops on the island
when he was on tour and searching for jobs that finding
clients had turned out to be the easy part. And he discovered that like his father, the former adman in New York, he
had a gift for the sell. He was still gone for a good portion of
the week, but with her own car and own friends, my
mother had an easier time than she had ever had before.

During that second summer, my parents and I took a trip
to the North Shore Animal League, where we looked for a
puppy. I had only been allowed to have fish before—a dog
needed structure and permanence, two things previously
missing in our lives. We picked out a shy little mutt with
silky black curls and a white belly. My father pounded a
stake into the lawn at the foot of the cement stoop out
front and taught me how to walk the dog and train her to
do her business outside. I named her Robin, because she reminded me of the bird, only in black and white.

The girls and I were planning a summer of canoe trips and fishing, dog walking, and creating a play. We'd already found a new fire trail to explore in the refuge and had a Marble notebook half-filled with ideas for the play when the phone call from our landlady came one afternoon.

"My daughter is going through a tough time. We need you to leave so that she can move in," Mrs. Kutch said into my mother's ear. Starting the following week, there would be workmen who needed access to fix up the house.

My parents were devastated. We had finally found a place where all three of us wanted to stay, and our boat was being tipped yet again. We had two months to find a new place to live.

Since we had moved to Shirley, interest rates had spiked. By the end of 1981, they had reached 20.31 percent. By 1983, when Mrs. Kutch delivered the bad news and my family started to look for a different house, much of Shirley had been boarded up. Families were unable to keep up with their mortgage payments, and all across town, pink eviction notices were being stapled to front doors. Parents and kids were forced to move in with relatives; entire living room and bedroom sets were sagging on front lawns, abandoned. Anyone who was renting was staying put, making rental properties like our house scarce or exorbitantly priced. The town's reputation was sinking even lower, and even I noticed how ravaged it had started to look.

It was in this atmosphere of skyrocketing interest rates and massive loan defaults that my parents needed to find a new house. There were hundreds in the area under foreclosure, and after a few meetings with Joe, our real estate broker next door, my parents decided to look into the foreclosure market.

Joe showed my parents dozens of houses. We toured different neighborhoods, but none had a wildlife refuge or Fourth of July block parties. The houses I favored were those with soap-opera details, like a spiral staircase or a Jacuzzi, but they were also usually riddled with termites or had some other major structural flaw. Each one was worse than the next—many needed new roofs, new plumbing, new kitchens, new walls. They were bad investments even at such low prices. Despite the bottomed-out real estate market, my parents were having trouble finding a place they could afford at all. They had, after all, sunk their entire savings into golf equipment. There was nothing left for a down payment.

Most of our neighbors in Shirley owned their own homes—more than half of them had come out to Long Island in the first wave of Italian immigrants in the 1960s when Walter T. ran radio announcements and newspaper ads in Italian that targeted recent immigrants who couldn't make ends meet in Brooklyn or Manhattan. Our neighbors asked around and kept an ear out for us, giving us leads on places they heard about in town. We were certain that we wanted to stay in Shirley, and my parents and I hoped that somehow we'd also be able to stay close to our little neighborhood. Although for most of my young life I had looked forward to our moves, and the new people and bedrooms and stories unique to each place, I suddenly couldn't imagine not living across the street from Jerry and Tina or next door to Joe and Maria and their boys. I didn't think I could the owner could be persuaded. The brown-and-white Cape Cod–style cottage was owned by absentee landlords who had endured a string of bad renters—a few years earlier an unhappy family had thrown bleach across the rugs, punched holes in the walls, and split the doors on the kitchen cabinets. After the landlords fixed the place up again, a girl I went to school with lived there with her mother and brother. The outside was usually a jumble of knee-high weeds, toys, and furniture.

Inside, however, the house showed promise. There were two bedrooms, and even a small room my father could use as an office, which he desperately needed as his business grew. There were two bathrooms, one upstairs and one down, a luxury that my family had never had before. And the backyard was huge by Shirley standards, with plenty of room for our dog, Robin, to run around. It was the most promising house we had seen so far, but when the owner proved willing to sell, my parents still found themselves without the money for a down payment. We were counting the days before we would become one of the families whose living room furniture ended up on the front lawn. My mother and I could always go to her parents' house in New Jersey, as we had in other times of trouble, but now we had a garage full of golf-equipment samples that my father's job depended on. We needed a house.

For the past few years, Jerry had been putting part of his paycheck from his work at the Brookhaven National Laboratory away, along with money he made from weekend jobs in the Hamptons, as part of his plan to leave the laboratory and start his own construction company. One night during a card game, Jerry suggested that he loan the money he had saved to my father. Jerry knew about the house around the corner that Joe had shown us, and he also knew that my family couldn't afford it yet. He wrote a check to my father for $10,000.

The loan wasn't open ended; Jerry charged my father 1 percent interest per month, which was a better return rate than if he had simply kept the money in the bank. My father used all of the money for the down payment. My new bedroom window faced the back of Jerry's house instead of the front. Staying in Shirley meant this would be the longest my parents had ever lived in one town since they were married, and the longest I ever kept any one group of friends, thanks to Jerry's generosity.

The entire neighborhood helped us move, driving our furniture around the block piece by piece in their pickup trucks and vans. I zoomed back and forth on my blue dirt bike along with the other girls, supervising and carrying small boxes when we could, picking up random items that fell out of the trucks as they bumped and rattled over the gravel road. My mother's spirits had quickly deflated the morning of the move when she saw the shape the family had left the house in. It looked as though they had gone out of their way to scratch and scuff the walls and rip light fixtures out of the ceilings, leaving jagged holes in the drywall. They hadn't even flushed the toilets.

Margaret's mother and Joe's wife—the same women who had welcomed us with rice balls and stories two years before, and who now let me wander in and out of their kitchens and homes, cooked me meals, and put Band-Aids on my scrapes if my mother wasn't nearby—showed up once again that morning, bearing bottles of bleach and mops instead of food. They stayed all day to help my mother clean our new home.

We concentrated on repairs and improvements first, like paint and light switches. The house was the first my parents had ever owned, and the first whose walls I could paint any color I wanted (seashell pink). By the second summer in our new house, my father began building a deck in the backyard with Jerry's help and widening the driveway to make room for the big diesel van my father's expanding job required. And with the help of two bonuses from big sales, my father slowly but steadily paid off Jerry's loan in one year. In turn, Jerry was finally able to quit his job at the Brookhaven National Laboratory and had started his own weather-stripping company. Everything was progressing as planned.

That September I entered second grade, and after the first few weeks, I realized with relief that moving around the block would not change too much in my life. I still stood at the same bus stop with Tina, Melissa, and Andrea in front of my old house, where we would spy through the chain-link fence on the inground pool, which had been promptly un-covered and filled with water when the landlady's daughter moved in. I started taking dance classes, taught by a local

mother in her basement, which was outfitted with a mir-
rored wall and ballet bar. Robin had healed and now had
the run of the new house, and it was my job to feed her
every morning and night. Third grade came and went, and
as the seasons changed, for the first time my stomach did
not cramp with the anticipation of moving.

My parents built their own routines. The second year at
the new house, my father pulled out the sloppy trail of
cracked and sunken red bricks that led up to the front door,
replacing them with wide slices of gray slate. My mother
painted the wooden shutters on the front of the house
Wedgwood blue, adding red wood cutouts in the shape of
hearts in the middle of each shutter. My father built a
matching wishing well out of plywood for the front lawn.
And at the end of the summer, my parents decided to replace the warped front screen door with a glass one.

This new door was my mother's main focus as Hurricane
Gloria made her way up the East Coast.

"Make it like a star, Kelly," my mother instructed. She
held the scissors out to me as I crouched on the stoop, yanking on the silver roll of duct tape. She was wearing a peach-
colored T-shirt knotted at the side and white canvas pants
rolled up mid-calf above her Keds. I had been unsuccessfully
trying to rip the tape with my teeth. The gummy strips kept
getting caught on my hands and hair, and on itself. But after
an hour, my mother and I had all the windows in the front
of the house crisscrossed with the silver tape, a human-sized
asterisk on the front glass door. If the glass broke in the

storm, the tape would hold the shards together for safe cleanup.

Mr. Manno, my fourth-grade teacher, handed out emergency supply lists that we were supposed to share with our families. It included safety instructions like staying in the basement during the storm. Our house had no basement, so the morning of the storm we followed Joe and Maria in our old station wagon and drove across town to Margaret's family's house, which had been built recently and had a good solid basement. Even though it had hardly started to rain, Margaret's mother, who was terrified of storms, was already in the basement by the time we arrived. Margaret and I held the front door open for Joe and my father, who maneuvered through with a stretcher they'd brought along, bearing Margaret's bedridden grandfather. They carried him into the living room, making him comfortable on the couch farthest from the window.

Outside, the blue sky changed to a smoky bruised purple. I watched as clouds tumbled beyond the living room windows in swift-moving plumes and streaks of ash and pink. The fierce wind made tree limbs and power lines flap, and when the electricity went out, I shrieked and giggled with the other kids in the house. The men smoked in the garage and played cards at the kitchen table, shadows of duct-tape crosses looming over the tablecloth. The women had already lit candles, and they retired to the hallway, away from the windows, listening to the radio above the wind. Reporters talked about overturned trucks and trees pulled from their roots and smashing into roofs. We kids spent the afternoon eating semolina cookies and alternating between our radio post and the basement, where Margaret's mother, Filomena, huddled, hands over her ears, curled and rocking in the corner.

The storm lasted most of the day, but in the early afternoon the wind quieted and the house stopped shuddering. We had read about the eye of the hurricane in homeroom: Even though it might look quiet and peaceful, the eye was actually just the storm holding its breath. Margaret and I were sitting in the hallway, gossiping and playing games, and when the wind quieted my mother waved me to the front door. She looked tired, her pale hair stuck loosely in a ponytail. She stood behind me, and as I looked out, the bright blue of the sky stung my eyes.

When I saw my father walking around the corner of the house to the driveway, my hands lunged for the doorknob. My mother dug her fingers into my shoulders and held me in place, explaining that he was just checking for damage and would be right in, but I pressed my nose to the glass between the strips of tape, knocking on the door and yelling for him to come back in before the storm started again. I knew how these things went. I had read about the dangers in school—one minute you are standing there in the false quiet and the next you are sucked up in the storm. My father walked to our car, halfway down the driveway, turning and waving once to me. Then he just stood there, looking up into the perfect sky, smiling. He had on a light blue plaid shirt, and when the rain started again and dampened his shoulders to black, he came back inside.

By the next morning, the storm had left, moving on up the coast and pushing out to sea, leaving the town under a heavy blanket of steamy mist. We returned home, relieved to see that the ocean had not climbed to our doorstep and no trees had crashed into our roof. Some of the other houses nearby hadn't fared as well, but the block had held up well compared to those even closer to the beach. Our glass door didn't even have a scratch.

The storm had badly damaged the county's electricity lines, and Shirley was left without power for ten days. At the time, the majority of families in town pulled water from their own private wells; but without electricity to power the water pumps, most of us had no fresh water. The list of necessary storm supplies they had given me at school had included bottled water, but we only had a few jugs, certainly not enough to tide us over for two weeks. Many families in town had to go to emergency shelters set up in school gymnasiums, or travel inland to relatives whose neighborhoods weren't hit as hard by the hurricane.

Once again, Jerry took charge. After Hurricane Gloria crashed into town, water was suddenly center stage. Signs sprouted up along the highway—big spray-painted slabs of plywood—that read, "Running Water Here" or "Feel Free to Use the Hose." Jerry had his own generator and was able to get his water pump working. His house was one of the only ones in the neighborhood with a gas stove, and it quickly became the hub of our two blocks. In the morning, the neighborhood adults lingered on his lawn and leaned up against his deck railing, waiting for the kettle to boil for their coffee. My mother trudged back over to heat a can of soup for lunch most days. But water was the object most people came searching for at Jerry's house.

Neighbors strung their garden hoses over backyard fences and bushes, different colored hoses connecting like links on a chain. We threaded the giant snake of hose from Jerry's front yard to our backyard, filling up anything that could hold water for drinking, flushing, and washing. Kids with everything from empty milk cartons to garden buckets lined up at the end of Jerry's driveway throughout the day. I had never really given much thought to how the water got to the tap in our kitchen sink before—it always just appeared. Sometimes it smelled like sulfur or tasted like tin, but most of the mothers just mixed it with orange juice concentrate or made iced tea.

As defrosting refrigerators and freezers were pillaged and grills fired up, the smell of storm and autumn was spiked with the mismatched summertime smell of barbecue. I was excited not to have to go to school and spent the days with the neighborhood girls, playing our usual games. Then I would go home for dinner—lots of peanut butter—while it was still light out, and my parents and I would read until the darkness strained our eyes, or I would go back outside to try to spot some bats with the circle. Everyone went to bed early those nights, and apart from having to lug a bottle of water and a candle into the bathroom if I had to go in the middle of the night, it was kind of fun.

The weeks after Hurricane Gloria felt like a holiday: Not only did school remain closed, but many of the parents stayed home from work. During this time, none of the parents talked about bills or asked us about grades, and the adults seemed softer, more inclined to touch and lean against one another, quicker to laugh. It was as if time had stopped, and our little section of the island had been forgotten, left out of the rules. In a way, these weeks were their own kind of eye in a storm—a maelstrom that few of us realized we would be swept up in.

A few months after Gloria, Jerry and his wife, Jackie, came over with a roll of blueprints. I always thought Jackie and Jerry looked like twins, brother and sister, with their chestnut hair and sharp movements. They spread out the blueprints on our kitchen table, one on either side of the roll, and showed us their dream house, which had a soaring cathedral ceiling and rustic details. My father had repaid the $10,000 loan, and Jerry's construction work was going well, so the couple had bought a piece of land down the block from us. Jerry would build most of the house with his own two hands, pulling in friends in construction to help with the parts he wasn't sure how to handle, which weren't many.

Jerry and my father talked about landscaping plans, and their daughter Tina and I tried to figure out if we would be able to shine flashlights into one another's bedrooms. We already had a set of walkie-talkies set up in our kitchens, but the new house would be even closer, and flashlight signals seemed more private. When the trees were cleared from the property, the neighborhood girls and I crisscrossed between the tree stumps on our bikes. After the foundation cement was poured, we dared one another to edge bravely over the concrete lip and look down into the black depth of the basement.

Jerry had most of the first floor framed out when he started to fall down. He would just be walking across a room or down his driveway and his legs suddenly would give way. Sometimes he wouldn't be able to get out of bed in the morning. He said that he felt frozen, and I imagined him like a Popsicle stick, hands stuck at his sides, legs rigid beneath the sheets, eyeballs open and unblinking. Some days, he was too tired to go to work, much less build anything.

Already a trim man, Jerry began losing weight rapidly. His jeans hung from his hips as if on pegs, and his skin, always so tanned and pliant, drew across his temples in waxy white stretches. He no longer looked like his wife's twin.

The doctors found tumors in his brain. My parents tried to explain to me what was happening to Jerry. They showed me pictures in books of the different parts of his body that were affected, tried to talk frankly about his chances. I imagined a chain of those spiny creatures daisy-chaining behind his eyes, hard little hands joined in a game of Red Robin. I didn't understand why the doctors couldn't carve the intruders out of him, the way they carved out his kidney stone. I thought about Jerry's ability to grow things deep within his body, and though my parents never lied about what he was facing, somehow I wasn't worried. I was convinced that even though Jerry was sick, he would get better. I knew that he was strong enough to push the tumors back out of him and cap them safely in a little black canister that he would then one day bring to the bat circle. And I swore that I would be the first one of the group to open my hand and accept the small shriveled creatures onto my outstretched palm.

Of course, I was wrong.

PART TWO

# RIDING THE WAVES

❖

*The headwinds were holding us in place in space.*
*We were flying, but not moving, visibility forever.*
*The ocean was down there waving.*

—Frederick Seidel,
"East Hampton Airport," *Ooga-Booga: Poems*

# CHAPTER FIVE

A report on community relations prepared in September 1991 for the Brookhaven National Laboratory by ICF Kaiser Engineers notes that "a number of BNL employees felt that the Lab administration needs to increase the attention it gives to employee health and safety." The report says that the employees were particularly concerned with low-level radiation exposure, resulting both from their direct work at the lab and simply from working on the Brookhaven National Laboratory property.

On a page discussing contaminated groundwater and public concern over long-term effects of exposure to past leaks at the lab of trichloroethylene, tritium, and radiation in general, the report says: "BNL employees concerned over work-related exposure related that, when they questioned the risks of certain activities, they were told by their supervisors that 'a little radiation won't hurt you.'"

❁

Jackie and my father took turns driving Jerry to chemotherapy. They would help him to the car, a young man turned old, his gait unrecognizable. His favorite shirt—red, with a bubblegum machine on the chest—swallowed his frame, billowing out like a sail on a boat. Hours later, the car would pull back into the driveway. We would stop our games on the street corner and watch as my father draped Jerry's arm over his shoulder and guided him up the steps of the deck Jerry had built with his own hands, into the cool darkness of his home. My father is not a big man—the muscles in his arms and legs are long instead of bulky, and he has the shape of a runner rather than a bodybuilder—but he made Jerry look like a child on those afternoons.

I don't remember what we talked about when Tina, Jenny, and I sat quietly in their living room, playing there instead of in the basement or Tina's room. Jerry would fall asleep, or chew ice cubes, or try to join in on a game. The winter was cold and quiet; no one ever banged the screen door at Jerry's house or rang the doorbell after dinner. As spring light started to peek through the blinds of the living room, however, there was a hopeful turn; the tumors in his brain were shrinking.

The neighborhood seemed to exhale in unison. We screamed louder during our games of softball on the corner, laughed more easily. My father was relieved, hopeful that his friend's suffering would be over soon. My mother was more wary.

"He still has a long way to go," she cautioned. But my father and I just figured we knew Jerry better than she did. Everyone in the neighborhood wanted to believe that he was almost through. The women kept cooking, taking turns every week dropping off food or plates of cookies to help take some pressure off Jackie. Everyone looked forward to the time when Jerry would be back on his feet, and with summer and the Fourth of July getting closer, there seemed to be an unspoken deadline for his recovery.

But the day Jackie and Jerry returned from what was supposed to be an appointment to discuss the next steps of his recovery, my parents sensed something was not right as soon as the car pulled into the driveway across the street. Over coffee in their kitchen later that day, Jackie explained that the doctor had deceived them. They had sat in their chairs, across from the oncologist, and heard him begin talking about the next round of treatment. When they said they didn't understand, that they thought Jerry was cured, the doctor clarified.

"I'm not talking about the tumors in your brain," he said. "I am talking about the tumors in your lungs."

The brain cancer was in remission but had metastasized into his lungs through a complicated rope-ladder of knotty lymph nodes. There were tumors along the ridges of his spine. It is unclear whether the doctor knew about these other tumors before Jerry started his first round of chemotherapy for the cancer in his brain and kept the news secret in case his patient might not choose treatment if he knew the extent of his illness, or whether they simply never checked for more tumors. Jerry only found out about the other cancer the day he thought he was cured.

Jerry's house was quiet for a time after that appointment. I didn't go over to visit, and Tina and her sister stayed inside. My father still made his daily trips across the street, and I eavesdropped from the hallway on his late-night conversations with my mother at the dinner table. Since Jerry had left his job at the Brookhaven National Laboratory, his benefits were basic at best. And with Jerry too sick to work any of his construction jobs for months now, the family had hardly any money to pay the hospital bills. The thought of more bills for an endless course of chemotherapy was daunting.

The next day in school, I asked my fourth-grade homeroom teacher if I could speak with him after class. I explained that my best friend Jerry had cancer, and that his family was having difficulty paying the hospital bills. I asked for permission to collect some money in class for him, and the teacher said if I brought in a jar and talked to the class about my friend that it would be fine.

I found an old coffee can in the garage that night and pasted a piece of loose-leaf paper I had decorated with drawings of Jerry and me across its rippled side. The next day in class, as my teacher promised, I talked for a few minutes about my friend Jerry and passed the coffee can around. We had about two dozen kids in class, and they filled the can with their loose change and weathered dollar bills. I left the can on my teacher's desk for a week, and then I took the coffee can home and handed it over to my parents, proud of my contribution. They helped me roll the coins after dinner and promised to give the money to Jerry.

The next day, my teacher called me up to his desk. He told me that he had spoken with my mother, who explained that my best friend with cancer was a forty-two-year-old man, not a child like me. And while he understood how difficult this was for me, I couldn't ask for any more money from the class.

Jerry and his family decided to continue treatment at all costs. As he grew sicker and the drugs that the doctors gave him to ease his pain became less and less effective, my father focused on alternative therapies. The men spent hours working on meditation and visualization. They breathed in unison, deep breaths in and out, counting backward and forward, imagining a cloud of relaxation moving up their bodies from their feet to their skulls. My father took books and tapes out of the library, learning how to lead Jerry to an imagined beach or field of flowers. His dream house sat unfinished and already overgrown around the corner as my father coaxed Jerry deeper and deeper into various types of trances.

A few times, in the middle of their sessions, Jerry talked about how he thought he got cancer. He had smoked, of course. But he was so young, and in these quiet moments, he confessed to my father that he suspected it was the work he did at the laboratory that had made him sick. He handled waste materials and had worried about some of the situations he had put himself in. He may have been the last one on the block to verbalize this idea—from what I could tell, the rest of the neighborhood already assumed the same. Everyone knew that Jerry's favorite joke was that he could glow in the dark. No one made that joke any more.

While I was growing up, the Brookhaven National Laboratory was a fixture of my imagination, as it was for the other kids in the neighborhood. Much like the proverbial monster in the basement, the lab obsessed us precisely because it was so close, and yet we had no access—we couldn't see the buildings or the scientists who populated them. The majority of the scientists lived on the north shore, or west of the laboratory—not in Shirley. The neighborhood fathers, like Jerry and Andrew, who spent their days there refused to talk much about what their jobs actually entailed, or what kind of work went on at the lab. Years later, I realized that this was not the result of some secrecy pledge they swore to on their first day of work but more likely because they didn't actually know what was going on in those clandestine reactor buildings any more than we did. They were support staff, not scientists. Andrew had gone to pharmacy school and worked in the computer support department, whereas Jerry, like most of our parents, had never gone to college at all and probably didn't remember the mechanics of fission from his high school physics lessons.

Lacking any real knowledge, we created our own version of the Brookhaven Laboratory. In my mind, the lab's buildings were made of a transparent igloo-like substance, and the rooms inside were full of metallic file cabinets, clinking glass test tubes, and notebooks full of secret codes. Men and women in crisp white lab coats and plastic goggles coaxed new species of frogs and lizards out of mottled purple eggs. Others hovered over milky glass globes of light, whose kinked antennae sparked blue shots of electricity into the dim, silent air. And the lab-coated scientists ate crayon-colored pills for lunch that tasted like chicken cutlets and chocolate cake. After Jerry's cancer, my imaginary lab became a much darker place, a small, sinister pocket hiding in the pines.

None of our parents ever discussed evacuation plans or the possibility of a nuclear meltdown so close to home. I'm not sure that our parents understood that there were nuclear experiments going on there. At the time, most people in the area were more concerned about another atomic threat: the Shoreham Nuclear Power Plant. Shoreham was located just north of the Brookhaven National Laboratory but did not share in the luck of having the natural barrier of the pine forest covering its progress. Shoreham had been a blueprint since the 1960s, when it became clear that Long Island's population boom was not going to slow down. Owned by the Long Island Lighting Company (LILCO), Shoreham received its license to build in 1973, and construction of the plant was soon underway. Many of the workers wound up buying houses in the Shirley area, knowing that the project's term would be a long one. However, within days of the Three Mile Island meltdown in March 1979, anti-nuclear activists were perched at the Shoreham site with protest signs. The integrity of Shoreham's design, particularly the outer shell—the plant's last defense against a serious loss-of-coolant accident, like the one at Three Mile Island—was questioned, and plant construction was plagued by mishaps and mistakes. One afternoon, my mother took me for a drive up William Floyd Parkway to see how close the nuclear power plant really was. It was unsettling how short the ten mile drive was. I remember my mother talking about Shoreham and shaking her head, saying it was put together with bubblegum.

Despite the protests, construction continued, and the Shoreham Nuclear Power Plant was declared finished in January 1984. LILCO and Suffolk County fought bitterly over evacuation plans for the island, which stalled the plant's opening. When Hurricane Gloria hit in 1985, the preposterousness of evacuating the island in any quick and organized way became clear; with only two major highways running east-west, the roadways would be impassable, and anyone caught to the east of the power plant would need a boat to escape. This reality hit Long Islanders hard, and a poll in *Newsday,* Long Island's main newspaper, that was taken a month after the hurricane showed that seven out of ten locals thought that Shoreham should not be opened. Less than a year later, as the County and LILCO continued to argue over evacuation plans, a fire and explosion at the Chernobyl Nuclear Power Plant in Ukraine released radiation into the environment. Although it has been calculated that 60 percent of the radioactive fallout landed in Belarus, a radioactive plume made its way west over parts of the Soviet Union, Europe, and eastern North America. Protesters printed new signs, with images of the ghost towns the accident left behind and bodies ravaged by radiation. Shoreham never opened, not even for a day.

Although it was clear to the public and Suffolk County by 1986 that the middle of Long Island was not an acceptable place for radioactive piles of nuclear material, this was not as obvious in 1947, when the U.S. Atomic Energy Commission chose to place the Brookhaven National Laboratory in the very same spot. Today, the Brookhaven Lab is balanced above Shirley like a boulder on a precipice. But it was never meant to be that way.

Originally, the national laboratory—the first to be founded for peaceful purposes—was meant to be built far from any heavily populated areas. The new laboratory's counterparts—both the Argonne National Laboratory in Chicago, Illinois, and Oak Ridge National Laboratory in Tennessee—were created during World War II to supplement the Manhattan Project in its quest to develop the atomic bomb. After the war ended in 1945, the Manhattan District of the Army Corps of Engineers, which ran the wartime A-bomb project, converted the Argonne and Oak Ridge labs into peaceful laboratories. By 1946, they were looking to build a new nuclear laboratory in the Northeast that would be near enough to the major universities to service them, but far enough away from any centers of population for safety, because of the danger posed by the nature of the atomic work expected to be conducted there.

Representatives from nine private universities in the Northeast—Columbia, Cornell, Harvard, Johns Hopkins, the Massachusetts Institute of Technology, the University of Pennsylvania, Princeton, the University of Rochester, and Yale—formed a group called Associated Universities, Inc. (AUI) in 1946 and began their campaign for bringing nuclear science to the Northeast. The Subcommittee on Site was led by Norman F. Ramsey, an associate professor of physics at Columbia University, and the group took three months to investigate the possible choices for location.

Proximity to a major university was the main require-ment when choosing the original pool of seventeen possible sites—Lake Zoar on the Housatonic River was a thirty-minute drive from Yale; Rocky Hill, New Jersey, was ten minutes from Princeton; and Fort Devens in Ayer, Massa-chusetts, was sixty minutes from Harvard. Of all the sites presented, the Long Island location was the farthest from a university, logging a bumpy 100-minute commute across a web of slow, local roads from Columbia University in New York City.

The Long Island site was the former Camp Upton, the very same camp that had originally brought Walter T. Shirley out to the island from his Brooklyn home during World War I, the same spot that lodged in Walter T.'s brain and reemerged like a sandbar in the tide, again and again, until he returned years later and started his namesake town. While the Manhattan Project was deliberating over the location of their new laboratory, however, Walter T. had yet to break ground.

On May 3, 1946, a subcommittee consisting of representa-tives from the universities chose Fort Slocum on David's Island as the place to build the national laboratory. David's Island is a mile offshore New Rochelle, New York, and this isolation was one of the main factors leading to the subcommittee's choice: Should the reactor have an accident, the island's seclusion seemed to offer built-in protection. However, the Manhattan District of the Army Corps of Engineers rejected the location after deeper investigation, concluding that "the greatest evil of the site appears to be its closeness to the mainland." There were also too many people living downwind of David's Island, namely those populating another island—Manhattan.

The subcommittee presented site after site for consideration by the Manhattan District of the Army Corps of Engineers from the list of seventeen, only to discover that each was unavailable or unattractive for one reason or another. Camp Shanks in Rockland County, New York, was slated to become a housing project; the military wanted to keep Massachusetts' Fort Devens running as an active base; and only a handful of buildings were available at the Fort Hancock site in Sandy Hook, New Jersey. As the subcommittee exhausted the list, it was soon left with only a single possibility: Camp Upton.

In a January 1948 document titled "The Founding of the Brookhaven National Laboratory," the selection process and requirements for the site are outlined in detail. Although there was a necessity to locate the laboratory so that visiting scientists could travel during the evening, spend one day at the laboratory, and be back at their own university the next, the report notes that "the far more compelling requirement that the nuclear reactors and electro-nuclear machines be adequately removed from concentrations of population was recognized increasingly as the site problem received study." Other requirements included the ready disposal of radioactive waste, the availability of adequate quantities of cooling water for the reactors, and the distribution of tainted gases from the stack of an air-cooled reactor. Colonel G. W. Beeler of the Manhattan District also spoke for the government in the requirement that the site be "five to ten miles from any populous area" and that the "drainage of the site must not seep into sources of drinking water because of the possibility of the concentration of radioactive waste."

Associated Universities, Inc. reflected in its founding document that although the final selection of Camp Upton was a compromise, it was a happy one, because it was understood that satisfying all of the requirements would be impossible. "It is near New York City, just beyond commuting range, yet the immediately surrounding territory is very thinly populated, with less than 100 people living within a three-mile radius and approximately only 17,000 within a ten-mile radius."

The barrenness of the site was keenly felt when the first scientists visited Camp Upton and were surprised at how much it resembled a classic ghost town. A droning ring of pine trees surrounded pools of mud, tattered and deserted canvas tents, and tangles of barbed wire from a stockade built to house prisoners of war. When the army camp closed, all of the supplies and most of the salvageable buildings had been auctioned off cheaply; some bidders even won whole houses, taking them apart and moving them to Queens. The buildings that were left behind were worn and weathered.

As the subcommittee members surveyed the surrounding area, they realized that the humble fishing villages and green wilderness that bounded the 5,300-acre retired military base—the very attributes that had captured Walter T.'s imagination—would be no help in wooing scientists to the area, whom the subcommittee imagined would want posh amenities with decent shopping and good restaurants. They decided instead to focus on those natural attributes that had so captivated Walter T. and chose to name the area Brookhaven. They thought the bucolic tone and suggestion of babbling brooks and pastoral idylls might appeal to the wives of scientists considering placement at the lab. In a way, it was the subcommittee's version of Walter T.'s idealistic "Town of Flowers" slogan for Shirley.

On his forty-third birthday, Jerry sat in a plastic chair at the end of his driveway. The chemotherapy didn't seem to be affecting the other tumors, and the cancer in his brain had returned. Jerry did his best to enjoy the July Fourth holiday and block party, but he had to return exhausted to his house before the customary cutting of his cake. The large sheet of vanilla and fudge sat on the rickety card table for most of the night.

That summer was charged with a feeling of inevitability. I had never known anyone who died, but by then, I had the feeling that I couldn't stop whatever it was that was coming. My parents had given me a small basket of capsule-sized Mexican trouble dolls. The directions said that you were supposed to whisper your troubles to the tiny figures or put a request into the little basket with their bodies and then hide the basket. I typed my messages and tore them off into bite-sized pieces. "Make Jerry better." I would refresh the request every few days with a new piece of paper. "Please help Jerry." If Jerry's own magic was failing him, I thought perhaps a different kind might work. But by the end of the summer, both my father and I had accepted what my mother already knew; we couldn't stop what was on its way.

The first nuclear reactor eventually built on the Camp Upton site was called the Brookhaven Graphite Research Reactor. During the years the reactor was constructed, between 1947 and 1950, the country's nuclear program was still top secret, shrouded in Cold War concealment. Built for research rather than to produce power, the BGRR was the first of its kind to be constructed for peaceful purposes: The scientists applying for opportunities to use the reactor would be conducting experiments designed to further science rather than simply bulking up the national atomic weaponry cache. Of course, from its earliest days, the reactor supplemented defense experiments conducted at other locations across the country: In 1996, the Brookhaven National Laboratory spent $23 million on defense-related work—and still does. Most research focuses on arms control and weapons disposal and is not classified, but a portion of the research is classified, or generates classified reports relating to national security and nuclear materials safeguarding.

A thirty-foot steel partition walled off the reactor's western face, preserving access for only those scientists who had been cleared by the federal government for experiments relating to national security and defense. In 1955, two years after President Eisenhower's 1953 Atoms for Peace speech, in which the identity and work of many of the country's atomic labs and experiments were revealed for the first time, the Brookhaven National Laboratory was officially declassified. To reflect this new era of openness, the thirty-foot steel partition was ceremoniously propped open. For the general public, however, little changed, and the compound remained clandestine and off-limits. Hardly any information about the nature of the lab's work or the machines housed there ever passed beyond the military-style gates.

By the time the first houses in Shirley were finished in the 1950s, their curtains hung and trim painted, the lab's first nuclear reactor was already humming away behind the tall barricade of pine tops.

But it was not until the early 1980s, during the much-publicized fight over the Shoreham Nuclear Power Plant, that discussion of the dangers of nuclear power on Long Island inevitably turned toward the Brookhaven Laboratory. By that time the facility had been operating nuclear reactors for almost forty years.

The Brookhaven Graphite Research Reactor only lasted about a decade. In 1960, nuclear waste from the reactor was accidentally pumped into a drinking-water well instead of the fill pipe of an underground holding tank. During some experiments to produce neutrons, the reactor also leaked radioactive slurry into the soil and groundwater. The reactor, aging and unreliable, was shut down in 1968. Leftover radioactive material from the Brookhaven Graphite Research Reactor was sealed in the boxy building. Seventy layers of contaminated graphite blocks are contained in a cube measuring twenty-five feet on each side. It would take 300,000 years for the radioactive material to reach levels safe enough for human interaction. That's longer than Long Island itself has even existed.

In 1960, meanwhile, Shirley was the fastest-growing community in Suffolk County. The town was exploding—Walter T.'s bridge to the beach was completed, and while the Brookhaven Graphite Research Reactor was shutting down, masses of Italian immigrants from the city, coaxed by the ads in Italian newspapers and broadcast over Italian radio shows, were flooding into town, so that the year-round population of Shirley more than doubled in the short span of ten years.

The Brookhaven project could have been stopped. The Atomic Energy Commission and the scientists themselves could have taken a look around and realized they were no longer on their own in the middle of the wilderness. A few hundred feet beyond the military-style gates of the 5,000-acre compound, newly arrived families were raking leaves, washing cars, tending vegetable gardens. Once the Brookhaven

Graphite Research Reactor had cracked open and leaked, and once the reactor had been decommissioned, the program officials could have looked back at their founding documents and reminded themselves that they were originally intended to operate ten miles away from any populous area. They could have packed up, or they could have recognized that the homes and neighborhoods sprouting up around their compound were too close to chance the radioactive nature of the work they were conducting and continued with only the non-nuclear experiments. But none of this happened.

Instead, the High Flux Beam Reactor came online in 1965. Unlike the boxy design of the Brookhaven Graphite Research Reactor, the High Flux Beam Reactor was housed in a large dome, smooth and concave like a forehead. The new reactor was built right next to the old one, and their slender, red-and-white-striped chimney stacks pointed into the air like twin fingers.

The High Flux Beam Reactor was supposed to restore the Brookhaven National Laboratory to the first tier of research facilities in the world, but it did not. Around the time my family moved to Shirley in 1981, the Brookhaven Laboratory undertook an initiative called Project Isabelle. Isabelle, yet another nuclear facility, would include a colliding beam accelerator that once more held the promise of making Brookhaven a player in the international realm of nuclear science again.

To make way for Project Isabelle's proposed 2.4-mile ring, the Brookhaven Laboratory bulldozed 200 acres of previously protected wetlands at the headwaters of the Peconic River in the 1970s. Tritium-tainted water, a radioactive byproduct of nuclear experiments, had been released into the river for decades, but these 200 acres had provided a protective barrier because they had filtered some of the waste. By 1979, fish and shellfish taken from the river were registering higher than normal levels of radiation in their bodies. In 1983, the Project Isabelle initiative was canceled after technical problems were discovered with the giant magnets necessary to make the device work. The massive, empty ring that had been burrowed into the middle of the Pine Barrens was so enormous that it was visible from space.

The Peconic River flows east into Flanders Bay, which is the body of water between the island's north and south forks (or between the jaws of the alligator). The headwaters of the Peconic River are located in the northern portion of the Brookhaven National Laboratory site in the vicinity of the sewage treatment plant. Two other rivers originate within the aquifer beneath the Long Island Pine Barrens; the Forge River, which is Shirley's eastern boundary, and the Carmans River, which is its western boundary and flows through the wildlife refuge that bordered my neighborhood. Both rivers discharge into the Great South Bay, on the edge of the Atlantic Ocean.

Along with these rivers, the Pine Barrens is also home to a recharge basin that serves Long Island's sole source aquifer. This aquifer supplies more than 3 million people with drinking water. The Brookhaven National Laboratory, with its Graphite Reactor, High Flux Beam Reactor, and failed Project Isabelle experiment, was sitting in the middle of the Pine Barrens, right on top of this drinking-water aquifer.

All of our nature walks in the wildlife refuge crossed the Carmans River. First with my father and Jerry, and then by ourselves, the girls and I would pull our Keds or jelly sandals off, sink our feet into the muddy banks, and cup our small hands as if in prayer to bring the cool water to our mouths. Sometimes we searched for frogs or box turtles while walking along the lip of the river, or we might just dangle our feet into the soft current from one of the concrete overpasses that dotted the river. All three of the waterways originating from the Brookhaven National Laboratory had canoe trails. When we used them, we tried not to tip into the murky water, with its slimy weeds and grasses reaching up to the surface from the dark depths, but usually we did. My father once lost his car keys in the Forge River.

The boys usually went clamming. They would stand at the edge of the riverbed or the bay, jeans rolled up to their knees and their feet buried in the silty muck, dragging their clam rakes. And the men loved to pack up before anyone else was awake and get into the water to fish for flounder. Jerry had a small aluminum boat, and he'd wake Tina up early on some mornings so she could bail the water out of his old boat while he fished. When the men returned home, slippery and tired, the wives would watch them gut the fish on newspapers in the driveway. Rolled lightly in flour and cooked until brown, these flounder were delicious, a summer staple of the neighborhood.

The first time I went fishing for flounder on the Great South Bay, I pulled in the first fish of the day and won a dollar from Jerry. I had been nervous and timid that morning, and it was cold when we launched the boats into the barely breaking sunrise. Years later, I tried to figure out how Jerry had orchestrated it so that I would catch the first fish. He must have known that it was the only way I would give in to the experience and relax, yet I can't imagine how he was able to make that fish jump onto my sparkling lure. He used to pretend to speak "fish." Now I wonder if he really could.

Many of the anti-Shoreham Nuclear Power Plant activists who had been focused on keeping nuclear energy off the island were shocked to discover that Long Island had been no stranger to nuclear reactors for more than forty years. The Brookhaven National Laboratory did not advertise its nuclear capabilities; instead, it made the local newspapers for awards, like the multiple Nobel Prizes in physics that had been won by scientists conducting experiments there. But as these experiments were performed, changing the way we look at the universe, another layer of atomic and nuclear research was impacting the surrounding communities.

Along with the awards, forty years of nuclear research resulted in quantities of radioactive and hazardous waste. A good portion of the waste was produced and dispersed according to environmental restrictions that were looser than they are today. The waste was disposed of by people like Jerry, who packed up or moved the refuse, readied it for shipment out of New York via trains or trucks, or buried it on the Brookhaven Laboratory property. Those less stringent waste-management policies resulted in releases to the environment, and spills and accidents released even more. Radioactive water and chemicals entered the soil, surface water, and groundwater. The only problem was, no one outside the compound's gates knew about it.

A few months before Hurricane Gloria, the Brookhaven Laboratory's sewage treatment plant released a higher than usual amount of tritium into what the community relations document calls "an on-site hold-up pond." I can only imagine what that must have looked like. A swampy green bog? A pool of clear, steaming water that looked as inviting as a hot tub? Regardless, some of the Brookhaven scientists expressed concern that this extra-high dose of radioactive waste might have moved into the groundwater. They feared that it might also be moving with that groundwater in the direction of some off-site residential wells.

Groundwater generally flows across the island either north or south, and the dividing line slices across the island in a thin spine; all groundwater to the north of this line runs toward the Long Island Sound. To the south, it drains into the Atlantic Ocean. This dividing line runs parallel to the North Shore, so most groundwater—including all that originates from the Brookhaven National Laboratory, since it lies south of this boundary—runs south. The majority of groundwater from the Brookhaven National Laboratory runs directly into Shirley and the neighboring town, Manorville.

The Suffolk County Department of Health Services was aware of the groundwater drainage patterns, so when it heard about the tritium dump, the agency began sampling the water from homes near the Brookhaven Laboratory. This sampling, of course, raised suspicion: No one in town had heard about any tritium release, and there had been no warning about the sampling.

The County found that tritium was present in some of the wells tested. Tritium is used in common objects today, such as exit signs, but it is also a nuclear material used in the fission process. Additionally, tritium is produced during nuclear weapons explosions. It has a half-life of 12.3 years, which is often held up as evidence proving its relative safety in the realm of radioactive substances. But, when one thinks about the true definition of a half-life—according to the EPA, the time required for half of the atoms of a radioactive element to undergo self-transmutation or decay—it is clear that while at first glance a shorter half-life may seem safer, this collapsed time span actually means that the substance is extremely radioactive since it is emitting its stored radiation at a rapid rate. And, of course, a quantity of tritium—like anything with a half-life—will exist infinitely as it halves itself again and again and again.

Although the tritium in the drinking water wells was found to be below public health and safety standards, tritium found in groundwater samples collected from off-site monitoring wells was measured at levels exceeding allowable concentrations. The presence of radioactive waste in the drinking water of these homes prompted periodic sampling and water testing from monitoring wells in the area. Today, an estimated 15,400 people obtain their drinking water from municipal and private wells that are within three miles of the Brookhaven National Laboratory.

In response to community concern, Suffolk County legislator Gregory Blass created a legislative task force. A six-person team, including Legislator Blass, his assistant, a nearby landowner, a representative from Group for the South Fork, and two researchers from the Stony Brook branch of the State University of New York's Marine Science Research Center, investigated the Brookhaven Laboratory's environmental problems and practices. In November 1986, they released a preliminary report. In it, the task force characterized the lab's waste disposal practices as examples of "careless neglect."

Two months earlier, in September 1986, Jackie put in an order for a hospital bed for Jerry. Regardless of how many pillows or layers of blankets his family stuffed beneath his withered frame, the couch had become incredibly uncomfortable for him. His fragile skin opened up too easily, and he bruised at the slightest touch. His bed would have been much more restful, but Jerry refused to move from the den. He wanted to be near his family, not shuttered away.

Jackie and my father were driving Jerry back and forth to the hospital a few times a week. Each time, the doctors would give him some drug or IV, last-ditch attempts to push the cancer out or quell his pain. And each time, the new drug or therapy failed, and they sent him home. But he refused to give up and was determined to fight until the end.

The hospital bed finally arrived. By the time it did, though, it wasn't much help. Within days, Jackie called an ambulance because she couldn't get Jerry into the car on her own. When the doctors told her they thought he only had a few hours to live, she called the neighborhood families. They left work and went to the hospital. It was a school day, and Joe arranged for old Uncle Lou to meet us all at the bus stop and keep us at Joe's until all of the parents came home. Margaret's older brother Sal was sent to pick up Tina's older sister from college.

We knew as soon as we saw Lou. He shuffled behind us, speaking Italian, trying to herd us all inside. Marie had left snacks out for us, and we took turns crying. Anthony, Joe's youngest son, let me borrow a rosary so I could join in, and I rolled the plastic beads between my fingers as he whispered the unfamiliar prayers.

The streetlights were just clicking on when I saw my mother's car pull into Jerry's driveway across the street. If it had been a month or so earlier, we would have been congregating on the street corner to count bats, remembering how Jerry used to come to our circle. Without speaking to the other kids, I pushed open the screen door and bolted from the house toward Jerry's, leaving one of my shoes on Joe's lawn.

Walking into the house, I thought for a moment that maybe I had been wrong; Jackie and my mother were sitting at the table, like always, coffee brewing, cups waiting by their hands. But the lights weren't on, and neither woman looked at me. I started to cry, and my mother held open her arms so that I could sit on her lap. The women continued to sit in silence, staring into the bottoms of their empty cups.

When Jackie had made her calls that morning, she had asked my father to pick Tina up at school before coming to the hospital. Although he drove as fast as he could, by the time he got her to the hospital, her father was already dead.

# CHAPTER SIX

We followed the paths between the crusty clefts of the bulldozer tracks, the icy latticework breaking through to slush and crunching beneath our feet with satisfying cracks. Each of us had a garbage pail lid, and we held them across our chests like shields. We made an army of six—four girls and two boys, now that Joe's sons Louie and Anthony were old enough to join our group—as we pushed on in single file.

Ahead of us, through the faint scrim of softly falling snow, the neighborhood fathers walked together in their work boots and jeans. Heads down, ungloved hands stuffed into their pockets, the men talked and nodded, and one or another would turn every so often to make sure we were still behind them.

"Come on, you slowpokes!" The men were smiling, relaxed on a morning when work was far from their minds. "The snow is gonna melt before we get to the sump!"

I stared at the backs of our fathers, straight and tall in a row, and I missed Jerry's form. It was our first year sledding without him. We had buried him in a quiet country cemetery in a small fishing village nearby a few months earlier. He had set it up so that we all went to his favorite fish restaurant afterward. I spent the morning of his funeral reading pamphlets made for children—one of them was "What Death Means"—flipping through mediocre illustrations and not finding the answers I needed.

I imagined Jerry walking next to the other fathers, in his tan canvas jacket and baseball cap, listening and laughing along with them. His daughters, Tina and Jenny, weren't with us either—after their father's death, the girls were kept close to home by their mother. I missed them all. The falling snow muffled the sounds in the forest, and our banter and cries felt sharp against the quiet of the trees.

After Jerry's death, an arctic gloom had settled on our neighborhood. Everything looked the same—Jerry's house was still on the corner, his beat-up blue pickup truck was still parked in the driveway—but it felt different, like a copy of a photograph instead of the actual thing. As we made our way into the wildlife refuge to go sledding at the sump, we all felt the change.

There had been construction going on behind our homes on the edge of the wildlife refuge over the past few months. Bulldozers had been pushing over trees and tearing out roots, smoothing wide paths that we explored each weekend when the giant mustard-yellow machines were silent, like dinosaurs frozen in time. But on that January day, we were surprised to find a seven-foot chain-link fence blocking access to the snowy sump. The large drainage ditch that we had been using as our own private bunny hill for the past few years was officially off-limits. One father short, our disheveled band of marshmallow-jacketed kids and confused fathers stood in a line, staring balefully through the fence. Grime we had kicked up from the melted slush beneath the thick coat of ice in the bulldozer tracks stained our ankles and calves.

Not knowing what else to do, we retreated home and packed into a few cars, caravanning to the on-ramp of the Long Island Expressway. A line of vehicles crowded the shoulder, and as we got closer, I recognized some other kids from school. Along the slope where the on-ramp swept down from the overpass to the expressway, an impromptu sledding trail had emerged, as it did every time it snowed more than an inch. A dozen men stood along the bottom edge of the slope, like a row of bowling pins. Usually, the kids' sleds bottomed out in the drainage gully a few feet from the cars whizzing by on the slick blacktop of the expressway, but the line of men acted as a safety net, catching any wayward sledders and out-of-control garbage-pail tops with their knees before they had a chance to slide out into the traffic. Since it was one of the only spots in town that bore any resemblance to a hill, the on-ramp was very popular, and by the afternoon most of the snow had melted into a mud-streaked mess.

After that year, we stopped sledding. Sliding down the hill with the other kids was okay, but we had lost access to our special spot, and sledding had in turn lost some of its appeal. When spring melted the snow, we tried to continue our nature walks, but soon a much larger chain-link fence appeared, encircling what seemed like acres of land that had been our prime hiking territory. Skeletons of giant houses rose from the dirt, and driveway paving got underway. A sign also went up along the William Floyd Parkway, a slab of plywood painted in subdued creams and ecrus with shadowy images of deer and quail. The letters spelled out "Woodlands," advertising a new development of luxury homes.

The talk started slowly at first, peppering our fathers' poker games and popping up during coffee and Entenmann's crumb cake and donuts in the Grace Lutheran church narthex when we attended on Sundays.

"I heard the new name is going to be Brookhampton," said a woman with a blonde bob and powdered sugar stuck to the corner of her mouth. I was hanging on my mother's elbow, letting her know I was finished with Sunday school and ready to go home.

A woman with purple eye shadow interrupted the blonde. "No," she said, shaking her head. "Not Brookhampton. That would just make people think about the Brookhaven Lab. No, I heard it's gonna be *New* Hampton. 'Cause we're the newest one, get it?" She stirred the drink in her Styrofoam cup with a long lacquered fingernail that matched her eye shadow, the tea-bag string catching around her knuckle.

Yanking my seat belt across my bony ribcage in the parking lot, I asked my mother what the women were talking about.

"Some people want to change the name of our town," she said, edging our sputtering Concord out onto the road. She sighed as we pulled to a stop at a crossroads. We both looked over to our right at a boarded-up house decorated with swooping black-and-red graffiti tags. It had been that way since we moved to Shirley six years before, and I had nearly stopped seeing the little house with the overgrown lawn and cracked stoop. The lot full of weeds and sucker trees to the left of the boxy house was dotted with junk and trash. Once, I'd seen a television set with its glass face smashed out, and another time, an armchair missing a leg was in the center of the lot. These bigger items were usually surrounded by black trash bags overflowing with garbage.

"I guess they think changing the name will change the town," my mother said, pressing her foot lightly on the gas pedal.

At school, Mrs. Gelfand handed out ballots to our fifth-grade class. She explained the rules: We could enter any name we wished, as long as it didn't include the word *Hampton*. The student who submitted the winning ballot would have the honor of being at the official renaming ceremony for Shirley and receive a $250 college scholarship.

Over the past few weeks, as the Shirley Chamber of Commerce floated possible new names for the town, any suggestions containing the word *Hampton*—such as Brookhampton and New Hampton, the front-runners I had heard in church—raised so much alarm in the neighboring communities that it was decided to just drop the reference completely. There was no possibility that the East Enders were going to allow Shirley access to their exclusive identity. The people who lived in Shirley were the people who built and weather-stripped the mansions on Dune Road, cleaned the Olympic-sized, heated indoor pools, landscaped the rosebushes and mowed the sprawling lawns, and served the $25 bowls of chowder and $10 beers at the Hamptons cafés and bars. They were not the ones who actually lived there.

The students were given a week. The contest was open to all schoolchildren within the town. I was enticed by the prospect of the $250 college scholarship.

"How many years will that buy, Mom?" I asked.

"Not enough," she snorted, and finished drying the dish she was holding. I had tried to talk to my parents about possible names during dinner, but it was clear that they weren't as excited about the contest as I was. I was never very good at winning things, but in third grade I had won a small white boom box in a raffle, and I was feeling very lucky about my chances.

"Do you really want the name of your town to change, Kell?" my mother asked. I was puzzled. I hadn't really considered the possibility. I had always loved the name Shirley, but I had just assumed it was a rule that it had to change.

"I don't know," I replied slowly. "I guess I want the town to stay Shirley, but I also want to win the contest."

My father had been quiet, but then he spoke, more to my mother than me. "The best thing this town can do is to get rid of its name. I bet property value would double in one year."

"The problem with this town is not its name," my mother said calmly to my father. Then she turned to me. "Good luck with the contest, Kell. Just don't get your hopes up, okay?"

The following week, I submitted a name—Nature's Way or some such offering—with everyone else. We had all been secretive about our ballots in Mrs. Gelfand's class the week before, but once we handed in our suggestions, we were anxious to hear our competition's choices and traded our town names over our scratched plastic desks. Some kids incorporated their own family's name into their ballots, like Mussettitown, or La Guidiceland. Others worked in the local Native American history, offering suggestions like Poospatuck Place, pulling in the name of the town's Indian reservation. We rated each other's names, certain the winner would be someone from our class. By the end of the following week, however, it became clear that no matter what we wrote on those ballots, none of us had ever really stood much chance of winning that scholarship money.

When Mrs. Gelfand announced the winner in class one morning, we were all disappointed that we didn't know her. Jennifer was an eighth-grader, and although most of us knew her family name because her father was on the school board, his daughters all went to a different elementary school because they lived on the other side of town.

More than 5,000 kids had lost out to this eighth-grader's winning submission: Floyd Harbor. Jennifer had incorporated the name of the town's colonial hero, William Floyd—who had owned a parcel of land nearby and signed the Declaration of Independence for New York State—with the classy image of a yacht club.

The name couldn't have been more off the mark.

Residents immediately began complaining about the choice. Not only did it seem suspicious that the winner's father was on the Board of Education and had links to the Chamber of Commerce, but the name Floyd Harbor also bore a striking resemblance to a nearby town on the North Shore called Lloyd Harbor. Women chatted with one another while folding T-shirts at the Laundromat, imagining all of the mail that would be lost with two towns having such similar names. Of course, Lloyd Harbor also had one more thing that Shirley didn't—a harbor.

A resident named Stan Prekurat wrote a letter to *Newsday*'s editor about the naming issue. "Shirley does have the following bodies of water—a river, a bay, a lake, a creek, an ocean and lots of pools. But where is the Harbor?" The week after the Floyd Harbor announcement was made, Prekurat started a group called the Committee to Keep Shirley Shirley. The committee quickly decided upon an apt slogan during its first meeting in Prekurat's living room: Where's Da Harbor?

Bumper stickers papered cars, and placards were stuck in store windows at the town's two strip malls and on front lawns. A blue-and-white version asked the Committee to Keep Shirley Shirley's question, "Where's Da Harbor?" And a legion of hunter green-and-white signs stated, "I Live in Floyd Harbor." People in town lined up on either one side or the other.

Joe was the first in our neighborhood to pound a sign into his lawn. Not surprisingly, he fell in with the I Live in Floyd Harbor group. Hawking homes in Shirley was difficult, and his real estate office, Cor-Ace, was the main force behind the big new development in the wildlife refuge behind our houses. He could sell a shabby house one block outside of the Shirley school district for more money in less time than he could the most well-kept cape in town. A name change would be much better for his business and his family.

From conversations around town, I gathered that we had an image problem. Living in Shirley said something about you. We glowed in the dark from the nuclear experiments at the Brookhaven National Laboratory. Our hair was teased higher and we had to put clothes on layaway, even at Fashion Bug. We bought three-day-old bread and cakes at the Entenmann's outlet. We talked louder and had bad grammar, said *undaweaya* instead of underwear, *liberry* instead of library. We preferred Spandex to natural fibers and smacked our gum.

Those in favor of the name change were looking to return Shirley's identity to its shiny, hope-filled beginning. For many people, like my own family and many of those around us, Walter T.'s dream of a Town of Flowers really had come true. The affordable real estate made it possible for my family to buy a house and raise me in a close-knit neighborhood. But every time I rode my bike around the corner and passed Jerry's dark house, I was reminded that the people in our town seemed to pay a different, higher price.

We would never have Walter T.'s Atlantic City of Long Island; there were no fancy restaurants or resort hotels in town, and it seemed unlikely there ever would be. But Shirley did have plans. A golf course was in the works, and so was a marina. These amenities, in concert with a new name, could revitalize the town and elevate its standing. No one would have to be ashamed to say they were from Shirley anymore.

Of course, the fact that anyone was ashamed at all was news to me.

As my parents quietly sparred at the dinner table over whether I should enter the renaming contest, a very different argument was running beneath the surface of the one I was hearing. My father had purchased a lot in Woodlands, the new development that had taken away access to our sledding sump. He had done so without my mother's full support. The deal was brokered during one of the neighborhood poker nights and sealed in Joe's office the following week. Our family now owned a plot of land right next to Joe's family in the middle of Woodlands.

The land was being developed by Mr. Coraci, the owner of Cor-Ace. My mother was not as confident as my father in the assumption that Mr. Coraci was going to be able to pull off the development. Woodlands had stipulations for homes unlike anywhere else in Shirley, and in order for a structure to be approved, the blueprints had to include at minimum a two-car garage, four bedrooms, and three bathrooms. My mother found it difficult to imagine that anyone who could afford to build a house of that kind would want to build it in Shirley.

My father assured her that he wasn't planning to build a house there, like Joe's family. Instead, he was just going to resell the land once the town's name changed and the price of the plot skyrocketed. The day after Jennifer's winning name was chosen, Mr. Coraci had stuck a second sign in the ground near the Woodlands one with the pictures of deer and quail. The new sign was neon green and said: "Welcome to Floyd Harbor!"

My mother just shook her head. "It's never going to happen," she warned.

The fight between the Where's Da Harbor and I Live in Floyd Harbor factions lasted for most of my fifth-grade school year. Chamber of Commerce President Judy Mezzapella-Illardo was quoted in a *New York Times* article suggesting that Shirley take the opportunity to shrug off its old stereotype. She acknowledged the town's shady past and that the throngs of houses abandoned by people who could no longer afford to pay their mortgages had sullied the town's reputation and image. "Many of them moved out in the middle of the night and left us with a nightmare," she conceded. But there was hope, she promised, and held up the new addition of the luxury development, Woodlands, as an example. "We are no longer a welfare haven," Mezzapella-Illardo claimed. "We feel a name change would remove the stigma of being from Shirley." Mezzapella-Illardo happened to be one of the first property owners in the Woodlands development. Jennifer's family had also recently moved into a freshly constructed house in Woodlands.

Stan Prekurat continued to pass out his Where's Da Harbor flyers and bumper stickers, and wrote another letter to the editor at *Newsday*. "If the 'new people with the new money' want so much to be a part of our community and give it new life," Prekurat wrote, "why is there a big fence going up around their development?"

The stigma of living in Shirley was especially difficult for me to understand because it was the best place I had ever lived. And as far as I could tell, everyone in my neighborhood agreed. While we had joked for years about glowing in the dark, no one yet knew the true extent of the dangers lurking behind the pine trees surrounding the nuclear facility down the parkway. And at the time, it never occurred to me that my family—or the other families in Shirley—didn't have a lot of money.

Most of our pleasures required no money. Playing outside in the wildlife refuge, the honeysuckle stems that we spent hours sucking on tasted perfectly sweet, and staring up into the pines as they rustled and whispered to us in soft voices was luxury enough. The magnolia tree on Melissa's front lawn bloomed as heartily and the waves of the ocean crashed as thunderously for our small group of scraggly girls as for any others. I had not yet been denied something I needed because we didn't have enough money, and, unlike my parents, I had not yet been denied entrance or acceptance anywhere because of where I lived.

For the longest time, I thought the yellow flame that glowed from far away on top of the small mountain we drove past on the Long Island Expressway was the Statue of Liberty. I would smile secretly at the bright spot from the backseat of our car, a star of fire on the horizon. But within a few years, I realized that what I took to be the lady's torch was actually an incinerator, and the small mountain was a landfill.

During the renaming controversy, the Brookhaven Lab was in the newspapers again and again for leaks and spills, and each new headline seemed to be a point for the I Live in Floyd Harbor side. In 1987, a suspicious homeowner had her well water analyzed and found volatile organic compounds, or VOCs, carcinogens often found in industrial and defense plants. Their volatility comes into play because of the ability of these chemicals—including the more carcinogenic VOCs benzene, toluene, and xylene, all three of which were found in the Brookhaven Laboratory's soil and groundwater—to vaporize and enter the atmosphere. The sample showed that the VOCs were present in a quantity below the levels that the state considered unsafe. A few weeks later, however, the New York State drinking-water standards were altered, and the VOC levels found in this woman's drinking water were determined to be above the new acceptable levels and thus dangerous to her health. The homeowner wrote to the Brookhaven National Laboratory and demanded that they supply her household with a water treatment system to reduce the levels of VOCs in her drinking water. Although the Brookhaven Laboratory hadn't yet officially been linked to the VOCs in question, it agreed to her request.

Meanwhile, the report created by Blass's Legislative Task Force had gained momentum. The task force had suggested that more studies be completed, and in a move that was a first for a federal research facility, the Brookhaven National Laboratory and the Department of Energy (formerly the Atomic Energy Commission) allowed the Suffolk County Department of Health Services onto the premises to have a look around, rather than relying simply on the documents and reports that the Brookhaven Laboratory gave to the county.

After the task force went public with its findings, the Department of Energy had quietly requested that the Brookhaven National Laboratory be included on the National Priorities List (NPL), a tally of the worst hazardous waste sites in the country. These sites are considered to have the highest potential for affecting public health, welfare, and the environment and have been identified for cleanup using money from the Superfund, a federal pot of taxpayer money.

Although the Brookhaven Laboratory had not been officially inducted into the list of the nation's most hazardous waste offenders—not yet, at least—a few months after Jerry died, the Department of Energy and the Environmental Protection Agency began to study the disposal practices of the Brookhaven Laboratory, focusing on the ways the facility treated and sluiced its nuclear and chemical waste. For more than thirty months, members of these government agencies took measurements and samples from the rivers whose headwaters started beneath the Brookhaven Laboratory's reactors and traveled south: the Carmans River, which surfaced in the wildlife refuge; the Forge River to the west; and the Peconic River, to the east toward the Hamptons. They pulled beakers and vials of drinking water out of the neighboring wells and removed chunks of soil from the ground, leaving big square footprints in their wake, as though some mechanical monster had stomped around the compound. They excavated more than fifty-five pits that had been used for the disposal of laboratory chemicals, radiated animal carcasses, and spent laboratory metal and glassware, pits that were dug and filled in during Jerry's tenure. Many of these materials were radioactive or chemically hazardous, and although the various contents were supposed to have been segregated, they had not been. The results of the study were not in yet, but everyone in Shirley knew they would not bode well for the town's future.

In the middle of a February snowstorm in 1987, a vote was held. The next morning, the results were reported over the radio: 1,325 people voted to take the name Floyd Harbor, and 671 voted to keep the name Shirley. For a few days, it seemed as though the town would actually get a new name.

I tried on this new identity. I practiced writing my new address over and over in my notebook, like a bride trying out her married name: *105 Arpage Dr. W., Floyd Harbor, New York.* The word *Arpage* had always sounded a bit French and fancy to me, and paired with *Floyd Harbor,* it conjured images of a terra-cotta villa on some craggy seaside, complete with a sound track of waves and the soft cries of seagulls. Of course, gulls passed over my house every day. But in my imagined Floyd Harbor home, their calls weren't as shrill, and they didn't shit on my mother's Concord.

Then I began to worry. What would happen to the bowling alley, Shirley Lanes? Floyd Harbor Lanes just didn't have the same ring to it. And what about our old house around the corner? I was always comforted to have moved just around the block, to a place where I could hop on my bike and be in front of the old house in three minutes flat. I tried that address out in my notebook: *101 Alcolade Dr. W., Floyd Harbor, New York.* The location looked foreign to me, like somewhere I had never been and never would go. My old house would be gone. In a way, *101 Alcolade Dr. W.* would cease to exist. It would be caged off and become part of someone else's town and memory, just like the sledding sump.

"But the price of our land will double," my father said, confidently. "Just watch."

The spring after it was walled off to us, Margaret, Melissa, Andrea, and I wedged our way through a gap in the security fence and visited our old sledding sump. Clumps of sticky condoms and broken beer-bottle glass in the corners of the sunken hole indicated we were not the first to explore the space. The four of us walked the perimeter and peered into the back holes of the drainage pipes.

After a few patrols around the sump, the other three girls were ready to leave, but I stalled. I wanted to draw each day out as long as possible before the end of the school year; sixth graders were relegated to their own school, an attempt to hedge the overcrowding issues in the district, which meant I wouldn't have any of my neighborhood friends on my bus or in my building. The four of us sat on the lip of the sump and stared. The chain-link fence around the sump was dwarfed by the towering pitch pines that the bulldozers hadn't ripped out yet.

We hung our legs over the edge like fishermen on a dock, bouncing our flip-flops on the dirt. The sides of the crater were now so sharply graded by the bulldozers that it would have been impossible to navigate a garbage pail lid across the snow down into the sump. The afternoon was quiet, and we could hear the low whir of traffic from William Floyd Parkway. Melissa lit a cigarette stolen from her mother's pack and passed it down the line. I decided we were probably too old for sledding anyway.

A few months after the vote, the U.S. Board of Geographic Names in Washington, D.C., declared Shirley's renaming vote unofficial because the Where's Da Harbor group had boycotted the polls. The U.S. Board of Geographic Names is the only governing body that can permanently change a town's name.

Some folks from the I Live in Floyd Harbor group refused to accept this loss. A few weeks after the decision came back from the U.S. Board of Geographic Names, the Floyd Harbor Pharmacy opened up next to Giaccolone's Italian Pork and Pasta Shop, and the Floyd Harbor Deli appeared a year later in another strip mall. When the Floyd Harbor Animal Hospital opened up three years after the name change was denied, a reporter from the *New York Times* asked the owner, Beth Etzel, why she chose the name. Etzel replied that she didn't realize Shirley wasn't destined to become Floyd Harbor.

"People told me that the name hadn't been changed because of some kind of red tape in Washington, and anyway, there was already a Shirley Animal Hospital," Etzel said. Coraci's electric-green Welcome to Floyd Harbor sign still stuck out of the ground in front of his Woodlands billboard, although both had faded from the sun.

My father put our land up for sale around the same time Etzel opened her vet clinic. Sales and construction in Woodlands had slowed, and the plywood shells of houses that had stalled in construction became haunts for teenagers to hang out, drink, and smoke. The shiny white vinyl siding of a few of the new houses was dotted with the looping cursive of graffiti tags. Like my father, most of the original investors in Woodlands had bought believing that the impending name change would reverse their fortunes. But the price of our land in Woodlands did not double, and even if the name had changed, there is no guarantee that it would have had any impact on the value of the land. A different name could not erase the fact that the town had a leaky nuclear laboratory in its backyard, postage-stamp-sized property lots, and no Main Street. One development of high-priced homes was not enough to change gutter-mouthed, tough-as-nails Shirley into an innocuous subur-ban playland, green-lawned and prim.

I liked riding my bike through Woodlands, whose black-top streets were still smooth from little traffic. I would pull up in front of our land, drop my bike against the concrete curb, and sit on a fallen tree. There was a small red-and-white For Sale sign nailed to a tall pitch pine that stuck out near the front of the property, and it was strange seeing my own phone number there, out in public, for anyone to write down and call. Next door, Joe's house was almost completed. They had designed a grand two-story structure with towering white columns on either side of the door, reaching up to a balcony on the second level. A brick chim-ney snaked up the side of the house facing our property. All of the trees in front had been ripped out and the lawn was a flat expanse of dirt and dead grass, a detail that in combina-tion with the lavish Romanesque columns made the empty house seem like some ancient relic, already used up and left to history.

A few months later, the structure burned to the ground. The fire started in the middle of the night, before construc-tion was completed and before Joe's family moved in, so thankfully no one was hurt. The next day, the neighbor-hood gathered in the street, staring at the steaming mess of charred wood and plastic that stretched across the singed lawn. All that was left standing was the brick chimney. Some of the bricks had been knocked out of place—still attached to the chimney but jutting out—so that it looked as if the pile of smoldering black debris had a ghostly staircase sprouting up from its middle, leading the way to some place out of Shirley.

# CHAPTER SEVEN

Shirley looked different to me after the Floyd Harbor debate. Instead of tracing the outlines of the delicate needles of the pitch pines, my eyes stuck on the trash that lined the edges of the refuge. At the beach that summer, I became obsessed with the beer bottle caps and cigarette stubs speckling the white stretch of sand crystals. I tried to move the litter from the small square of beach where I wanted to spread my towel, only to churn up more of the lipsticked stubs and rusty caps with each turn of the sand. Riding my bike through Woodlands during early weekend hours, I uncovered remnants of parties from the previous night, with charred plywood and collections of brown forty-ounce bottles of beer, drained and left in precarious pyramids or smashed and glittering across a freshly poured cement step. The amount of garbage overwhelmed me.

Living in Shirley—or rather, living in Shirley and liking it—became a guilty pleasure, like dismissing a song on the radio in front of your friends, only to go home and play it on repeat in the privacy of your bedroom. The knowledge that other people looked down on our town was piercing. For the first time, I felt ashamed and embarrassed about where I lived.

In the face of this strange new identity, the wildlife refuge became a place of solace for the girls in our group. Woodlands had changed the geography of the neighborhood, shrinking the expanse of the refuge and forcing us to explore new paths and trails. Growing up, we would search for marsh marigolds to hold under our chins or try to identify the cries of songbirds. Now our explorations had the added pleasure of Virginia Slims and pilfered wine coolers, wedged inside the elastic waists of our shorts, cold against our stomachs. We felt safe in the refuge—safe to walk around by ourselves, and safe from the watchful eyes of the neighborhood adults. The only warning our parents had ever given us about the refuge was to watch out for hunters who occasionally stalked the pheasants and waterfowl.

Blue-and-white signs, decorated with the silhouette of a large bird in flight, dotted the perimeter of the refuge, listing fines for hunting. But this never really dissuaded anyone in the town. Melissa's father, Ritchie, hunted in the refuge regularly. He would travel for a month or two, working as a steamfitter, usually in the Carolinas or Virginia, and then stay home the rest of the year, fixing vintage cars in the driveway or building his model trains in the basement. When a car hit a deer on the block, Ritchie was the first on the scene. He arrived with a purse of knives, and what he couldn't slice and dice on the street he bundled up in a tarp to take home and work on in his garage. Melissa's freezer was always full of Saran-wrapped chunks of red and brown meat.

A slice of bright orange in the morning fog, Ritchie would head to the refuge, shotgun slung over his shoulder, his big black boots clomping. He smoked a pipe, and a faint bluish-gray cloud trailed behind his head. Ritchie was handsome, with lips always twisted into a playful grin, and he was big—his shoulders broad and his hands like baseball mitts—and I was intimidated by him. One afternoon, I watched him sidle home, the long, loose body of a pheasant draped across his back. I thought of how Melissa said the birds were pretty when he brought them home, with blue and purple feathers, and long arching necks like swans. Later that day, I crossed the street to her house to see if I could catch a glimpse.

There were three cars in the driveway, all in different stages of repair. I picked my way around them and climbed the stairs of the wooden deck that Ritchie had built the year before. My finger was about to hit the bell when I heard a low, soft sobbing from the backyard.

I turned the corner and stopped. Melissa's blonde hair was in her usual pigtails, and she was sitting in a green plastic lawn chair. She wore her father's orange hunting jacket, much too big for her. She had the bird, which was more than half her size, balanced upside down in her lap, spiny black legs resting on her shoulder and slick purple head dangling between her knees. There were piles of blue and white feathers on either side of the chair, and she was crying, shoulders shaking with each pull, her chubby hands black with blood. She had already cleared a small section of the bird's rear feathers away, leaving the gray stippled skin exposed, obscene-looking.

She raised her head and stared at me through her hot tears, scowl pulling her mouth down, and she yanked another feather and threw it at me. The feather made a wild loop in the air, returning to Melissa as it landed slowly, resting on her right foot.

As a child, I had no concept of the true size or purpose of the refuge. I thought the rickety observation blinds nailed up in the trees were forts, not realizing that the reason the paths didn't grow over was because they were fire trails, kept clear by the forest service in case trucks needed to reach flames deep in the belly of the trees.

The refuge was even older than the town of Shirley. Originally private duck-hunting grounds owned by the Wertheim family, the land was donated to the U.S. Fish and Wildlife Service in 1947, the same year the Manhattan Project decided on Camp Upton as its location for the laboratory. Bisecting the refuge is the Carmans River, wide and chilly and full of fish, second in size only to the Peconic. Red maple swamps and honeysuckle brambles run along the river's length and make parts impassable. At 2,550 acres, the forest is about half the size of the Brookhaven National

Laboratory compound and runs along Shirley's western border, walling us off. It was a refuge in more than name; at the time, I felt protected by that wall of trees.

The news came second- and thirdhand from older brothers and sisters. *Her throat was slit from here to here,* Melissa's brother said, dragging his finger under his chin from one ear to the other. *He used a foot-long kitchen knife and then smashed her head in with a log,* Andrea's sister told us.

A fifteen-year-old girl had been found, barely breathing, by a park ranger in our beloved refuge one Tuesday mid-morning in May. Her body had been pierced fifteen times by the sharp blade of a knife, leaving her with wounds in her back, arms, and stomach, along with the cut across her neck. Her fingers were also sliced and bloody where she had grabbed at the knife to stop him from plunging it into her again.

Jeff, a sixteen-year-old boy from the neighborhood on the other side of the Woodlands development, had called the girl at 6:30 AM that Monday, asking her to cut first period and meet him under the bleachers instead. Jeff and the girl were in the ninth grade together at the junior high school. The police and the boy's attorney called Jeff her boyfriend in a few statements to the press, but the girl told the authorities they were just friends.

Jeff was quiet, with a muscular build and strong back and a head of bushy black hair. All of the men in his family—including his father and younger twin brothers—were under five and one-half feet tall, with short thick legs and long sinewy torsos. They gave the appearance of a tribe of Centaurs when they stood together, as though the top halves of their bodies weren't quite meant for the bottom halves.

Jeff's voice still had the high-pitched strain of mid-puberty. He also spoke softly, adding to the girlishness of his speech. His hazel eyes were offset by his black hair and mocha skin, and he was cultivating a downy scruff of mustache.

On Monday morning, Jeff and the girl met beneath the seats of the old sagging bleachers off the fields shared by the high school and the junior high. There was only a month left in the school year, and the warm weather made everyone buzz with the anticipation of summer. The sun-washed bleachers faced the school from the far end of the fields, providing perfect cover for the students tucked underneath the unsteady rungs. A chain-link fence surrounded the fields, but someone had unraveled an opening between the tight metal stitchings of the fence just behind the bleachers. Every morning, students congregated there, drifting over in small batches from the big yellow buses, walking slowly, pirouetting every once in a while to be sure they weren't being followed by a security guard. Once under, some kids smoked cigarettes or puffed on joints, others made out. The bleachers offered a quiet, dark asylum from the early morning sun blazing down. Soon after the girl met Jeff there that morning, he led her through the hole in the fence.

Margaret, Melissa, Andrea, and I met up as soon as we could near the corner of my old house, at the seam where the glossy new pavement of Woodlands met the rocky gravel of our street. Our fifth member, Tina, was still spending most of her days inside, close to her mother and sister. Their house has been put up for sale, although the three of them had withdrawn so far from the neighborhood that it felt as though they'd already left. The idea of a new family in Jerry's house was only one of the many changes facing the neighborhood: Since the construction of the development began, we had been entering the refuge through a path that ran behind the new houses. Smaller trails broke off from this path, leading to Carmans River. The main route was wide and kept clear of debris by the park service. We stared at the mouth of our path, certain something was about to jump out at us from its cool darkness.

We compared the stories that we had heard. The other three girls all had older siblings in high school, so they had more information, albeit contradictory. One had heard Jeff and the girl were dating, another had heard they weren't. One was certain the girl was paralyzed, and another thought she was making a complete recovery. The newspapers weren't giving the name of the girl because of the combination of her youth and the sexual nature of the attack, but the whole town knew exactly who it was.

We stared into the depths of the forest with fear.

"My mom says I can't go in there anymore," I whispered.

"My mom told me there are rapists and killers in there now," Margaret said.

We stared longingly at the path. The trees were budding and the felt-soft leaves of the wild strawberry patches that lined the edge of the forest were turning bright green. We could smell the honeysuckle bushes, strong and sickly sweet.

"My dad said it was a hunter who found her, not the park service," Melissa whispered. "He said she was out there all night, by herself, and nobody found her for, like, twenty-four hours. She couldn't scream because her throat was cut."

I had heard this part already—that she had spent an entire day and night on the floor of the forest. This idea was more acutely painful to me than the stabbing itself. I had been thinking a lot about the girl out there all by herself, wishing I had taken a walk through the woods that afternoon, wishing I could have found her sooner than the man who heard her cries Tuesday morning.

"I heard they had sex in the trees," Andrea said. We sat on the edge of the lawn of my old house and threw stones at the back of the stop sign. On the silver back of the sign, one of the older kids had used a fat black Sharpie to draw a cartoonish figure of a naked woman running, disembodied hands reaching after her.

That night in my bed, half a mile from where the girl had spent her night out in the woods, I let the bright stars of the cloudless sky outside my window burn into my brain, and then I shut my eyes tight. I could still see the stars against the black of my lids. I reached out across my blankets and pretended to hold the girl's hand. After she woke up from the blow to her head from the log, hours later, it would have been dark. I imagined her stomach growling from hunger, even as pieces of it poked out of the gash in her belly. Maybe she wished for a breakfast of Corn Flakes, yellow cereal and white milk against the blue of her favorite bowl.

I cried for her, sorry that no one had actually been there that night to hold her hand or protect her. I prayed that when she woke up after her head had been smashed in by the log, she was stretched out on her back so that, even as she lay, bloody and crushed on the floor of the forest, she might have watched a flock of bats above her dancing in the moonlight, like the girls and Jerry and I used to do.

She was only three years older than me.

Jeff was taken in by the police almost immediately after the girl was found. His bail was set at $200,000 bond or $100,000 cash. The family had lived in Shirley for twenty years, Jeff's lawyer argued that afternoon. Jeff's father worked as a sales-man for a wholesale hardware-supply company to support his wife and five children and was an active member of St. Jude's, the town's Catholic church. After a few hours, the bail was knocked down to $100,000 bond or $25,000 cash. The church congregation and neighborhood friends raised $15,000 in under two days, enough in combination with the family's $10,000 life savings to get Jeff out of jail for a week until the initial hearing. They took donations after Sunday services.

Newspaper articles ran accompanied by his black-and-white photo—first, from his school yearbook, then stand-ing in the courtroom in a jumpsuit and handcuffs. In both, he looks like a child, his smudge of a mustache the only fea-ture betraying his teenagehood. Standing outside the courtroom barely a week after the attack in the woods, Jeff's attorney told reporters, "From what we understand, she's been around. She's had boyfriends before."

The day he was arrested, Jeff had told the police that he attacked the girl because she had made fun of him after having sex that morning in his house. But in the courtroom, he was changing his story, suggesting that he stabbed her when she wanted to have sex with him and he didn't. The attorney's comments were the first nod to the new version of events.

"This girl definitely, in our opinion, was the aggressor," the attorney said. "From what we understand, our young man was a virgin, number one; and number two, she started being aggressive with him, sexually and physically."

The newspapers didn't mention that Jeff was on both the junior varsity wrestling and football teams, or that the girl just barely topped 100 pounds. Between the church's support, the girl's anonymity, and the lawyer's insinuation that she got what she had coming to her, the town seemed to have made up its mind. Shirley cast its lot, and quietly stood behind its errant son.

As fifth grade ended and summer began, there was an awkward celebration on the block. We were happy to be free of school, but without the cool darkness of the refuge to play in, the girls and I weren't entirely sure how to spend our time. We played kickball or SPUD halfheartedly in the street, jumping limply through sprinklers on front lawns. The beach was off-limits for most of the summer because every few weeks, medical waste was washing up on the shorelines of New York and New Jersey, and many of the beaches were shut down as health hazards. Even when they were open, our parents didn't want us in the water or even walking the sandy beaches, afraid that a hypodermic needle would puncture our feet. This was also the first summer that we did not have our annual Fourth of July block party to look forward to. The neighborhood had decided it would be wrong to throw the party without Jerry, his birthday celebration having become so integral a part of the holiday. On the Fourth of July, families cooked on their own barbecues in their backyards, and a few kids lit some sparklers at the end of the block, watching the jerky embers slowly fizzle out in the dark.

As summer progressed, however, the lure of the refuge grew stronger. We were tired of scraping our knees against the hard gravel when we fell. We missed following the Monarch butterflies along the paths and lifting the soft branches of the pines in search of turtles. But every few weeks, another piece of news would trickle down through the older kids or our parents about the girl, and our longing would be quashed.

Her right leg had indeed been paralyzed—Jeff had slid the knife deep into the small of her back, slicing through her sciatic nerve. The delicate skins of her spleen, kidney, and liver had all been punctured. The doctors had to stuff her intestines back into the hole in her abdomen wall, as if they were rewinding a ball of yarn.

By July, however, we couldn't hold ourselves back any longer. Melissa and Tina weren't with us, but Margaret and Andrea and I decided one morning that we were going to return to the refuge. We promised each other that we wouldn't go near the place where the girl had been stabbed. The park service had closed the trail where the attack had happened, but some of our friends had said they had broken through and found the spot. Holding hands, we entered the dirt path.

Everything looked the same. From the main fire trail, we could see the backs of the houses being built in Woodlands. We decided to go to Carmans River, veering off the fire trail onto one of the smaller paths.

"I have a wrench!" Andrea suddenly yelled out. Margaret and I giggled nervously on either side of her.

"I have a *big* wrench!" We joined in on Andrea's incantation, imagining the rapists and murderers cringing in fear on the edges of our path.

Although the day was hot, the wide branches above us kept the trails cool and shaded as we moved through the forest, alert and on edge. We loosened our grip on one another, but we still held hands as we came up to the water. There were some yellowed magazines and bags from McDonald's along the reeds, and beer bottles littered the path. The trail took us to a spot on the river where a simple metal bridge had been built, just high enough so that canoes could float underneath. We lined up along the bridge, took our sneakers and socks off, and let our legs dangle over the side above the water, the way we used to when we were little. Every few minutes we strained our ears, listening for anything out of the ordinary, and after a short while, we put our socks and sneakers back on and turned to go.

As we headed back out toward our path, we spied a balloon tied to a post near a broken white Malibu bottle and more brown and green beer bottles. The wind blew, turning the face of the balloon toward us. Black letters spelled "Happy Graduation!" against a shiny silver background. There was still enough helium in the balloon to keep it barely afloat in the air, like an animal struggling to lift its head to the sky.

A few weeks after the brave refuge expedition with the girls, my friend Jodie and I were hanging out at my house after a youth-group treasure hunt around town (verses from the Bible were hidden in lawn ornaments or local businesses owned by people from our church, and even in the hand of a statue of Mary in front of St. Jude's Catholic Church). Jodie's father appeared at the end of our driveway in his old van, twenty minutes early. Jodie and I walked out together, and he told us that a boy had just been killed on their block, just on the other side of Woodlands. I asked him the boy's name as Jodie climbed into the passenger seat. "Tommy Kearns," her father said. "He was riding his go-cart and a car came and smashed him and drove away."

I stood at the edge of my driveway thinking about Tommy long after the van disappeared around the block. I had sat next to him in history class the year before—his last name was near mine in the alphabet. I remembered watching as a friend of his tried to copy from his test paper during class. Tommy had been the one who got in trouble when he tried to explain to his friend that he couldn't copy from his test, but he never betrayed the other boy to the teacher. Tommy had spiky brown hair and fair freckled skin. His smile was fast and full, a surprise for his small and delicate face—the force of it made his eyes almost disappear. I had just seen him a month ago, I thought. He couldn't be dead.

I went into the house and told my mother what Jodie's father had said. Over the next few hours, through phone calls and the news, we found out that it was true. Tommy had been riding up and down on his block in a go-cart he built himself. He was looping close to the edge of the street to make a U-turn when a car came speeding around the corner. The driver crashed into the small toy of wood and plastic, barely braking, and then continued down the block. He never came back. The impact had broken Tommy's neck, and the neighbors watching said it looked as though he was just stunned—the go-cart looked fine, hardly a splinter, and Tommy was still in his seat with his helmet on. But his neck lolled back at an angle that just seemed wrong. One of the men nearby took off his jacket and spread it over Tommy's head while another ran to the boy's house to get his parents.

Even though Jerry was young—no one expects someone in his early forties to die—the months the neighborhood had spent watching him shrink further and further away from himself had helped me prepare for his death. No matter how much I thought about Tommy, his death just didn't make any sense at all. If a boy from my history class had to die, why couldn't it be the jerk who was trying to cheat? Or someone else who deserved it, even if only a little bit more than him? Standing in front of the boy-sized casket at the wake, I was scared to look at Tommy's face. Instead, I stared at his hands, and the delicate knob jutting out of his thin wrist, like a gumball stuck beneath his skin.

That summer I had been spending a lot of time with my friend Annemarie, who lived in a small shoe box of a house on the William Floyd Parkway. Although she was only three blocks away, her family wasn't part of our neighborhood. We had been in the same classes since second grade and had become close. She was taller and more athletic than I was, with hazel eyes and a pretty mouth.

We had an easy friendship for the most part, with few of the dramas that mark most adolescent relationships between girls. Our mothers got along well; her parents took me on a trip to the Ice Capades and my father took us on canoe trips down the Carmans River. Annemarie's parents had come to Shirley when her father got a job as a steamfitter at the Shoreham Nuclear Power Plant. He worked at the plant for years, moving to different sections of the building as construction was completed, until the order came down to abandon the project. When Shoreham was shut down, Annemarie's family decided to stay in Shirley rather than moving again.

A few years after the project, Annemarie's father became sick. He had lung cancer that had spread throughout his body, and whenever I walked into her house, I was reminded of Jerry's home during those last months—the darkness, the quiet. The doctors had removed Annemarie's father's voice box, but the cancer was still growing, seeping into other parts of his body. He was a tall man, very strong, the kind I imagined walking with a railroad tie slung over one shoulder, a sledgehammer hanging from his other hand. Like Jerry, this man sat on the living room couch, a couch that was too small for him, under layers of blankets. Annemarie, her sister Jessie, and I would watch television in the room with him, and sometimes he would ask us for the remote, or to switch channels. His wife and two daughters kept moving through the house, hardly ever staying still, as if they hoped that one day he would jump up and start moving through the house with them, healed. I'd watched Jackie do the same. A few months after Annemarie buried her father, his best friend, who had also worked as a steamfitter at Shoreham and lived nearby, also died of lung cancer.

I thought about Jerry and Annemarie's father, and I thought about Tommy and the girl left out in the woods with her throat slashed open, and even about poor Jeff and his family. I didn't understand. In the past, I would have taken a walk through the wildlife refuge to allow these thoughts to unfurl within my head, but now there was no comfort to be had in that place. Just as the refuge walled Shirley off from the rest of the world, the refuge had been walled off from me, joining the other places in town—the Brookhaven National Laboratory, the street where Tommy was hit, Jerry's dark house around the corner, Annemarie's quietly desperate living room—that had become full of fear for me.

After the name change was revoked, it was almost as though everyone gave up trying to improve Shirley. The plans for the golf course never materialized, and no one talked about a marina anymore. Small spats erupted between the neighborhood families. Jerry's widow, Jackie, finished the dream house and moved her two daughters, Tina and Jenny, inside, keeping them there as much as possible and withdrawing from the neighborhood. They sold their old house around the corner, and when a new family moved in, the neighborhood women didn't cook their rice balls or bring over tinfoil-covered sheets of lasagna. They didn't suggest the best place to get a haircut or offer to take the new family's mail in while they were on vacation. For the next few years, each family on the block grieved in its own way for Jerry, but more than that, the families grieved for the way the neighborhood used to be.

Everyone seemed resigned to the deaths, as if they were simply one more part of living in Shirley. Most of us didn't have any other experience to compare with ours, and so even those who held the growing list of losses up to the light, turning it this way and that as if looking for cracks in a porcelain plate, had no way to gauge the degree of brokenness.

Driving us to the beach or the movies, Andrea's mother would read to us from pastel pamphlets at stoplights, quoting scripture and terrifying us with tales of the end of the world. "If the Redeemer came right now, at this very moment," she would ask, one hand on the steering wheel, "Would *you* be ready?"

My mother responded by asking me to help write her obituary. We sat at our old oak dining table and considered what we would want people to remember about her, where she would want her service to be held, and where she would be buried. She sketched out her headstone on a piece of loose-leaf paper I pulled from my three-ring binder and decided that she would want a heavy blanket to cover her inside the casket, because she was always cold.

This was her homework. After watching Jerry die—in the hospital, in excruciating pain, without his daughters by his side, and exactly the opposite of the way he had wanted—my mother was so distraught by the toll the death took on Jerry's family that she searched for systems that might offer a family going through the same thing more comfort. She found Elisabeth Kubler-Ross's book, *On Death and Dying,* in the library, and when she opened it in the middle of the stacks, a bibliography of a dozen other books relating to the topic fluttered to the floor. Over the course of a few months, she bought or borrowed them all, and learned about hospice, a service that provides advocacy and support to terminally ill patients and, most important, to their families through a team of workers who make visits to the home. The closest hospice was run by Brookhaven Memorial Hospital, and my mother had joined a three-month training program to become a volunteer.

The hospice was small and the caseload heavy. As my mother grew more and more involved in the program, death became a constant topic at our dinner table. She had patients, most of whom were dying of cancer, as young as three months and as old as eighty-three. Sometimes she simply sat, holding a hand or talking to the healthy family members about the weather, or taxes, or anything but the disease that was eating away at the insides of their loved ones. Other times she spoke of the frank realities—financial, physical, and emotional—of death and dying.

I understood why my mother was drawn to the work, just as I understood that it was something I could never do—I was unable to see the hope involved, only the fixed promise of death. But my mother soon began taking on extra responsibilities, doing paperwork at the office, organizing events. There were only two full-time staff members at the hospice, and within a year the director, Lynn, asked my mother if she was interested in becoming the director of volunteers. It was a new position, and when she accepted the offer, my mother became the third official staff member of Brookhaven Hospice.

My mother always included me in her volunteer work. Throughout my childhood in Shirley, I spent afternoons helping her fold clothes at the nearby thrift store, deliver holiday food baskets from the church, and pack grocery bags with diapers and week-old English muffins at the neighborhood food pantry, a dilapidated trailer in the parking lot of the town's junior high school. Hospice was no different. She put me to work after school, doing paperwork or filing, stuffing envelopes, and making signs and banners on poster board—everything but becoming involved with the actual patients.

The hospice office was just a room in one of the hospital's dank administrative outposts. Folding card tables and carpetboard walls separated the room into three areas, carving out space for two work stations and a meeting spot.

My mother became close friends with the other two women working at the office, both registered nurses. The first few years my mother worked there were filled with paperwork, constant petitioning of the hospital for more funds and visibility, educating doctors about the hospice program, and setting up fund-raisers and walkathons. But this persistence paid off; within that time, the hospice staff swelled and its offices expanded, taking over more dank and windowless cubbyholes in the same building. The number of patients also expanded.

By the time I had entered eighth grade in 1989, cancer had become a constant in my life, moving from something that happened to a few people I knew to part of daily conversation. This may be why I didn't really notice right away when everyone else started talking about it, too.

It was simply another part of the Shirley curse: People accepted the illnesses as more bad luck. Years later, state cancer registries would show that the reason cancer felt so prevalent within our neighborhoods at the time was because, in fact, it was.

Three years after Jerry died and the first preliminary report was released by Blass's Legislative Task Force, the Brookhaven National Laboratory was officially proposed for the National Priorities List—that tally of the worst hazardous waste sites in the country—on July 14, 1989. The list is refreshed annually, and as some sites are cleaned up and moved off the list, new ones are added. Since the time the task force report had been released, the Suffolk County Department of Health Services had been conducting environmental tests on the compound property, and the results were not good.

Along with the tritium they had already found in the groundwater and drinking-water wells, other radioactive elements, including cesium 137 and strontium 90, were found in the fish in the Peconic River, and in its silt. Some of the radioactive leaks that the testing found had gone undetected for years, dating back to the mid-1960s, when the Brookhaven Graphite Research Reactor was decommissioned. According to the Environmental Protection Agency, which determines what sites are deemed dangerous enough to be put on the National Priorities List, about three tons of waste were deposited in an on-site landfill, including a small percentage of waste that was hazardous and radioactive. The waste dumped at the landfill ranged from contaminated clothing and equipment to radioactive animal carcasses. A plume of 1,1,1-trichloroethane, a metal degreaser, and other volatile organic chemicals (VOCs) resulting from spills and equipment rinses were found in the groundwater. On-site monitoring wells showed evidence of tritium, aromatic hydrocarbons, chloroform, and strontium 90. All of these toxins had been sinking deep within the ground beneath the pines, as well as into the recharge basin of the drinking-water aquifer below.

The Brookhaven National Laboratory's safety and environmental practices and impact on the surrounding population had been under review for quite a while. David Schweller, who headed the Department of Energy office at the lab for most of the 1980s, found the management of the Brookhaven National Laboratory too focused on science, at the expense of assuring safety and protecting the environment. Associated Universities, Inc., the management company of the Brookhaven National Laboratory, had, for example, continued to insist that the site was legally exempt from Suffolk County water regulations until 1987. Schweller's memos on the growing environmental troubles at the lab were ignored by both AUI and the DOE hierarchy. "I was told we're here to do science and to peddle my papers elsewhere," he said in a report.

In 1989, however, Admiral James Watkins was named secretary of energy and became focused on DOE facility compliance with Occupational Safety and Health Administration (OSHA) regulations. He dispersed "Tiger Teams" of scientists, geared to focus on safety, health, and the environment, to all of the DOE's properties, including most of the country's national laboratories. After a Tiger Team visited the Brookhaven National Laboratory in early 1989, it immediately recommended the site for the National Priorities List. Although the team report determined that the pollution and contamination at Brookhaven were not as severe as many of the department's other nuclear facilities that expressly produced weapons—Savannah River in South Carolina and the Hanford Reservation in Washington state, for example—the environmental issues were more dangerous because of its location on top of a major aquifer, in the middle of a densely populated area.

On November 21, 1989, the Brookhaven National Laboratory was officially accepted on the National Priorities List, along with four other national laboratories that were proposed on the very same day, including Oak Ridge National Laboratory in Tennessee, Savannah River National Laboratory in South Carolina, Lawrence Livermore National Laboratory in California, and Idaho National Laboratory in Idaho. Once the facility was placed on the National Priorities List, the federal government took over and the testing continued, as wave after wave of diminishing property values and embarrassment washed over the town of Shirley. I read articles in local newspapers talking about different pollutants found at the laboratory, and it seemed that they discovered some new leak every month, including soil and drinking water contaminated with cesium 137, europium 154, plutonium 239, and radium 226.

The words used in the newspapers reminded me of the stories that had run on the Chernobyl reactor meltdown

# PART THREE

# THROUGH THE PINES

**a·tom·ic** *adj*

1. based on or using nuclear energy
2. extremely small
3. used to describe a proposition, sentence, or formula that cannot be analyzed into a coherent structure

Although the levels of nuclear waste in the drinking water at the elementary school were found to be within standard safety limits, parents were outraged that no attempt had been made by the Brookhaven Laboratory to contact them about the leak. Nor had the Brookhaven Laboratory ever contacted any of the school authorities. When questioned, the laboratory simply said that the county had been monitoring the well and was aware of the presence of tritium in the school's drinking water. The Brookhaven Laboratory contended that it was the county's responsibility to report the results, not the lab's.

An off-site tritium plume flowing east had been discovered as early as 1984, and more plumes flowing south were also found. According to a description of the off-site plume, known as Area of Concern 23, sources of tritium at the laboratory include: the High Flux Beam Reactor, the Medical Research Center, the Linac-Isotope Production Facility, the Biology Building, the Physics Building, the Chemistry Building, the Decontamination Facility, certain Department of Applied Science Buildings, and the Liquid Radioactive Waste System. These plumes continued to be monitored and although the residential wells tested contained levels of tritium below the drinking-water standard, the idea of our well water having even half a teardrop of nuclear waste swimming in it had me shortening my showers and staring suspiciously at the glass of water next to my plate at dinner.

In eighth-grade earth science class, I learned about the basic water-cycle pattern. We used sponges and small Plexiglas boxes to replicate the process of clouds forming from condensation above the ocean or a lake; once the sponge-clouds reached their saturation points, they released the water they had collected through a spray of rain, refilling the water table and allowing the water to eventually cycle back to the lake or ocean, where it would be picked up by clouds once more.

The process of the rainwater being released from its cloud and hitting the ground reminded me of my parents' morning coffee ritual; the rainwater percolates through the ground like our tap water through the coffee grinds. Pollutants from the surface move with the rainwater through the sand and sediment, which acts like a natural filter, cleansing some of the contaminants, the same way that coffee grounds or the occasional pebble got caught in my parents' coffee filter. Pollutants with smaller molecules, however, like most chemicals, don't get caught, and they continue to travel with the water through the sediment. These chemicals were like the silty sludge that ringed the bottom of my parents' coffee mugs.

In 1987, the year before I took earth science, I spent a few weeks sitting on the edge of the lawn watching a flock of squealing, birdlike machines bite into the street in front of my house. It was summer, and a few of the other neighborhood kids also watched the men force the chomping machines into different shapes, tearing up the road and making way for tunnels that would hold the new pipes piled at the foot of the street. Our water often smelled strange, and many people in the neighborhood boiled it before drinking or masked the earthy, metallic taste by mixing it with orange juice or powdered Tang. My mother had petitioned the neighbors to pitch in for a municipal water hookup after stories about the Brookhaven National Laboratory's pollution and some old leaking oil tanks from a defunct gas station on the other side of the highway hit the news.

As I watched the men work at the gravel and dig their craters in front of the lawn, I was surprised by the wafer-thin layer of pavement, and I spent the next few months pining for X-ray glasses so I could see through the blacktop that was covering the secret world of pipes and rocks and hollows beneath my block. I ran in for glasses of water or to the side of the house for the garden hose when the workmen got thirsty. The project lasted almost a month and left behind a two-foot-wide strip of smooth charcoal-black pavement running down half the block—perfect for roller-skating.

❖

Long Island is simply a jumbo sandbar. Composed mostly of the rocky residue of two terminal moraines, the island is made up of debris dumped 11,000 years ago by the Wisconsin Glacier. Although most of the glacial evidence is not visible to the untrained eye, traces of this debris are present on the rocky beaches of Montauk Point, the easternmost tip of the two-pronged island. Montauk's cliffs are striated, like a zebra's jagged stripes, with dark clay deposits from the last Ice Age that alternate with thick bands of light gray and white sediment. The craggy rocks and boulders that make up a large part of the landscape of Montauk's beaches were broken off from New England bedrock and pushed onto

Long Island by slow-moving mountains of ice gliding along the coastline.

This particular glacial history created highly fertile soil in the Northeast. Because Long Island's soil comes from glacial outwash deposits, the heavier sediment, which is gravel, landed in a clump, whereas the lighter fragments such as sand and silt spread out with the melting ice. This combination of materials produces a light and fertile sandy loam that allows water to flow easily through the different layers of sediment. Of course, this type of soil also makes the land more vulnerable, because contaminants, chemicals, and pollutants are able to move through the ground at an extremely quick pace.

All drinking water used on the eastern end of Long Island comes from rain or snow that has fallen on the land's surface and has traveled down through layers of wet sand to the aquifer. The further underground one travels, the older the water. At the deepest level, the water beneath Long Island is thousands of years old and pristine. Most of the water eastern Long Islanders get through their taps is a few decades old and generally entered the aquifer twenty-five to fifty years prior to drinking. This makes the legacy of contamination, wartime metals, and nuclear experiments a very real threat to the island's drinking water today.

There are three levels of aquifers beneath Long Island, and they sit atop one another, separated in some spots by clay layers. The aquifers slope downward toward the southern side of the island, like a dinner plate tipped slightly toward the Atlantic Ocean. A layer of bedrock, the impermeable base that all continents are built upon, runs beneath the aquifers.

Imagine walking out into the Atlantic Ocean from the South Shore of Long Island. The sand beneath your feet would slope down, following the general slant of the bedrock as it subsides and land gives way to ocean. The three aquifers pile on top of this bedrock, like a sand painting, following its slant. The topmost level is the Upper Glacial Aquifer, the primary source of drinking water for the East End of Long Island. This aquifer is the most porous of the three. The next level down is called the Magothy Aquifer, and a layer of clay which is less porous is slathered between the two aquifers. This clay doesn't exist beneath the island, though; the layer of clay only begins where the island ends and slopes out toward the ocean, leaving a perfectly permeable partition between the two aquifers underneath the island itself. The final and deepest level, before hitting the bedrock, is the Lloyd Aquifer, which houses the purest water. This aquifer has never been harvested for consumption on the East End of the island, but the Suffolk County Water Authority recently petitioned for permission to tap this source of clean water in an effort to blend it with the more polluted water from the Magothy. It is unclear, once tapped, how long the Lloyd Aquifer could support the drinking water needs of the island.

Years earlier, my mother had made an appointment with the county to hook our house up to the municipal water well, which could be monitored regularly for safety. The morning of the appointment, however, we were busy packing our station wagon and getting ready to head to Margaret's house in preparation for Hurricane Gloria. And after the hurricane, which caused more than $300 million in damage to the island alone, the county had more important things to attend to than our water hookup. But my mother had a feeling in her gut that something was not right with our water, so she kept calling. After a few months of relentless calls, another appointment was scheduled.

During one of many phone calls she had with the county, my mother had been told that, according to town maps, there was a main municipal line at the end of our block. But when the workmen searched for signs of that line along the wildlife refuge at the end of the block the day of the appointment, they realized there was a mistake. A new water company had recently replaced the old one, and apparently the maps were in desperate need of revision; the map showing the main line's course down our street was completely wrong. The municipal pipeline actually stopped short at the highway on the opposite end of the block, a few hundred feet away. If my parents wanted municipal water, they would have to pay thousands of dollars to snake a connection line all the way down the block directly to our house.

My parents did not have any extra thousands for this procedure, so they set about petitioning neighbors to change the water collectively. But my mother knew that if she wanted to get municipal water for her family, she would have to bring the neighbors some kind of proof that there was, in fact, something wrong with what they were drinking.

My mother hired a private company to test our water. She found the company in the phone book, and a technician came with plastic vials and checklists, collecting water from the taps in the bathrooms and kitchen.

"Well, ma'am," the man said over the telephone a week later. "It looks like we've got a case of free ammonia on our hands."

My mother quickly processed these words, but could find no connecting definition in her memory. "Free what?"

"Free ammonia," he repeated. "Sometimes it's called urea. It's from septic systems."

My mother blinked, switching the phone from one ear to the other.

"Urea, as in urine?" Her voice was unsteady as she tried to make sense of what the man was saying.

"That's the one," he said. "It's from pee."

Before World War II, when potato farms instead of housing developments dominated Long Island's landscape, the local governments decided that each household should be allowed to pump its own water from a shallow well on the property. Sewage and wastewater would be dispensed through individual septic tanks, also on each separate property. This is common practice throughout the country, and it works perfectly well when land gradations are taken into account and wells positioned uphill from the flow of wastewater that leaches naturally from septic systems.

This system works particularly well in farm country, where household plots consist of multiple acres. But as subdivisions crept in and much of Long Island became suburban, keeping this system functional proved difficult. The average plot of land in Shirley is .13 acres. This means that for every square acre of land in town, there are seven or eight septic systems and seven or eight drinking-water wells working below the ground. Chances are pretty strong that some of the wastewater being pumped out of a house will get pumped back in again.

The implementation of septic systems and wells is also more complicated on Long Island because the land is almost completely flat. This quickly became obvious as the water source beneath the more populated areas of Queens, Brooklyn, and Nassau County was irreparably polluted early in the suburban push eastward. The aquifers that naturally stored drinking water beneath these sections of Long Island were soon overwhelmed by the flow of household detergents, industrial toxins, and the high number of septic tanks seeping sewage into the water supply. Between the 1920s and 1940s, the boroughs of Brooklyn and Queens gave up the well system and have been pumping their water in from reservoirs located in upstate New York ever since, along with the rest of New York City. Large municipal sewage systems treat the waste and pump the treated wastewater into the Hudson River, New York Harbor, and Long Island Sound.

In Nassau County, centralized sewers were installed a few decades after Brooklyn and Queens made the switch. In the 1950s, Nassau also began drilling its drinking-water wells deeper, tapping into the older and purer aquifers as the water closer to the surface became polluted. Most of Suffolk County, on the eastern end of the island where Shirley is located, still operates on the well and septic system today.

It took about a year, but my parents were able to convince the neighbors to sign petitions requesting that our taps be hooked up to the municipal well. My mother's discovery of free-ammonia contamination, and the assumption that nearby wells could also be swimming in the toxic urine by-product, convinced the surrounding households that this was a necessary expense. The cost of connecting our houses to the municipal well was spread out among a few consenting neighbors on one half of the street.

The new water that ran through the taps from the pipes these men installed was, and still is, referred to as "city water" in the neighborhood. New York City's water, which is drawn from reservoirs in upstate New York, is touted as some of the cleanest and best quality in the country. It didn't matter that it would be almost structurally impossible to build pipes large enough and deep enough to link city water to the shallow eastern end of Long Island. Ultimately, I believe, after the months and months of petitioning and fighting for the municipal hookup, my family, along with the rest of the families on the block that pitched in, just wanted to believe that what they were getting was indeed the pristine city water they had heard so much about.

In reality, all municipal water in Suffolk County is pumped from a well within a twenty-mile radius from a person's house. Instead of being pulled from a well right next to our house, we now drank water pumped from a larger municipal well nearby. And while the municipal well was under the surveillance of the Suffolk County Water Authority, there are hundreds of contaminants in tap water that the federal government doesn't regulate, and which utility companies are not required to monitor, including tritium and strontium 90. This new water also did not come from anywhere markedly different than the water we were drinking before. It still originated from the aquifer whose main recharge basin sat in the Pine Barrens beneath the Brookhaven National Laboratory.

Our new water had the same strange, tinny taste as the old water. The only marked difference was the smell of chlorine that the taps now emitted, a smell similar to the one that made my nostrils flare at the local pool where I took swimming classes. Along with that, small turquoise clumps of stone now peppered our water. My father installed mesh nets on all of the faucets, and it was my job to clean them once a week. It was a satisfying chore, unscrewing the tiny nets and dumping the blue rocks out onto a tissue.

The rocks of chlorine were added to the water supply at the municipal well. As with its use at the local pool, chlorine is employed as a disinfectant to reduce viruses and bacteria in the drinking-water supply. The chemical is a common tool in keeping drinking water safe: It can kill microorganisms from diseases such as typhoid fever and cholera on contact. Most households did not have the glut of chlorine stones that my family did; we were at the end of a line, a dead end of sorts, and so the rocks tended to collect. The chlorine clumps looked like candy Nerds, and their color reminded me of the Native American jewelry I coveted at the pow-wows my family took me to in the Catskills. The rocks seemed precious and primal, and it made me sad to flush them down the toilet each week. But we felt some sense of safety with our new "city water." Many others around us on the island, however, were also beginning to regard the water being into their homes with suspicion.

I don't remember the first time I heard about the Long Island Breast Cancer Study Project, but it was probably in the mid-1990s. Overnight, it seemed like everyone was talking about breast cancer on the island.

Margaret had started working at a deli a few blocks from our house when she was in seventh grade. She started as the sandwich maker and register girl, and as she got older she moved on to slicing cold cuts. The owners were a first-generation Italian couple and Margaret was friendly with the wife, Marie. One day, when Margaret was working by herself, Marie brought a folded and dog-eared form in and handed it to Margaret.

"The paper, it says negative!" Marie was on the verge of tears; she could barely read or speak English and was asking for Margaret's help. Margaret looked at the form letter and the doctor's office letterhead. "I looked it up in the book and the book says negative is bad. Margaret, negative is bad, right? I'm going to die, right?" Marie looked at the young girl expectantly.

"No, Marie. Negative usually means bad, but in this case it means good!" Margaret tried to explain that sometimes, negative means positive. Later that night, in my backyard over hot dogs, Margaret told me that Marie must have been carrying the piece of paper around with her for a while.

"The date was from a few months ago," Margaret said. "When do you think she was planning on telling her husband?"

During the years leading up to the Long Island Breast Cancer Study Project, many of my mother's friends and acquaintances from town had some type of breast disease. My mother had started collecting ceramic angels, and she would give them as gifts to her friends as good-luck charms during their recoveries. When she was not at the hospice office, she was driving women to their chemotherapy sessions or doctor appointments.

Cancer of the breast and lung were the most common illnesses among my mother's patients at Brookhaven Hospice. Lung cancer came packed with guilt—if there had been a ribbon for lung cancer, it would most likely have been nicotine yellow. It would be another decade before activists began piecing together the link between low-level radiation and the island's incredibly high rates of lung cancer—among smokers and non-smokers alike—and thyroid cancer. The lungs and the thyroid gland are both highly sensitive to radiological exposure. In the meantime, the pink ribbons were pulling in the money. And the money pulled in the politicians.

Officially, the Long Island Breast Cancer Study Project was a multibillion-dollar scientific effort mandated by Congress to determine whether there were environmental contaminants to blame for the high rates of breast cancer among women on Long Island. Unofficially, it was a study that caused many women on Long Island to hold their collective breath as they waited for the results of the dozen separate tests to tell them why they were getting sick and what they could do to prevent it.

The massive research project began with a group of activists on the island, a collection of women who were participating in activism or politics for the first time in their lives. In response to a startlingly high rate of breast cancer on Long Island in comparison to the rest of New York state and the country, two scientific studies had been released within three years of each other, one by the National Institute of Health in 1987 and another by the New York State Department of Health in 1990. Both studies concluded that a combination of high socioeconomic status, heredity (especially in relation to the Jewish population on the island), and high-fat diets was to blame for the elevated breast cancer numbers in the area.

Many women who had breast cancer at the time felt let down by these studies; the answers seemed vague and off target, not convincing enough to explain the unsettling number of women on the island being struck by the disease. Some of these women decided to take matters into their own hands.

The first breast cancer advocacy organization, and the organization that remains the most well known on the island today, was started by breast cancer survivors Fran Kritchek and Marie Quinn. In 1990, according to statistics, one in nine women had breast cancer on Long Island. Kritchek and Quinn named their organization "1 in 9" after the statistical ratio, and within a year the group went from a roster of two to a gathering of 300 for the organization's first protest on the steps of their local courthouse in western Long Island. The group of women, holding banners demanding more money for research into the breast cancer rates on Long Island, was featured on the cover of *Newsday*, in a full-page color photo. By 1992, 1 in 9 held its first walkathon and received a $35,000 grant from then-Senator Norman Levy. This grant was the group's introduction to the power of politics. Their membership numbers and the media attention also drew the attention of local politicians, and the group went on to become one of the most powerful political activist organizations in the country.

In West Islip, a few towns west of Shirley, another woman was inspired to take action on her own. Lorraine Pace had struck up a conversation with her seatmate on an airplane in 1992. He was a mortician in Suffolk County and during their conversation, he told Pace that over the past few years, the young women on the East End of Long Island who were brought to his funeral home all seemed to be dying from breast cancer. When she returned home from her trip, Pace went directly to her doctor and requested a biopsy of a lump in her left breast that she had been aware of for a few years. The results confirmed her worst fear—the lump was cancerous and the disease had spread to her lymph nodes. Pace was fifty years old, never smoked, was not on hormone replacement therapy, had only used birth control pills for two months, and had no family history of breast cancer. She had also had regular mammograms since her early thirties and had lived within the same zip code for forty-seven years. Her cancer could not be explained by the two studies that had recently come out about breast cancer on the island. Then she learned that twenty women in her small West Islip community were also living with breast cancer, and most of them were living on dead-end streets, like she was. Pace began a simple kitchen-table project that would ultimately draw national attention. She made a map.

For eighteen months, Pace painstakingly drew out streets and measured properties to scale as she underwent chemotherapy and radiation treatments. Word of her project grew as neighbors came to visit her and saw the map spread out on her table. She started getting calls from friends and neighbors, and then from strangers, all offering their services to assist with the information collection and mapmaking. The press became interested, and after a few months Pace formed the West Islip Breast Cancer Coalition with the help of her husband, John. Volunteers passed surveys out at supermarkets and placed them in mailboxes, and a local priest, Father Tom Arnao, encouraged his parishioners to fill out the questionnaires. After a year, Pace had collected responses from 69 percent of the West Islip population and had a detailed, color-coded map with clear areas of breast cancer concentrations. As press coverage increased, women from across Long Island began calling Pace, asking for assistance in starting their own mapping projects. Pace's cancer went into remission, and she started another activism group called Breast Cancer Help, Inc., an organization dedicated to encouraging other areas to conduct mapping surveys to better understand the relationship between the environment and breast cancer.

Meanwhile, in the town of Manorville—a town east of Shirley that also borders the laboratory—a human resources director for the local post office took action when diagnosed with cancer. In 1993, after having twenty-nine benign tumors removed from her breasts over the course of many years, Diane Sackett Nannery was told that her thirtieth tumor, which grew along one of the jagged scars on her right breast, was most likely benign, just like the others. Her doctor told her there was no need to remove the tumor, but after a few months, the forty-year-old Nannery opted for surgery based on a hunch that something wasn't quite right. By the time the tumor was removed, the cancer had spread to her lymph nodes.

Angry at her doctor and frustrated by a series of insurance problems, Nannery wrote an article for the postal newsletter about her story and the importance of choosing the right insurance plan. After the article ran, Nannery learned that eight employees at her post office had been diagnosed with breast cancer in the six-month period before her own diagnosis. Like Pace, Nannery resorted to activism during her months of chemotherapy and radiation treatments. She thought about the stamps at her office for the American Heart Association and other diseases and decided to try to get a stamp dedicated to breast cancer.

Nannery's proposal was formally rejected by the U.S. Postal Service twenty-six times. Giving up, however, was not in Nannery's nature. The Postal Service accepted and approved her twenty-seventh proposal and by February 1994, only a few months after Nannery started her campaign, the Postal Service launched the breast cancer stamp project, officially releasing the first stamp in June 1996.

As Nannery recovered from her breast cancer, she received invitations to speak at conferences and events, first on Long Island, and then nationally. Through her communication with New York senators and representatives about the breast cancer stamp, she quickly became recognized as an activist who had the ear of local politicians, and people sought her support for many projects. Nannery, new to activism, decided early on that she would strive to remain nonpartisan both politically and within the realm of breast cancer activism, marking her voter card "Independent" and never joining any partisan political organization.

Nannery, Pace, and the 1 in 9 organization were seen as the main catalysts of the Long Island Breast Cancer Study Project. Pace's ten-foot, color-coded map was used first by the media as proof of the epidemic, and then by scientists in the beginning stages of the Long Island Breast Cancer Study Project as a way to envision tackling the very tricky task of conducting an environmentally-based study. Nannery's close relationship with Senator Alfonse D'Amato from their work on the breast cancer stamp gave the women an ally within the U.S. Congress, an ally who was also luckily up for reelection and particularly interested in securing votes from women. The ability of 1 in 9 to collect hundreds of women on courthouse steps was also instrumental in getting media coverage for the cause, which in turn piqued the interest of many other local politicians.

Women across Long Island were hopeful when, in June 1993, the U.S. Congress voted in favor of a study to investigate the possible relationship between the environment and breast cancer on the island. An official mandate, Public Law 103-43, directed the National Cancer Institute and the National Institute of Environmental Health Sciences to conduct the study. This public law called for the investigation of contaminated drinking water; sources of indoor and ambient air pollution, including emissions from aircraft; electromagnetic fields; pesticides and other toxic chemicals; and hazardous and municipal waste. Funds were originally slated to come from both the National Institute of Environmental Health Sciences and the National Cancer Institute. The law contained a time frame of thirty months for the study, and the women of Long Island prepared for the two and one-half year wait before the findings would be reported to Congress.

In the meantime, until the results were released, everyone talked about their own theories. Around the same time the newspapers began reporting on the advent of the Long Island Breast Cancer Research Project, I was starting my senior year in high school and was nominated for the Homecoming Court. The nearly 700 students in my grade nominated ten girls for queen and ten guys for king, and then a panel of teachers determined the winners after looking at each student's academic record and extracurricular activities. They interviewed each candidate, and four teachers asked me questions about school spirit and what I planned to do after graduating. I gave them the answers I had practiced at home with my mother, and just as the interview was coming to an end, one of the teachers motioned to the pink ribbon on my jacket.

"Is that for breast cancer?" he asked. I nodded, quickly planning an answer to his anticipated question. I would talk about my volunteer work and list the walkathons and fundraisers I had helped my mother with. I had heard that his wife had recently been diagnosed with breast cancer, and I wanted to impress him with my list of breast cancer fundraising activities.

"What do you think is causing all the breast cancer? Why do you think so many women in our community have breast cancer?"

I thought it must be a trick question. Everyone knew that it had to do with water, or at least that was what everyone in town talked about when they discussed cancer. But I wanted to separate myself from the pack, and I knew that all of the other contestants would say water, too.

"Power lines!" I blurted out. I had just read yet another article in the newspaper about possible causes, and this one stuck in my head because I had never considered it before. While most of America's power lines were buried beneath the ground, power lines were built above ground in Long Island because the landmass was so shallow. I explained this theory. "It is the electromagnetic fields that come out of the power lines." I watched the teacher's eyebrows knit together above his eyeglasses.

"Power lines, eh? Well, thank you, Miss McMasters," he said, without looking at me. I was dismissed.

Walking down the hallway, trailing my hand along the line of lockers, I replayed my interview. I slowly realized that I should have gone with my first instinct and said water. It never occurred to me that the teacher wasn't looking for an answer that was different. I just wanted the scholarship, the same way I had wanted the scholarship during the name-change debate years earlier. The teacher was looking for an answer that conveyed a true understanding of the epidemic that was affecting the women of the town. He wanted to save his own wife with an answer that pulled away from the PR and the walkathons and the pink ribbons. But at the time, I was only concerned about how things looked on paper, and not about the actual women who were dealing with the disease, the ones, like his wife, who did not know if they would be survivors and just wanted to know what had gone so terribly wrong. Even though many of my mother's friends had the disease and some of the neighborhood women had benign lumps, no one close to me had breast cancer yet. Besides, all of the pink-ribbon posters and pamphlets talked about survivors, women like Diane Sackett Nannery and Lorraine Pace, who were young and vibrant and blonde. From what I could tell, once someone had breast cancer she immediately became a survivor. I didn't know the statistics on the women who did not survive. Nor did I know that since the organization 1 in 9 had been formed, the cancer rate in my hometown had changed to one in seven. Shirley never had any breast cancer support groups. There were no women in town scribbling out maps of the town in between chemotherapy appointments.

Most of the studies included in the project were conducted by scientists at major universities in the Northeast. When I searched the documents of the main case-control study of the Long Island Breast Cancer Study Project, I discovered that most of the data on women with breast cancer were pulled from hospitals including Stony Brook in Suffolk County, Mount Sinai in Nassau County, and Sloan-Kettering in Manhattan. Numbers and records from Brookhaven Memorial Hospital, where most of the people in my area would have gone for treatment, were not used in the study.

As mandated by Congress, weekly meetings were set up so that the activists who had been so influential in bringing the Long Island Breast Cancer Study Project to life could have a hand in determining the scientific direction the study was to take. Each week, the activists came with lists of hundreds of chemicals to be tested, including pesticides, household cleaners, gasoline, and aircraft fuel emissions. The overwhelming majority of activists believed that there was some environmental factor specific to Long Island that was causing them to become sick, and just as everyone in my town had a theory about how the pollution was being transmitted, the activists had plenty of theories about which chemicals might just be the culprits.

At the beginning of the Long Island Breast Cancer Study Project, the 1 in 9 group brought in epidemiologist Dr. Jay M. Gould and radiologist Dr. E. J. Sternglass of the University of Pittsburgh Medical School to search for areas with particularly high spikes of breast cancer. After examining the state's breast cancer incidence rates for every town on Long Island, the doctors discovered what they called a "cluster" within a fifteen-mile radius of the Brookhaven National Laboratory, including the towns of Shirley, Bellport, and Yaphank.

As the thirty-month deadline drew closer, the scientists involved in the Long Island Breast Cancer Study Project realized that they would not be able to complete the study in the given time, so they requested an amendment to the time frame outlined by the law. An expansion was granted. And although Congress had mandated that the National Institute of Health finance the Long Island Breast Cancer Study Project, after the thirty-month deadline was thrown out, the Department of Defense stepped in and funded the majority of the project.

Although it falls under the auspices of the Department of Energy, the Brookhaven National Laboratory is also funded primarily by the Department of Defense. And as the Long Island Breast Cancer Study Project continued on its way, the initial stages of Superfund testing at the Brookhaven National Laboratory were being completed. Out of more than thirty nuclear and hazardous wastes found by the Superfund in the groundwater and soil of the Brookhaven National Laboratory, only DDT was on the scientists' lists to be tested by the Long Island Breast Cancer Study Project. They were hoping to determine that there was a direct link between DDT—whose dangerously carcinogenic properties environmentalist and biologist Rachel Carson had pinpointed in her groundbreaking book, *Silent Spring,* nearly half a century earlier—and breast cancer in particular. There was no doubt that DDT caused cancer; the scientists were hoping to show that if exposed, a woman was likely to develop breast cancer in particular.

In October 1993, our football team lost the Homecoming game. My father walked me onto the football field at half-time to wave at the crowds in the stands with the other nominees, and my mother escorted my friend Dino, whose own mother wasn't well. Between the game and the dance later that night, my boyfriend J. brought his white-collared shirt to my house so my mother could iron it for him. His mother was recovering from a brain aneurysm—

he and his brother had come home one night to find her on the bathroom floor, convulsing.

The high school gym was decorated with green and gold streamers, the school colors. My hair was permed and I was wearing a push-up bra and high heels with the new dress my mother had helped me pick out at Macy's. Margaret, Andrea, and Melissa were all in college already—Margaret at State University of New York (SUNY) Stony Brook, Andrea at SUNY Albany, and Melissa at C.W. Post, further west on the island. We had heard that Tina—whose family had, in the past few years, moved out of our neighborhood and then out of our town—had gone to a design school, but I didn't know where it was. I was feeling left behind again and lonely, and I clung to J.'s hand in the gym. His lanky frame looked even thinner and longer in the baggy suit he had borrowed from his older brother. I was hoping to win that night; I wanted to add "Homecoming Queen" to my carefully constructed list of awards and activities on my college applications.

I wanted to get away from the town, and get away from the entire island. I had my sights set on Vassar, in upstate New York. My parents had spent weeks over the summer driving me to colleges in the Northeast; I had been set on Wellesley, whose pastoral campus looked to me like a postcard, until I was placed with a girl who only talked about her boyfriends at all the surrounding schools during a campus visit. On a whim one weekend, my parents drove me upstate to look at Vassar, and as soon as I stood in the shade of the long-limbed London plane tree on the main lawn, staring at the castlelike spires that topped the Gothic library, I knew where I wanted to be. I listened to the tour guide say that the campus was an arboretum with more than 200 species of trees and loved how much the place reminded me of my wildlife refuge at home.

J. wasn't planning on going to college, although I had dragged him to take the SAT test anyway and was collecting a secret pile of applications I had half filled out for him.

When we all filed into the auditorium, J. escorted me onto the stage when my name was called and then found a seat in the audience. Ten girls stood smiling nervously, not touching, on the left side of the stage, and ten boys stood to the right, arms slung around one another's shoulders, knocking their palms into the back of each other's heads. They announced the runners-up first, and then the winners, of which I was neither. Some of the girls started crying right on stage. I held back my tears until the auditorium had mostly cleared out. I found J. and crumpled in his arms. Margaret's parents and my parents were standing nearby in the aisle and watched as I wept, clucking softly and offering their support. I knew J. was uncomfortable with me carrying on the way I was, but I didn't care. I kept crying—about pink ribbons and crowns and college applications—until I wasn't sure what I was crying about anymore.

# CHAPTER NINE

J. and I were fighting. Again. I was tired of his incapability of driving anywhere without a can of Budweiser between his legs and he was tired of my being such a prude. We had been together on and off for three years, and while at first his group of friends—the skaters with their scabby elbows and stringy asymmetrical haircuts and the surfers with their leather necklaces and wristbands crusted with sea salt—was new and exciting, by senior year I was growing tired of the same old parties in the same old desolate hideouts.

There was no youth center or meeting place aside from the bowling alley, where I was not allowed to go because of the number of fights after dark. So kids from Shirley mostly hung out somewhere outside. Woodlands was the hangout closest to my house. My mother had been correct—years after its creation, not many people had built houses in the development. Every weekend there was a lineup of cars along one road that was tucked in against the refuge. The first time I went there, Melissa drove us in her thrumming 1976 Camaro (black with a red racing stripe), nosing the car against the bleached white concrete curb. I remembered finding the pyramids of beer bottles and ribbons of sparkling glass along the sides of the streets during my morning bike rides when I was younger.

The boatyard was closer to J.'s house. Set off on its own away from any houses, it was the best place for bonfires. We faced the water of the bay, and the smell of the skunky weeds competed with the cheap beer and puddles of puke and piss. Cars would crank up their stereo systems and sometimes we would just dance around the fire. Couples would pair off and climb into the backs of pickup trucks or cars, and every so often the rest of the group would surround the car and rock it back and forth, laughing at the fogged-up windows.

Many nights started out at the Poospatuck Indian Reservation, around the corner from the boatyard. Located along the Forge River, the Rez was a scruffy collection of stark concrete block houses and trailers. The Poospatuck was the smallest Indian tribe on the island, with around 250 residents. A smoke shop was set up at the entrance like a guardhouse, and I would wait in the car while J. bought cheap cartons of cigarettes for his mother and a pack or two for himself. Sometimes, if they needed something more than cigarettes, a car filled with J.'s friends would continue past the smoke shop and drive deeper into the Rez, tires kicking up dust like in an old Western movie. Once a car passed a certain point, dogs appeared out of nowhere, chasing the crunching tires, running alongside the vehicle as if it were their pack leader.

On the other side of town, at the end of a tight, bumpy block named Cranberry Road, there was a rickety wooden dock that jutted out into the bay. A circle of dirt and cracked pavement surrounded by cattails and frothy muck served as a small parking lot. White headlights from cars arcing over the Smith Point Bridge toward the beach sparkled across the black water at night, and if no one was playing music you could hear the metallic snap of the flag clanging against its pole in front of the beach parking lot across the bay. The dock's old wood was soft and splinter free, scarred with years of names and dates. In the darkness, the pitted boards felt like Braille under my fingertips.

I worked at the concession stand at the beach most summers; a neighbor managed the place, and because he was also the coach of the boy's high school basketball team, he hired any team members who needed a job to work the grill while Margaret and I oversaw the till. Sometimes J. would pick me up at closing, and the boys from the team would tease me while he waited outside smoking cigarettes in his cutoffs, his shaved head in sharp contrast to their preppy haircuts and sweat suits. I loved his tight bare chest and the small iron-cross tattoo he had drawn on his right bicep with a sewing needle and a pot of India ink after drinking too many beers when he was thirteen. The cross trailed off toward the back of his arm, skewing the proportions so it looked like a fun-house mirror reflection—one of the four spokes of the cross hung limp and loose, a broken arm. After work, we would walk down the beach to the section reserved for camping if one of our friends had paid for a slot, or head toward the nude beach in the other direction to start a bonfire, careful to bury the coolers full of beer in case we were bothered by the cops.

On the summer mornings when I woke up after a night at one of these places, I would curl my nose into my hair first thing and breathe in the stink of bonfire, bug spray, and sea salt.

My favorite days with J. started at 5:00 AM, when he or his brother would pick me up on their way to the beach to pull a "dawnie." I loved running out to the car when the light was still dim and the sun just about to break, squishing into the car full of surfboards, a waxy fin poking me in the side, The Cure or Nine Inch Nails blasting. By the time we got to the beach, the sand was still cold, and I would sit with my knees tucked into my sweatshirt and watch the water lift the boys up and then down, losing myself in the rhythm of the ocean and the bobbing of their bodies, black and slick in their wet suits against the searing blue of the sky. Their calls to one another mixed in with the crying of the seagulls, and when I closed my eyes I could barely tell the two apart.

At night, we went to hangouts with J.'s friends or made out in his car under the bridge until the cops came to clear out all of the couples who were parking, along with anyone they could catch doing drugs. Once, during a house party, J. and I slipped into a bedroom. As I sat on the edge of the single bed, J. silently unscrewed the bottle caps from our forty-ounce bottles of beer and set them on a nightstand. He produced a thin white kitchen candle from the pocket of his jeans, and when he snapped it in half, it sounded like a bone cracking. He lit the two candles with his cigarette lighter and let some wax drip into the caps before sinking the candles into the white liquid, holding them steady for a moment before letting them go. We were quiet while he did this, but the music from the party on the other side of the door pulsed through the walls. He pulled his T-shirt off, and at the moment when his head and arms were hidden in the fabric above his head, I held my breath. The light from the candles made him glow—and I never imagined a back could be so beautiful.

Other nights, we sat for hours in the parking lot of Taco Bell, where J. worked. The boys wore their uniforms of shiny black flight jackets, white T-shirts, jeans, and Doc Martens, with their heads shaved to stubble or shaggy and long—there was no halfway point. They drank until they puked, taking turns retching in the ratty row of shrubs separating the parking lot from the street. J. would stumble back, his half-smoked Marlboro Red still pinched softly between his fingers. The girls—a collection of girlfriends and a group of younger, chubbier girls whom the boys called "the Hogs" and who were always happy to step in when a girlfriend wasn't there—sat on the cement blocks. We stretched our legs out in front of us, bumming cigarettes from the boys and sharing wine coolers or Zima or bottles of beer, waiting to be driven home.

One night, after a fight with J. during a house party, I was sitting in a basement by myself, watching television and listening to the noises of the party upstairs. The owners of the house were away; their daughter—one of the Hogs— was supposed to be sleeping over at a friend's house. Instead, she called her cousin Mike, who invited a bunch of people over. About fifteen minutes after we got there, the friend's sister had called; the parents were threatening to return unless their daughter called them at their hotel from her friend's house as planned. She had been gone for half an hour when two houseplants came crashing down from the landing into the basement, the pots cracking open just behind my chair.

I went upstairs to see who had pushed the pots over, but the house was empty; I wondered if the bass of the techno music shuddering through the house had shimmied the pots over the edge. I looked through the back door and in the orange glow of the porch light saw a pair of plastic lawn chairs floating in the aboveground pool. Three guys had the matching table hoisted on their shoulders, beers in their outstretched hands, and they chucked it into the pool with the chairs, umbrella and all.

I spotted the shiny stubble of J.'s head at the end of the porch. He had one hand slung in his jeans pocket, the other holding his usual bottle of beer and cigarette clamped between two fingers. Some other boys were wheeling the barbecue closer to the pool when he turned around and came inside.

"We should leave," I said. He walked past me without even flicking his ice-blue eyes in my direction and went to the fridge, pulling the tab on a fresh beer.

"In a bit," he said, and walked back outside. I went down-stairs to the basement again to pout. I was in the middle of sweeping some of the spilled soil into one of the cracked pots when the party moved back inside. I walked upstairs and saw J.'s brother spray painting the inside of the oven with his tag, SIB–47, which stood for Strong Island Boys, the number corresponding to his house. A crash in the living room sounded like glass had been smashed. The phone rang and Mike announced that his cousin was on her way back from her friend's house and wanted us to leave. People started heading out the door, and J. and I walked out of the small bungalow to his baby-blue Bonneville. I slid in, care-ful not to put my foot through the rusted-out hole on the passenger side, and J. loaded a few more bottles of beer in between us. His friend Kyle came stumbling out with a beer in one hand and a white platter covered in tinfoil balanced on his other palm. Kyle put the platter on the long scratched-up hood of the Bonneville and held up a pudgy finger.

"Wait just one more minute," he said to J. "I forgot some-thing." The other cars, an old Camaro and a rusty sedan, revved around us and took off. A few minutes later, Kyle came out with a fork and knife, a paper napkin, and a jar of mustard. He grabbed the platter from the hood and almost fell into the backseat.

"Onward!" J. drove while Kyle peeled back the tinfoil to reveal half a roast beef.

Kyle was finished with most of the roast by the time we got to Cranberry, the long skinny road leading to the small broken-down dock falling into the bay. Halfway down the road, we passed a group of people—some in their sweats and robes, clearly just out of bed—on a lawn. The entire group stared accusingly at our car as we passed by. Kyle waved from the backseat.

"What the fuck is up with that?" he said to the air. J. and I shrugged. We weren't speaking.

When we pulled into the cramped and pot-holed circle in front of the dock, two other cars were already there. We got out, and one of the guys, whose nickname was DeeWee (as in DWI), because he had so many drunk driving charges, told us that he had shot at a street sign with his shotgun.

"But it missed!" he laughed. "It fucking missed and it hit a car, man!"

I realized that the people we had seen in their robes and nightgowns were not just on a lawn. They had been circled around a car that was parked on the street at the end of the lawn. I turned to J.

"We are leaving right now." The others looked at J. to see what he would do.

"In a minute," he said dismissively, turning back to his friends. I got back in his car to wait. I stared out into the blue-black bay water and tried to focus on the sound of the small waves against the shore instead of the cracking open of more beer. Within five minutes, blue and red lights lit up the bay and dilapidated dock, sparking off the aluminum beer cans the boys quickly chucked into the reeds.

DeeWee's girlfriend, Cindy, came over and knocked on the driver's window. I opened the door and slid over so she could get in the front seat. She was a few years older than me and I liked her. She worked at a liquor store and always brought along nips of peach schnapps to share with me.

"You didn't hear anything, right?" she said. She looked scared. I nodded.

"Okay," she paused, watching as one of the cops pushed DeeWee toward the trunk of his car. Another cop dragged a beer cooler over to the patrol car. "DeeWee wants me to say I was driving. If he gets another DWI, he'll go to jail," she whispered, looking straight ahead. She had a porcelain, girlish face with a crown of curly blonde ringlets.

"I told him not to shoot that damn gun. I don't know what he was thinking." She turned and looked at me. "Do you think I should say I was driving?"

I bit my lip. Kyle's parents had been away for a few weeks a month earlier. I had visited his house twice with J. during that time, and DeeWee had shown up, each time with a different girl. They would smoke some pot at Kyle's kitchen table, then go upstairs to the master bedroom. After a while, they'd come back downstairs and the girl would leave. Then DeeWee would go into detail at the table.

As I debated whether to tell Cindy about DeeWee's cheating on her, one of the cops lit up the dashboard with his flashlight. He asked Cindy to sit in the patrol car, and he talked to me through the window.

"How old are you?"

"Sixteen," I said in a very small voice.

"What's your name?" He had a notepad out and was writing things down.

"You're not going to call my parents, are you?" I asked, terrified. My grades hadn't slipped a notch, and so far I had been successful in keeping the realities of my nights out a secret, thanks to a combination of breath mints and perfume.

"Do I need to call your parents?"

I told him my name and what I knew, which wasn't much. I said we were the last to get there, and that we had passed a crowd on the street. He told me to smarten up and went back to the circle of boys, whose eyes had been burning into the back of my head the whole time.

In the end, Cindy didn't own up to driving DeeWee's Camaro. The cops pulled a shotgun and a pair of brass knuckles out of his trunk and loaded him into the patrol car. He stared at Cindy as if she had murdered his mother while the car pulled away. J. drove her to a friend's house afterward, and we left as she was making plans to go to a pawn shop in the morning to try to hock some of her gold jewelry to post his bail.

DeeWee and Cindy broke up after she bailed him out. I missed her during our nights out, one of the only other constant female presences in the group. A few months later, J. and I were driving on William Floyd Parkway, a few friends in the back seat, when she pulled up next to us at a stoplight. The boys in back yelled hello to her through the window, and I could see that her old Corvette was packed with girls. Cindy was slapping the steering wheel in time to a loud drum solo, and I could hear the shrieks and giggles of her friends even over the blaring stereo. She smiled at us and waved and then pulled away, fast.

The boys all agreed that she looked amazing, that they heard she was doing great. I was silent in the passenger seat, stomach churning with envy, wishing I was in her car instead of J.'s, that I was speeding off somewhere.

She hadn't even looked at me.

By 1994, I'd reached the second half of my senior year. I had received my acceptance letter to Vassar and was preparing to leave the town, but many of my friends were going to be staying home. Mel got arrested in the Taco Bell parking lot with 200 sheets of acid in his backpack; Stacey got pregnant and kept the baby; Mike got into a motorcycle accident that tore up his wrist, so he lost his football scholarship to college; Sarah got pregnant, and Melissa had to drive her to the clinic for the abortion because Matty wouldn't even talk to her in the hallways.

A few weeks before school ended, my Advanced Placement calculus teacher had all his students decorate a ceiling tile in the classroom with the name and logo of the college they were going to the following fall. I traced out the female image from the folder I had bought at the Vassar school store when I visited—a seated woman in flowing robes with a book in her lap and what is probably a laurel branch in one hand, the glimpse of a Romanesque building behind her. I colored the tile in rose and cream. The ceiling was covered with SUNY school logos, and most kids, like me, were staying in New York state, if not on the island. One ceiling tile had the University of Scranton written across it in block letters, another had American University, and I wondered where those schools were. J. and I had broken up again, for good this time, but I heard that he had gotten into a technical school in Boston. Those last few days in class I spent most of the time staring up at my tile, pleading with the statue's calm and serene face—made cartoonish in my hands—to get me to the place she represented as fast as she could.

That summer, the girls came home from college and the neighborhood felt whole again. We worked at our summer jobs—Melissa and Andrea worked at the Splish Splash water park, Margaret made sandwiches at Sam's Deli, and I put away books and helped senior citizens make photocopies at the public library. After working at the beach concession stand with Margaret every previous summer, the library's air-conditioning and the fixed solidity of the Dewey decimal system was a relief compared to the sweat-soaked, suntan lotion-drenched dollar bills and grease spatter of the beach. After we got home from work, the girls and I would revert to our childhood patterns, milling outside after dinner at the end of the block, sitting at the end of each other's driveways, making plans for the night.

As long as the four of us were together, it wasn't important where we were going. Ever since Melissa had bought her 1976 Camaro, we had been piling in and driving out of Shirley, without much thought to the direction. When we went east, we walked the sidewalks in the small Hamptons towns or peeked through the thick green hedgerows as we drove past, announcing which house we would own when we were older. Or sometimes we'd take the train to Manhattan, without any goals except to say that we had been there, usually spending the afternoon circling the blocks around Penn Station, smoking our Virginia Slims and feeling dangerously adult.

One night after a party, Melissa drove us to Smith Point Beach. She parked and we kicked our shoes off and trudged through the sand to the shoreline. I let my eyes adjust and stared at my friends. I tried to memorize Melissa's relaxed giggle as she sat at the edge of the water and Margaret's small hand steadying me as I stumbled over a piece of driftwood. The moonlight caught in Andrea's black hair the same way it sparkled across the cresting waves, and I imagined that from a distance we must have looked like demons, the red embers of our cigarettes lighting up like eyes.

On the way home, the muffler dropped out of Melissa's Camaro as we crossed the bridge. We pulled over, collapsing into one another as we laughed, trying to recover the rusty old parts from her car that now littered the road. The metal disintegrated in our fingers as we scooped up the pieces, dispersing into the night like grains of sand.

At the end of the summer, my parents helped me pick out plastic crates and a mini-fridge. We loaded up the car and drove the careening curves of the Taconic Parkway until we saw the signs for Poughkeepsie. At Vassar's main gate, the heavy stone guard tower loomed over our car as we waited in line with the other freshmen families dropping off their kids. A bright yellow and white plastic sign happily sang its announcement: "Welcome Class of 1998!" I thought of that ceiling tile stuck in the corner of the calculus classroom and of the regal woman with her books and serene knowledge. The campus was surrounded by a low wall of heavy stone, like a parapet protecting a castle. I looked at those solid stones with greedy eyes, waiting anxiously until our car pulled through the gate and we were on the other side.

For the next four years, most of my life took place within those walls. I didn't miss waking up to the salty smell of the beach in my hair or running my fingers over the pockmarked wood at the Cranberry dock or traipsing through the wildlife refuge to dangle my feet in the Carmans River. I learned to simply answer "Long Island," or "the East End" when other students asked where I was from.

The summer after my first year of college, I worked during the day and went out with the neighborhood girls at night as usual. But the town looked different when I came home. The third step still creaked when I ran upstairs to my bedroom and my father's gardens bloomed as brightly, but it was as though a curtain had been torn down and I was seeing Shirley for the first time.

We spent a lot of our evenings at the nightclubs in the Hamptons. None of us were of legal drinking age yet, but we just waved to the bouncers and they let us in—most of them were boys who had gone to our high school. We parked for free in the staff lot, and inside we were sure to find a bartender we knew. One night, between the strobe lights and thumping music, a tall woman dressed in a pair of tight jeans, her breasts spilling out of a black halter top, tottered over to us. She held a wooden box out in front of her, and as she came closer I realized the box was attached to a thick leather strap that circled behind her neck, like a horse's bridle. The box was half full of glass test tubes.

"Mara!" Andrea shouted over the noise. The girl waved, flashed a bright smile, and walked toward our group. I kept staring at her until I realized why her apple cheeks and smooth skin were so familiar to me. I had been in awe of her—she was in all AP classes, always got the lead in the school plays, and had even been in the high school Rockettes kick line.

"Hi!" she waved, careful not to upset her box full of glass and alcohol. A clutch of crumpled dollar bills was stuffed in the corner of her crate. We all stood there catching up, stories competing with the thumping music. I studied Mara's face, and she looked older than I remembered, tired. Some guys in khaki pants and boat shoes came over to Mara, leering into her cleavage as they opened their wallets. I looked at her forced smile as she handed them shots of liquor, and then I scanned the room, finding the familiar faces of the bartenders and the bouncers we knew from Shirley. For the first time, I saw the difference between us and the real

Hamptons crowd, dancing in their strappy heels and lip gloss and collared golf shirts.

During my sophomore year at Vassar, my parents moved. They wanted a house that was smaller, now that it was just the two of them. Robin, our dog, had died. For the past few years, her body had been riddled with benign lumps the size of chicken eggs that finally collapsed her windpipe. My parents had considered leaving the town earlier, but my father was determined not to move until he had saved enough to cover my entire college education. And although they considered leaving town, they did not want to leave the area— my parents had friends, my mother especially, that they did not want to move far from. So they called Joe again, who showed them a unit in a rustic townhouse community bordering a lake just two towns east of Shirley. It felt strange driving home and getting off at Exit 70 instead of 68, and I missed my neighbors and friends, but I also felt a strange relief not having to drive into Shirley, not having to call it my home.

But Shirley pulled me back. There seemed to be a funeral every few months. Pat, a boy I had dated in ninth grade, was killed a few blocks from my house when he rode his motorcycle into the back of a parked UPS truck. Anthony drowned in his parents' pool, which was suspicious because he was more than six feet tall and cleaned pools for a living. Angel died of AIDS. Shannon caught meningitis during her freshman year at SUNY Stony Brook and died a day after her parents took her out of school and put her in the hospital. Joey's mother died after she had an aneurysm, and a year later Joey himself died of a heart attack. Shawn had managed to move to Queens with his brother and score a promising job at a fashion magazine, but he killed himself about a year after he left Shirley. Ralph killed his mother-in-law and burned his wife's family house down. Jay took too much acid one night and was put in a mental institution, his brain fried. Jason overdosed on heroin, and two years later Al did as well.

These wakes became a kind of morbid reunion. I would come home from college, put on mascara and a black turtleneck, and borrow my mother's car to drive to the funeral home. Margaret and I sometimes went together, and we would fix our lipstick in the rearview mirror before leaving the car.

In 1996, about a year after my parents moved, I was down in Texas, visiting my college boyfriend, helping his mother grate cheddar cheese while we made dinner. They had a television in the eat-in kitchen.

"We have confirmed reports now that TWA Flight 800 has crashed just off the coast of Long Island. We have a reporter standing by in Shirley to give us the rest," I heard the announcer say. I stared at the screen. The picture flipped from the news desk to a beach scene, where there were hundreds of people standing at the edge of the water. As the camera panned over the sand, I recognized the Smith Point boardwalk and the glass doors of the concession stand where I had worked for four summers.

"Oh my God," I said, hand still firmly gripping the block of cheese. "That's where I grew up!" My boyfriend and I stared into the television as the reporters listed the number of people on the plane and the rescue efforts that were underway. No one knew why the plane had dropped out of the sky, but there were reports of eyewitnesses seeing a missile hit the plane before it exploded in midair.

I flew home the next day, my fingertips cramped from holding the armrests so tightly. That night, I drove to Shirley and met up with Margaret and Melissa, and we decided to drive to the beach. As we trudged over our usual path from the parking lot, we could see a few small groups of people at the edge of the water. Toward the ocean some light caught our eye, and we realized that the space underneath the boardwalk—where the burnouts and metalheads used to sit with their boom boxes, sweltering in their jeans and boots—was glowing with candlelight.

There were letters wrapped in clear plastic sandwich bags thumbtacked to the wood beams of the boardwalk, and dozens of bouquets of flowers, both arrangements from florists and roses still in their plastic deli wrap from 7-11. Someone had left a teddy bear propped up on a piece of driftwood, and there was a necklace hooked onto a nail sticking out of another beam. The plane had been on its way to Paris, and there were young students from a school group on the plane. Candles—the kind with images of religious saints painted on the tall glass fronts—dotted the landscape of memorabilia, and the three of us went around with our lighters, relighting the candles that the wind had blown out. Some were impossible to keep lit—every time the wick caught, it would smother just a moment later—and this seemed hopelessly sad to us.

We sat on the cold sand with our arms around one another, sharing cigarettes and staring at the blinking red light of the aircraft carrier where the wreck divers were flinging themselves into the water in shifts. No survivors had been found.

Smith Point Beach was set up as a headquarters. William Floyd Parkway was lined with news vans, and every night I sat with my parents and watched our old town flash across the television screen. I had an internship that summer working on a congressional campaign for Nora Bredes, a working-mother-turned-activist from the North Shore who had been instrumental in keeping the Shoreham Nuclear Power Plant from opening in the 1980s. Firefighters and men who volunteered for the coast guard came into her office for the rest of the summer with stories about the rescue effort: The military seemed more interested in the plane parts than the body parts; they had set aside an air hangar to try to piece the plane back together and figure out whether it had been a missile or some internal malfunction that made the plane drop; the reason the identification process was taking so long was that by the time the divers reached the bodies, the crabs scuttling along the bottom of the ocean had already gotten to them.

Four years earlier, on November 24, 1992, Shirley had made local headlines for another crash—this one further up the highway and closer to the Brookhaven National Laboratory. As the sun was setting, some people driving along the Sunrise Highway watched as a red metallic object spun over the island and then wobbled uncontrollably, crashing down inside Southaven Park. Eyewitnesses reported that the craft looked like a UFO, and neighbors close to the park saw flashing lights in the sky and heard rumbling noises before they saw an explosion and black smoke curling like a signal in the air above the tree line.

The men from the local fire department were surprised to be stopped at the entrance of the park when they arrived to answer the 911 calls of neighbors. The Brookhaven National Laboratory's fire brigade had been the first to arrive, and although the fire was clearly still burning, Brookhaven officials wouldn't allow anyone other than Brookhaven National Laboratory personnel beyond the park's borders. The next day, signs were posted along the perimeter of Southaven Park announcing that it would be closed for the next week due to a private duck-hunting party.

Suspicion set in immediately. The Brookhaven National Laboratory trucks remained posted at all entrances until the week's end. The local neighbors and eyewitnesses from town who had seen a saucerlike object careening through the night sky had already appeared on television, and the mysterious nature of the Brookhaven National Laboratory just fueled the fire of speculation. A local UFO research group—Long Island UFO Network, or LIUFON—came to inspect after the park was reopened to the public, claiming that a fresh patch of scorched earth, trees bent in an odd formation, and high readings on their Geiger counters proved that the crash had indeed been a UFO. High levels of radiation were recorded by LIUFON, and neighbors reported that they had experienced multiple power surges in their homes. The group offered the theory that the Brookhaven National Laboratory had used a particle beam to zap the craft as it hurtled over the nuclear facility's campus and that the lab's fire brigade had been dispatched to collect the bodies of the aliens and hide the saucer itself.

People from Shirley were interviewed night after night on the news, most agreeing with the theories LIUFON had put forth about the Brookhaven National Laboratory having shot the craft out of the sky. The spokespeople from the Brookhaven lab hardly needed to respond; it seemed clear to almost everyone except the people from the town that the scenario was preposterous.

The possibility that the red metallic craft had originated from the lab, and was possibly an experiment gone wrong, was never raised. Instead, LIUFON, which had been in existence for five years when the Southaven park UFO touched down, shared with the press the information it had accumulated since its inception: Most of the reports and UFO sightings the group investigated centered in the Shirley area. The group's founder, John Ford, said, "Historically, UFOs have been seen wherever there is a research facility, nuclear power plant, or major military installation. Someone is certainly keeping an eye on our scientific and military development." A Southampton psychic was also interviewed, and she, too, felt that the Brookhaven National Laboratory area was an epicenter for alien activity. "They are watching the nuclear submarines in the Long Island Sound, but . . . they are trying to protect the subs from damaging the earth or its people," she suggested.

At the time, as a tenth grader, I was more than ready to believe that an alien spaceship had landed in my town. I loved the idea. I had watched the news and scoured the papers for additional reports, completely unaware that most everyone else was laughing at us.

The fiery crash of TWA Flight 800 brought the "UFO" from four years before skidding back into collective consciousness. Hundreds of eyewitnesses in town offered their accounts, the majority of them claiming to have seen a streak of light traveling toward the plane before the tail broke off and the first explosion shattered the air. Theories of terrorists launching shoulder missiles from the Long Island seashore made their way across the wires, and talk of our own government taking the plane out by mistake also heated up. The Southampton psychic may have been onto something; at the time of the crash, there had been two nuclear submarines just off the coast of the island. Reporters latched onto this fact because the submarines had materialized at the crash site within minutes. The possibility of a routine training exercise mishap was also posited.

The airline and government officials, however, did not like all of this talk about a missile shattering the belly of a commercial plane. For every Shirley resident who swore to having seen a missile shoot up into the sky toward the plane, an official reminded reporters about the hysterics the town had displayed years before when these same people swore they saw a UFO crash into their local park.

"The plane malfunctioned," the officials maintained. "There was no missile." More than 200 eyewitnesses signed up to be interviewed during the long process of piecing the plane back together. None of the people who said they saw the flash of light moving toward the plane were interviewed. None of them made the official report. Instead, the National Transportation Safety Board created a video simulation to explain how the eyewitnesses must have mistaken the exploding plane tail, which thrust away from the plane and plummeted to earth, for a missile launching into the sky.

Memorial services for the 230 people who lost their lives on the plane were held on Smith Point Beach. The space underneath the boardwalk became clogged with trash and dead flowers as time went on. The letters grew wet and moldy in the rain and seawater, the stuffed animals—more and more bears were lined up every time I went to visit the site—becoming mottled and dirty. The blinking red light of the aircraft carrier was visible from shore for the rest of the summer. In time, people came back to the beach, paying their parking fee and stripping down to their bathing suits in front of the makeshift memorial, oiling up under the bright sun as it glinted off the steely frame of the ship.

# CHAPTER TEN

Smith Point Beach was transformed into a memorial for the hundreds of plane crash victims, but the town was overflowing with memorials of its own. Just as I often came home every few months to go to the wake of a friend, my parents also returned to the town for funerals.

During weekly phone calls with my mother, I would stare out my dorm-room window as she talked about the women she knew who were going through radiation therapy or mentioned another friend who had found a lump and was waiting for the results. Many of the women, like Diane Sackett Nannery, the woman who created the breast cancer stamp, found benign lump after benign lump every few months or every few years before cancer developed. Others had lumps that were malignant from the start. That was the strange face of breast cancer on Long Island.

At the turn of the twenty-first century, statistics estimated that one in four Americans would experience cancer during their lifetime. However, cancers are also statistically expected to happen much later in life; the average age of a breast cancer patient is fifty-six. Linda, one of my mother's best friends, worked at Brookhaven Memorial Hospital and told my mother stories about all of the young women coming in who were sick; one girl was just twenty-two years old and needed a double mastectomy. Few of the patients came from families with a history of cancer.

Although the Long Island Breast Cancer Study Project held out hope for some women, others didn't live long enough to hear the results. And more and more people were getting sick. A New York State Health Department map showing breast cancer incidence in New York state by zip code for the time period 1993–1997 highlights Shirley in different shades of lavender and plum, showing the town's breast cancer incidence as between 15 percent and 100 percent above the expected rate. Shirley is also covered in diagonal lines on this map, as is the whole of Suffolk County, a marking that according to the key shows "an area of elevated incidence not likely due to chance." Lung cancer at the time was also 50–100 percent higher than expected, and thyroid cancer was seen in women 20–29 percent above the state rate, and more than 30 percent the state rate in men. The thyroid gland and breast tissue are particularly sensitive to radiation exposure; the only proven cause of breast cancer, aside from heredity, is radiation, and the only known cause of thyroid cancer is exposure to radiation. Lung cancer is often easily dismissed as a smoker's disease, but in recent years scientists have discovered links between lung tumors and exposure to radiation. The American Cancer Society found through studies of survivors in Nagasaki and Hiroshima that the risk of developing lung cancer becomes 50 percent higher after high-dose radiation exposure. Studies on American Indians from the Navajo Indian nation who mined uranium ore in the 1940s and 1950s for the U.S. atomic weapons production program, as well as uranium miners in Canada and the Czech Republic, have moved the U.S. National Research Council's Committee on Biological Effects of Ionizing Radiation to conclude that the radiation exposure they received during the mining work was a cause of their high lung cancer rates.

Tucked away in my own little world at Vassar, I tried to seal myself off from the stories my mother told me. Instead, I took in the news about women I had known for years as if they were simply more of my mother's hospice patients. I had seen what my mother's work required: I often pictured her sitting next to the shrunken body of a stranger in a bed, holding a hand whose skin felt fragile and thin, a tissue-paper flower. I could imagine her filling a bathtub with water just warm to the touch. I knew exactly the way she would rub the washcloth across her patient's back, shoulder blades poking out like the edges of dinner plates, and I knew the way she would hold her patient's chin up, making sure the shampoo didn't get into her patient's eyes as she poured cups of water over the small, unsteady head. These were the same hands that cared for me as I was growing up.

I was not the only one to look on my mother's work with awe. Earlier that year, Brookhaven Hospice had created an

Angel Award in her name, and they hoped to give the award annually to someone who embodied the grace, munificence, and warmth that were my mother's hallmarks. She also traveled to Poland and Russia the same year with a small group of hospice experts from America—hospice was a new concept in these countries, and my mother's group visited makeshift wards in rural farmland, where the nurses and nuns didn't even have aspirin to combat the patients' pain, relying on music therapy and meditation instead. Since Jerry's death, she had become like Atlas, carrying on her back the weight of as many sick people and their families as she could. But now there was something different in her voice—the sick people were no longer simply clients, but her close friends.

It was only when my mother told me that her best friend, Linda, had found a lump that I allowed the reality of her news to seep through the wall I had constructed. But even after she found out that the tumor was malignant, I simply sent cards from the Vassar gift shop and then waited impatiently by the phone for my mother to call me after Linda's mastectomy, her reconstruction, and her re-reconstruction after the first one failed.

There were no plane crashes or UFO sightings or dying friends within my walls at school. And that was how I tried to keep it, for as long as that was possible.

Others, of course, didn't have that same luxury. A few months before the plane crash in 1996, a father from

Manorville, which shares a border with both Shirley and the Brookhaven compound, noticed that his three-year-old daughter was slurring her words and drooling more than usual. Randy Snell and his wife took their daughter Lauren to their pediatrician, who found a lump under her tongue. The doctor told them it was nothing to worry about, suggesting they schedule surgery to have it removed at Stony Brook University Hospital. They arrived with Lauren on the appointed day and sat in the waiting room while their daughter was taken in for a procedure that was expected to take forty-five minutes.

Two and one-half hours later, a nurse brought them into a conference room and sat them down with an oncologist. The doctor told the Snells that their daughter had a rare cancer of the soft tissue called rhabdomyosarcoma, and that it typically hit 1 in 4 million children a year.

I spoke with Randy eleven years later in his branch manager office at North Fork Bank. A soft-spoken man with graying hair and bright blue eyes, he recalled that the oncologist had told them it was an aggressive cancer. "He said there was a 40 percent survival rate, which seems accurate from all the kids we met. My daughter was one of the lucky ones. We went to a lot of funerals."

After her initial operation, the family spent thirty-one straight days in the hospital. The Snells shuttled their toddler through three jaw surgeries after removing the tumor, nine months of chemotherapy, and six months of radiation.

"They finally declared her cancer free. There is a waiting period, and then they tested her every six months. It felt like a time bomb." In the hospital, Randy met and became close to William Theobold, another father whose small son was declared cancer free at the same time as Randy's daughter Lauren. Four months later, the cancer returned. Two months after that, the boy was dead.

At the time, Stony Brook was treating twenty children with cancer. Randy was surprised to find that four of those children had rhabdomyosarcoma. During his daughter's treatment, Randy researched more and more, finding conflicting numbers regarding incidence, but even the lowest rate he found—four children in 1 million—didn't match up with the numbers he saw when he looked around the chemo ward. Given the statistics the doctor had reported to Randy, it should have required a community of 16 million children to produce four simultaneous cases of his daughter's cancer. In 2000, there were only 352,842 children under eighteen living in Suffolk County. Just over 88,000 of those children were under the age of five.

During his research, Randy found a report by Dr. Seymour Grufferman of the University of Pittsburgh, one of the nation's leading specialists on rhabdomyosarcoma. The report concluded that the only known cause of the rare cancer—which begins as a tumor and enters into the soft tissue—was low-level radiation exposure.

Randy continued to research the cancer. When he looked beyond Stony Brook Hospital, he found eight other kids in the area with rhabdomyosarcoma. They all seemed to be centered in mid-Suffolk County. Randy contacted officials at the New York State Health Department and told them he thought there might be a problem, hoping they would give him the names of other families whose children had rhabdomyosarcoma on the island so that they could get together and figure out what was happening. They told Randy that they were unable to give out names at the local level because of confidentiality issues. They also declined an opportunity to look into the possibility of a cluster, because, Randy says, it was their policy not to act unless there were more than five cancers within a single zip code. So Randy kept counting, relying on word-of-mouth and leaks through sympathetic nurses and doctors, and learning as much as he could about his daughter's cancer.

"I thought to myself, where did she get this? At the time, I didn't know anything about the lab. I thought BNL was a lab with white coats and test tubes. I had no idea there were reactors there."

A few miles away from Randy's house, some neighbors on Carleton Drive in Shirley began meeting in each other's basements and dining rooms around the same time Lauren was going through chemotherapy. The street—nicknamed Death Row because so many of the people living there were sick with cancer—bordered the Brookhaven National Laboratory's property. Barbara Osarczuk, who had lived in the same house since 1968, had nine benign tumors around her thyroid and windpipe, cancer in her right breast, and two benign tumors in her left breast. Other neighbors had breast cancer, uterine tumors, congestive heart disease, and children with birth defects and learning disabilities. Debbie Hughes, whose son, Kenny, also had rhabdomyosarcoma, lived nearby and started coming to the meetings. Every week, more people from northern Shirley joined the group.

The people at the meetings felt certain that they knew what was making them all so ill: the Brookhaven National Laboratory. Carleton Drive was literally first in the line of fire for any air or groundwater pollution released from the facility, and although the Brookhaven National Laboratory denied being responsible for the elevated cancer rates in the area, the people meeting on Death Row knew that something through the pines was not right.

No one in the group was surprised when local newspapers reported in early 1996 that multiple underground plumes containing concentrations of hazardous waste exceeding federal and state drinking water standards had migrated beyond the borders of the Brookhaven National Laboratory. According to the U.S. Department of Health and Human Services, volatile organic compounds (VOCs), including 1,1-dichloroethylene (DCE), carbon tetrachloride, trichloroethylene (TCE), 1,1-dichloroethane, perchloroethylene, 1,1,1-trichloroethane (TCA), chloroform, and the pesticide ethylene dibromide, were found in wells.

The waterborne TCE, 1,1-DCE, and 1,1,1-TCA were of the greatest concern; aside from ingestion, all would readily turn into vapor during household chores, such as showering, hand washing clothes or dishes, and watering lawns or vegetable gardens. The routes of exposure of most concern for these chemicals, which were typically used as solvents and degreasers for cleaning metal, were inhalation, ingestion, and skin absorption. The Environmental Protection Agency maximum contaminant level for TCE at the time was 5 ppb, or parts per billion. Some monitoring wells tested registered 110 ppb. The chemical 1,1-DCE registered at more than double the EPA maximum contaminant level, and TCA was found at 340 ppb in residential wells. The New York State maximum contaminant level for TCA in 1997 was 5 ppb. Today, the EPA's standard is 0.02 ppb, a level arrived at, according to the EPA fact sheet on the chemical, because "given present technology and resources, this is the lowest level to which water systems can reasonably be required to remove this contaminant should it occur in drinking water." The short- and long-term effects of exposure to these chemicals include kidney, liver, and lung damage, toxicity to a developing fetus, and damage to the nervous and circulatory systems. And cancer.

The Brookhaven National Laboratory put together radio announcements publicizing an offer to connect hundreds of residents to municipal wells free of charge. These announcements, however, were often the first the residents heard about the problem and didn't give any indication of which blocks qualified for the hookups, just that there would be hookups in the area south and east of the facility. More than 600 people showed up at a meeting held in an auditorium at the Brookhaven campus, most simply trying to figure out if their house was on the list of homes slated for "city water." Brookhaven spokespeople tried their best to talk over an angry crowd, also answering questions about a recent fire in the High Flux Beam Reactor that had resulted in seven employees receiving low doses of radiation and a venting of tritium by the reactor stack. The spokespeople from the laboratory maintained that the underground plumes were not harmful and that their offer to hook the homes up to municipal water was simply the act of a good neighbor.

One month after the Brookhaven National Laboratory admitted that these plumes of chemical waste had traveled offsite, Barbara Osarczuk and her group filed a $1 billion class action complaint against Associated Universities, Inc., the management company that was overseeing the Brookhaven National Laboratory. Among their team of lawyers was famed attorney Richard J. Lippes, who had gained national esteem after the multidecade suit he fought and won for Love Canal, a small, blue-collar town near Buffalo, New York. Also on board was Jan Schlichtman, who had recently exploded into public consciousness as a main character in the book *A Civil Action,* which detailed Schlichtman's hard-fought victory in favor of the residents of Woburn, Massachusetts against local chemical companies.

In both Love Canal and Woburn, hazardous wastes infiltrating the local drinking water were connected with the high rates of miscarriage, illness, and cancer found in the adults and children of the surrounding communities. There were fifteen chemicals of the 248 ultimately identified from the Love Canal waste site that were considered most fatal or carcinogenic; the Brookhaven National Laboratory shares six of those fifteen highly hazardous chemicals: benzene, tetrachloroethylene, toluene, TCE, xylenes, and PCBs. In Woburn, TCE was also highlighted as the major chemical culprit.

However, neither the Hooker Chemical and Plastics Corporation at the Love Canal site nor W.R. Grace and Company and Beatrice Foods at Woburn were federal entities. They didn't have the backing of the Department of Energy and the Department of Defense. These facilities were not winning Nobel Prizes in physics for the outstanding national research they did. And no one from these companies would have asked a parent of a child with cancer, as Randy Snell says a federal investigator did of him, "Didn't you ever think that you'd have to live with additional risks because of the good this lab has done for the community?"

Randy ultimately joined forces with Barbara Osarczuk's group and even became the treasurer for a time because of his background in banking. A few months after the class action suit was filed, the High Flux Beam Reactor was closed for "routine maintenance."

Roads in northern Shirley had been torn up for months as the pipes were laid for connections to municipal water, which even the Brookhaven National Laboratory spokespeople called "city water," just as my neighbors had years earlier. Randy had kept up with his rhabdomyosarcoma scorecard, and by this time had tallied sixteen children with the rare cancer, all within a fifteen-mile radius of the

Brookhaven National Laboratory. Just as the breast cancer activists had done before him, Randy drew a map, marking the spots where a child with rhabdomyosarcoma lived with an X.

"There were two instances where two children living on the same block had been diagnosed with rhabdomyosarcoma," Randy says. "But the scientists at the lab kept saying, 'That's not how science is done—if you put a bunch of dots on a map you can always make a cluster.'"

Clusters are historically difficult to pinpoint, and scientists often point to what is widely known as the Texas Sharpshooter Effect for perspective: A traveler driving through a town in Texas notices on almost every barn he passes that there is a target with a single bullet hole that goes exactly through the center of the bull's-eye. At a gas station in town, he asks the attendant about what he assumes is the town's amazing sharpshooting ability. The attendant laughs and tells him the shooting was the work of one man. Hardly a sharpshooter, this man would shoot through the side of a barn and then paint the targets around the bullet hole.

But as Randy stared at the bull's-eye the X's created on his own map, and as nurses in the hospitals took him and his wife aside, whispering words of support and telling him that they were onto something, the Texas Sharpshooter Effect didn't seem to add up on Long Island. Instead, I imagine Randy felt more like someone playing tennis who, despite all effort, continually hits the ball straight at the opponent on the other side of the net. As much as Randy didn't want the X's to continue lining up the way they were, each mark he placed on the map kept going right into the same fifteen-mile radius around the Brookhaven National Laboratory.

Randy's rhabdomyosarcoma group and the class action group quickly found themselves flanked by other factions that opposed the Brookhaven National Laboratory. Most of the members were people like Randy—not politicians, not activists, simply concerned citizens—but what at first felt like momentum quickly gave way to infighting. And Randy knew that if he was going to win his fight against a federal giant, he needed some serious backup.

This backup did arrive, though not in the form Randy expected. During the maintenance scheduled for the High Flux Beam Reactor, a leak in the machine's spent fuel pool was discovered by the Brookhaven National Laboratory. When the reactor was built, it was common practice to take the precaution of outfitting the pool with a second metal liner. To save money, designers had only included a single liner in the High Flux Beam Reactor's underground storage pool. Suffolk County regulations actually required this second liner, but the Brookhaven National Laboratory did not have to comply with this regulation since it was a federal facility. The Superfund investigation team had also included a second liner as a high-priority item in their list of suggestions to improve safety at the site, but the fortification had been put off for two years.

A spreading plume of tritium was detected beneath the spent fuel pool. Rather than reporting the leak immediately, however, lab officials allowed the tritium to continue to seep into the ground for months until all of the spent fuel rods from the pool could be removed and shipped to another national laboratory site in Savannah, South Carolina. Investigations would discover that the leak had been dispensing radioactive tritium into the groundwater for more than twelve years. The plume stretched south toward the Long Island Expressway. In illustrations printed in newspapers at the time, the tritium stretched out like an underground hand reaching toward Shirley.

Officials on the Brookhaven National Laboratory PR team were more prepared for the meeting they held in their auditorium on the tritium leak than they had been for the previous meeting on the chemical waste plumes. Local politicians and activists had already called for the permanent shuttering of the High Flux Beam Reactor. With the reactor itself at stake this time, the Brookhaven National Laboratory printed up flyers to make sure that the people coming to the meeting understood that the research the machine allowed was incredibly important. A flyer entitled "The H.F.B.R.: Solving Real-Life Problems Through Science" pointed out the many scientific benefits of the nuclear reactor, including "better medicines," "improved technologies," a "cleaner planet," and even "new cancer treatments." Community members, many of whom were suffering from cancers they felt came from the waste originating from the laboratory's reactors, were deeply offended by the handouts.

Randy remembers the community meetings on the chemical waste and tritium leaks as an exercise in frustration, as scientists whose presence was meant to offer expert opinion became defensive and terse. "One person asked about all the mercury that had recently been found in the Peconic River, and whether it was from the lab. The scientist up front responded: "Yes, it came from the lab, but when I was a kid I played with the mercury in my thermometers and I'm fine, I don't have cancer."

More than the ridiculous answers and inability to admit that something might not be perfect at the lab, it was the arrogance that really infuriated Randy and others at these meetings orchestrated by lab officials. The meetings were meant to be a public forum, but the scientists repeatedly retreated into obscure technical answers and jargon. One of the community groups that Randy belonged to was called Citizens for a Cleaner Brookhaven, and most of the group members came from the Shirley area. It was the responses and reactions that the people from this group received from the scientists that inspired Randy to take a more public position in the fight against Brookhaven.

"I had public speaking experience, and I wanted to be a voice for people who might not have the ability to speak. A lot of Shirley was not able to speak up for themselves," Randy says. "I mean no disrespect. Understand that. But there was a class issue and just lower education involved." The scientists from the lab picked on people at these meetings. "I remember one person asked a question and mispronounced the word *tritium*. And the scientists just jumped all over them. They said, 'You don't even know how to pronounce it, how can you say this is harmful?' It was degrading."

At one meeting after the discovery of the leak in the reactor's pool, one scientist stood up and offered to guzzle tritiated water at 100 times the drinking water standard to prove that the radioactive waste flowing into the water was safe. He was never called upon to follow through with his dare. And he was never pressed about whether he would have fed that same glass of tritiated water to his three-year-old daughter. Nor was he asked to do so daily for months on end.

By 1998, Randy had collected the locations of twenty-seven children with rhabdomyosarcoma in Suffolk County. He had also joined forces with a group called Standing for Truth About Radiation (STAR), which was based in Manhattan and backed by money from Hamptons fund-raisers thrown by East End residents Alec Baldwin and Christie Brinkley. Both had long been involved in cancer research on the island; Baldwin's mother was a breast cancer survivor. The organization had also pulled in a young local lawyer as counsel. Scott Cullen, in his late twenties at the time, had grown up as one of the few who experienced life inside the heavy military gates of the Brookhaven National Laboratory. His grandparents had both worked at the lab in service positions—his grandmother in tech support and her husband in security. He spent summers swimming laps in the lab's pool and picnicking on the grounds. "It had a college-campus-like atmosphere," Cullen remembers. "And the arrogance that goes with it—there was this overriding sense that they knew best."

This was the catalyst for the coordinated effort that Randy had been hoping for, the way to unite the rather raw and disorganized local groups. Beyond that, he saw STAR as his only hope to compete effectively against the federal government. Many of the other homegrown activists were skeptical of STAR at first, and of the Hamptons money behind it, but eventually most people changed their minds once they witnessed the group's ability to raise awareness and gather research and experts together.

"All of a sudden, [the activism effort] went from housewives to a higher level," Randy says. "We would never have been able to get an audience with a senator on our own. But Alec Baldwin? Christie Brinkley? They absolutely could. And that was all that mattered to me."

Scott Cullen and STAR's team of nationally recognized scientists, including Jay Gould, director of the Radiation and Public Health Project, and Nobel-winning Helen Caldicott, took the lead. Baldwin appeared on the Montel Williams show with Caldicott and *A Civil Action*'s Jan Schlichtman. Parents of some of the children diagnosed with rhabdomyosarcoma, including Randy, were interviewed on the show about their experiences, and Shirley residents Debbie Hughes and her eight-year-old son, Kenny, who was in remission, explained their theories that the radiation exposure responsible for Kenny's cancer must have come from the Brookhaven National Laboratory. A taped response from the lab showed scientist William Gunther, standing with the High Flux Beam Reactor stack towering above him. Gunther smiled and reported that tritium in wells was below the drinking-water standard, and that the main plume that was twice the limit was still within the site's boundary.

The camera then panned back to the sunken face of a man named Brian who sat hunched in a chair. His eyes were hollowed out and he talked about his hope for a Childhood Cancer Awareness Week. He had just lost his five-year-old twin boys, Luke and Zachary, who had a rare form of leukemia and had been in the same ward as Randy's daughter Lauren. Brian stared out into the crowd, as pictures of the boys flashed on a screen behind him. Then the show flipped back to the smiling face of Mr. Gunther.

The High Flux Beam Reactor remained closed until more testing could be completed. Then, in March 1997, during routine Superfund testing, drinking water near the decommissioned Brookhaven Graphite Research Reactor showed levels of radioactive strontium 90 as high as 566 picocuries per liter (pCi/L)—more than seventy times the federal standard of 8 pCi/L. Meanwhile, the Brookhaven National Laboratory continued to place ads in local newspapers calling for support to reopen the High Flux Beam Reactor, and to increase its power from 30 megawatts to 60 megawatts.

Rather than supporting the Brookhaven National Laboratory's request to reopen the reactor, the Department of Energy removed the site's founding managers. The oversight body Associated Universities, Inc. was ousted because, according to Energy Secretary Federico F. Peña, the group put science before environmental safety. While it searched for a new management company to take over the $400 million contract, the Department of Energy came under scrutiny itself; the House Science Committee requested a report by the Government Accountability Office (GAO, formerly the General Accounting Office), the nonpartisan audit arm of Congress, looking into the history of oversight at the national laboratory. The GAO findings were severely critical of the Energy Department, charging that they should be held responsible for failing to detect the twelve-year-old tritium leak and that they should not try to shift the blame onto Associated Universities, Inc.

Although the Department of Energy maintained that the tritium leak was not a health hazard and that all levels of the nuclear waste found in residential drinking wells were below federal standards, Congress voted to decommission the High Flux Beam Reactor.

The idea that the tritium-laced water was safe to drink seemed to be a theme in the Brookhaven National Laboratory's defense. The federal government drinking-water limit for tritium was placed at 20,000 picocuries in the 1976 Safe Drinking Water Act, a level that was upheld in 1991 and is still the acceptable limit in the United States today. A picocurie is one-trillionth of a curie, a measurement of radioactivity named after Marie Curie that is equal to the amount of radioactivity emitted by 1 gram of pure radium.

In addition to the projected $460 million needed to clean up the Brookhaven National Laboratory site through the

Superfund, the Suffolk County Water Authority put $20,000 into an advertising campaign in an attempt to assure its customers that their drinking water was safe. Half-page ads appeared in *Newsday* and *Suffolk Life,* and the water authority began monthly testing for tritium at ten municipal wells closest to the laboratory. But how safe was a glass of water containing 20,000 pCi/l? And how much tritium was an acceptable amount to be drinking daily over a long period of time—for example, the twelve-year known time period of the leak? "Their dose reconstruction is simply BS," says former STAR counsel Scott Cullen about the Brookhaven National Laboratory's contention that the leaks of chemical and nuclear waste were not health hazards.

The Institute for Energy and Environmental Research (IEER) holds that there is no threshold for cancer risk from radiation, and therefore no exposure level is necessarily considered safe. The EPA's limit of 20,000 pCi/L does not mean that the agency condones someone drinking water that tests at 19,999 pCi/L. In fact, the EPA defines safe as zero known risk. The 20,000 pCi/L is what is known as a maximum contaminant level (MCL). The EPA also establishes maximum contaminant level goals (MCLGs). These are levels at which there is zero known risk, defined by the EPA as "the maximum level of a contaminant in drinking water at which no known or anticipated adverse effect on the health of persons would occur, and which allows an adequate margin of safety. Maximum contaminant level goals are nonenforceable health goals." MCLGs for all radionuclides, including tritium, are zero.

The EPA fact sheet on tritium states that "as with all ionizing radiation, exposure to tritium increases the risk of developing cancer." Anything above 0 pCi/L, then, is not safe—because "safe" means zero risk.

Randy's daughter Lauren may not be able to have children because of the radiation and chemotherapy she received as a toddler. She had three more operations on her jaw when she turned sixteen to correct the damage and stunted growth resulting from the high level of radiation her mouth received as a child. When I spoke to Randy in his office in 2007, her doctors were debating whether they would have to pull all of her remaining teeth and fill her mouth with implants. But Randy still considers Lauren to have been incredibly lucky. "We would make friends in the hospital and then they would die. There aren't too many of those kids alive."

Many children who survive cancer lead full lives as adults, but many have irreparable damage to the heart from the chemotherapy drugs. Others are left sterile. Often, the amount of radiation used to suppress their cancers sparks secondary cancers that surface years later. "I remember one night at the hospital with the twins," Randy says, talking about Zachary and Luke, the five-year-old boys with leukemia. "They had so much chemo in their little bodies that even a cough could rupture a blood vessel. That happened one night, and all the parents on the floor were just running around, getting as many towels and blankets as we could to try to stop the bleeding."

Randy felt some satisfaction at the announcement that the High Flux Beam Reactor would not be starting up again. The Brookhaven National Laboratory maintained that the decision was financial and that the federal money should be put toward other, stronger machines operating around the country. "I hoped they would admit they were wrong," Randy says. "But I took the closing of the reactor as their admission of guilt." Over the years that he had fought the Brookhaven National Laboratory, Randy had lost friends and, like many of the activists, struggled with his family life. Neighbors who thought he should simply shut up and stop saying bad things about the town would accost him in his driveway or at the supermarket, blaming him for the plummeting property values. What they did not understand was that their property values had already dropped, not because of Randy but because of the town's proximity to a leaking nuclear laboratory. The damage had been done long before Randy ever opened his mouth to talk about his daughter.

He found it was useless to try explaining to these neighbors that he was speaking out not only for his family, but for theirs as well. People who worked at the Brookhaven National Laboratory also looked unkindly on him, worried about job security and most likely their own image—no one wants to line up on the side of the bad guy. "I was enemy number one," Randy says. "I've had death threats. The calls were traced to the Brookhaven National Laboratory. When they found the guy, the lab people just said, 'We spoke to him, and he's not going to do that anymore.' If that happened in my office, there is no way that person would still be working!" When I asked if he would have done anything differently, he looked at the framed photographs of his children that run along one of the file cabinets in his office. "My only regret is that I wasn't wealthy enough to devote my entire time to the fight. I still had to take care of four girls and my wife," he says.

I was on the phone with my mother again. The Vassar campus was covered in snow, and I was getting ready for the last midterms of my senior year. I knew the moment I picked up the phone that something was wrong, and after I put the phone back on its cradle, I walked to the bathroom and threw up.

My mother was supposed to be exempt. All of the talk at the dinner table, all the hours she spent sitting at the deathbeds of strangers, all of the walkathons and fund-raisers, all of the damp washcloths and bloody bedpans—I thought these things were supposed to work like some kind of talisman, a protection against the very thing she had so welcomed into her life these past ten years. I thought that my mother's willingness to bring cancer to our dinner table night after night was assurance against it coming to our house of its own will. But the talisman had not worked. She had found a lump.

When I was sixteen, a dermatologist had to remove a mole on my arm. The doctor biopsied the spot in the office and my mother stood behind the nurse as she swabbed the area with alcohol and gave me a shot of anesthesia. Instead of looking at my arm, I looked at my mother and tried to match my breathing to hers. I couldn't feel anything, but I could smell the burning skin and hear the metal-on-metal scrape of the doctor's tools. I was just beginning to relax when my mother's face turned pale and waxy and she gripped the side of the doorway.

"Mom?" My eyebrows went up. The nurse turned in my mother's direction.

"Uh-oh. Better get her out of here," the nurse said, and grabbed my mother by her elbow.

A few minutes later, my mother returned with a small cup of juice and a cookie in her hand. She smiled at me and sat down in a chair next to the door. She looked like a child with her juice and cookie. She stayed in the room, but she didn't watch the rest of the biopsy.

I teased her that afternoon. She regularly witnessed some of the ugliest aspects of terminal illness, yet she couldn't handle her own daughter's blood! Alone in my dorm room, I thought of her smiling at me after she came back into the room. I had no idea whether I could do the same for her if she needed me to.

I postponed my midterms and took the train home. I stared at the dark lines of the Hudson River as the train rushed toward the city, and then through the scraggly arms of the pines as a different train brought me out to Long Island. It felt strange not to get out at the Mastic-Shirley station, and

I suddenly wished that we could go back to our little house near the refuge. I wanted to return to the time when I was a child surrounded by friends as I swung at a papier-mâché donkey in my front yard, not a young woman going home to her sick mother.

I thought of the long white scar on my mother's neck. When I was in third grade, my mother had a tumor on her thyroid gland. It was benign, but half of her thyroid had to be removed along with the growth. My father drove me to visit her before and after the surgery, and a doctor took a piece of paper from my coloring book and drew a picture of a butterfly.

"Your mother's thyroid looks like this," he said, pointing to the pen drawing. He drew a line down the center of the butterfly's body, slicing it in half.

"We have to take out this wing, but your mother will still have this other wing." I looked at the paper and I looked at my mother, somehow smaller under the scratchy white sheets in her hospital bed. I could see the small knob of tumor that pushed through her skin halfway up her thin neck. When she came home, the scar was an angry red at first, but she sliced off leaves from her aloe plant, cracking the thick pulp open and smearing the gummy juice on her incision every morning and night. As the scar healed, the line turned white instead of fading into the rest of her skin. My scars do the same thing. In the summers, when she is tan, the scar looks even whiter against her browned skin, like a piece of butcher's twine. I wondered if this was what the scar on her breast would look like.

My father picked me up at the train station. He was quick to smile and joke, say the surgery was no big deal, everything was fine. But his eyes looked tired, and when he rubbed them the purple skin of his eyelids rippled into folds where he had pushed the skin to the outside corner, and the folds stayed there. He had been working so hard for so many years; as he had hoped, he had been able to pay for all four years of college. He had become more handsome as he aged, the salt and pepper in his hair an attractive contrast to the blue in his eyes, but more than a decade of working as a traveling salesman had left its mark.

He had brought my mother back from the hospital that morning and had to go away overnight for business, which was why I was home. I could tell he was nervous, just wanted this to be over and for his wife to return to normal. When we went into the house, there were flowers on every surface of every room; all of the women my mother had driven back and forth to radiation appointments and sent angels and flowers to over the years had returned the favor. The house smelled thickly of lilies.

Recuperating upstairs in her bedroom, my mother looked tired, but she was smiling. We spent the day in her bed, passing magazines back and forth, dozing and watching taped episodes of the *Oprah* show. I made soup from a can and toasted some bread, the same meal she made me when I used to stay home sick from school as a child. The shadows grew longer across the walls, and I knew we would have to change her bandage soon. My mother motioned to the bathroom door.

"Okay. Let's get this over with!"

I followed her into the bathroom, where she leaned her back against the counter, edging her right shoulder out of her white terry-cloth bathrobe.

"You don't have to do this, you know," she whispered to me.

"I'm fine, I'm fine!" I lied. I tried to smile. I was terrified to look at my mother's breast.

The robe hung across her body like a sash. She bent her neck and tried to look at the place where they had removed the lump. She cupped her breast beneath her ribs with her left hand, and for a moment it looked like she was holding a baby to her chest. My eyes traced the bright blue vein that ran from her neck to her nipple.

The yellows and greens of the bruises clouded around the edge of the bandage. She worked the sticky edge with her fingertips until she'd gotten most of it free. Blood crusted along the jagged teeth of the sewn-up incision. I looked at the thin white half-moon across the base of her neck and tried to imagine this new incision healed and faded instead of raw and pink.

"It doesn't hurt," she offered, looking at my face. "Not really."

I turned the brown bottle of peroxide over in my hand and soaked a cotton ball, trying not to look at my mother's face. I knew if I did I would cry. I slathered antibiotic ointment onto a fresh gauze pad and handed it to her.

"I can't reach it, Kell. Can you press it on for me?"

Her voice apologized as she asked me. I tried to think of her breast as a knee or elbow. I remembered once when

Margaret and my mother and I went for a bike ride when I was little, and I fell before we even got around the corner. The rough gravel had skinned layers off the top of my knee, leaving a slick white patch where the skin used to be. I watched, stunned, as little rivulets of blood pooled on the white patch and started to drip down my leg. My mother left our bikes on the side of the road and picked me up, my head to her shoulder and her arm under my legs. It was summer, and my mother wore a light yellow blouse and white pants. I tried to hold my bloody knee away from her, and she kept telling me to relax, not to worry, it was just blood. But she was too pretty to get blood on.

I snapped back to the bathroom and her purple and yellow clouds of bruise and did my best to press the bandage gently over the stitched incision where the doctor had pulled out a hard mass the size of an almond. The doctor had called earlier to tell us that the mass had been benign. We should have been happy. But we knew how breast cancer worked on Long Island. Our relief felt very temporary.

CHAPTER ELEVEN

One of my favorite pictures of my mother was taken in August 1976. I've been in her belly for about eight and a half months, and her stomach swells like a sand dune beneath a paisley shift dress. She is on a weathered wooden deck and waves crash in the ocean in the background. She is turned away from the photographer, my father, and only half of her dreamy, close-lipped smile is visible in the frame. Long white-blonde hair, uncombed, spills down her back, and her hands are brought together above her belly, as though she is holding a communion wafer. Her back is straight, and her shoulders and arms are thin—so thin at first glance, one might not realize that she is pregnant. The blurry white body of a seagull shimmers in front of her, and the bird's wings are outstretched, silver tips blending into the waves behind him, as if trying to hold himself steady to catch the piece of bread my mother is about to throw to him. The day is overcast, and the picture is mostly a smear of blues and heavy grays.

My parents were in Montauk for the weekend. They had rented a motel room, the kind where you can drive right up to your door, the kind we spent our first night in when we first moved to Shirley. Even before I was born I was linked to the island, to the push and pull of the waves, to the sea salt drying on my skin, soft as powder. I've always loved it. It has always felt like home.

After I graduated from Vassar, I moved to the city. With the exception of one year when I shared an apartment on Spring Street in Manhattan with a friend, I technically continued to live on Long Island for ten more years as I moved between apartments in Brooklyn and Queens, both geographically still part of the island. So it made sense that when my new husband and I decided it was time to buy a house, we looked to the east.

Mark and I spent our honeymoon in a motel in Montauk, similar to the one in the picture of my mother. Holding hands, skin tight with sunburn, we scoured the postings in the windows of the local real-estate agents during our walks along Main Street. It quickly became clear that we wouldn't be able to afford even a small summer cottage, let alone a real home.

Over the next few months, we looked at places on the North Fork and in the less-expensive Springs area of East Hampton, but nothing was in our price range. One night, after yet another unsuccessful weekend of house hunting, we returned to Brooklyn, discouraged and tired. We walked to our favorite Mexican restaurant for some fish tacos and sat along the orange-and-brown tiled wall, sipping from a pitcher of margaritas and munching chips and guacamole. One of the owners, who was friendly with Mark, came over to the table, and we started talking about our difficulty finding the house we wanted on the island for a price we could afford.

"Well, you guys are clearly looking in the wrong places," he said simply. "I just bought a place out there, and let me tell you—this town is going to be the new Hamptons! Our house is near a big park and we have a lawn and everything, so it is perfect for my little girl. We are minutes from the beach, and it was *cheap,* man!"

He had us on the edges of our chairs. Where was this magical place?

"Well, it isn't quite there yet. Some of the neighbors are pretty rough around the edges, but we get a kick out of the bizarre Virgin Mary statues and plastic flowers and other crap people put out on their lawn. But they just opened up a golf course and are talking about a marina, and I think when that happens the place will really explode," he said. "It's just before the Hamptons, on the South Shore. It's called Shirley. You should really check it out!"

He laughed when I told him I grew up there. "Then you already know," he said with a smile.

A few days later, my mother sent me an article from *Newsday* that talked about "artsy city dwellers trickling into towns in South Shore others have dismissed." The article highlighted a rental permit law that had gone into effect in 2000 that required landlords to maintain their properties as one of the reasons for Shirley's resurgence, but the president of the Citizens Action Coalition, Grace Ionnidis, was skeptical of a boom anytime soon. "We have a lot of crack, a lot of heroin, domestic disputes, loose dogs, quality-of-life issues, unregistered vehicles, unlicensed drivers, a lot of DWI cases," she was quoted as saying. But the Brooklyn crowd didn't care. One homeowner said that the contractors she tried to get to come out to her house all groaned, as if to ask why she had to buy there. "It seems to have this bad reputation, but we're like, 'Hey, we live in New York City . . . That's not an issue for us.'"

I had driven Mark through Shirley and the Mastics before, and we both agreed that Smith Point Beach was more beautiful than any of the private Hamptons beaches we had been to. But I didn't know if I could live there again.

It had been fourteen years since I'd left, but the town itself seemed relatively unchanged. The strip malls still dotted William Floyd Parkway, and many of them were empty and abandoned, just as they were on our first day in town. There was a new Home Depot, and the library had expanded. A public golf course had indeed opened, and its seventy-foot chain-link fence towered above the tops of the pine trees along William Floyd Parkway. The Woodlands development was finally full, although the gloss on the blacktop was gone and the houses, which always seemed like mansions to me growing up, no longer looked especially luxurious.

Some of the old neighborhood was still intact. Strangers had just bought our old house on Arpage, and Mrs. Kutch's daughter no longer lived in our first house around the corner. My parents had moved away, as had Melissa's. They had followed their daughter out west, to Phoenix, where she was teaching art to elementary students and had recently had a baby girl. Margaret and her cousins, Joe's sons, all lived in the city, and the four of us met for drinks and breakfasts and dinners regularly. Margaret had been my maid of honor, and I stood up for her in the same spot at her wedding. All of Margaret's family still lived in the neighborhood, and her older brother and uncle had also moved into houses within the two-block span of the original neighborhood. Andrea had moved back to her childhood home in Shirley with her parents and was working as an occupational therapist nearby.

One night in 2007, while her parents were on vacation in Florida, I went to Andrea's house for dinner. She cooked spaghetti with homemade sauce and we split a bottle of red wine. Her kitchen was still laced with the familiar fragrance of vitamins, which I now recognized as the earthy scent of health food.

"The Mayos' house across the street is for sale," she said, with a conspiratorial note in her voice. "I'm thinking about putting an offer on it." I knew she was enjoying living at home with her parents—much to everyone's, including her own, surprise—but a permanent move across the street was pretty serious.

"Well, you know me, Kelly. I love it here, but I'm also terrified. I go to my doctor every other month thinking I feel a lump. No matter how safe they say the water is, there is no way I would drink anything but bottles." She took a sip of her wine. "I mean, I would love to live across the street. Love it. I love this neighborhood, and I loved growing up here. But I just feel like if I stay—if I actually buy something here—I'll get cancer. I'm terrified."

All of the neighborhood girls have said that they expect to get a lump at some point. I can't help but feel the same way. None of the multiple studies over the past few decades have been able to give us any answers about why so many of our mothers, friends, and neighbors are getting sick. Even when the Long Island Breast Cancer Study Project finally released its findings after an interminable ten-year wait, the findings weren't much different than the findings from the studies this huge multi-million-dollar project was supposed to replace.

The main hope of the Long Island Breast Cancer Study Project was that the Geographic Imaging System—the in-depth, electronic system of mapping women with breast cancer on the island—would be the basis for a true environmentally based study, a more comprehensive version of the street-by-street maps the activists had made of their own neighborhoods showing where cancer was occurring across Long Island.

At the beginning of the study, the Brookhaven National Laboratory was given $542,997 to work out the feasibility of a Geographic Imaging System, a computerized geographic mapping program that would mimic and expand the hand-drawn and color-coded town maps pinned to the walls by the activists. In the interim, the Long Island Breast Cancer Study Project turned into a geographic modeling project, which used statistical aggregation rather than the actual data collected to determine cancer incidence. In other words, individual women with cancer became statistical smears and averages instead of the points on a map of Long Island as intended by the original plan. All specificity was lost, as was the hope for a true geographically-based environmental study.

The year before the Long Island Breast Cancer Study Project findings were released, the National Cancer Institute completed the Geographic Imaging System, but not in time to be used in the Long Island Breast Cancer Study Project to create a geographically based environmental study, the kind of study the activists thought they would be getting.

The other hope for the study—that it would be one of the first to include the voices of the activists who had fought so hard for it—was also erased. Each week these activists, almost all of whom were women, drove to the meeting hall and met with the scientists, but with each meeting their hope dwindled. The lists of hundreds of items that the activists brought to the attention of the scientists—the majority of whom were not from Long Island—were hardly considered. The activists were looking for substances specific to their lives and lifestyles—chemicals they used at home, pesticides sprayed in their streets and over their homes for mosquitoes or bugs in the potato fields, waste products from the aerospace projects conducted by Grumman and other Long Island–specific industries. The activists were shocked when it was announced that the cornerstone study of the

with the exception of DDT, none of the dozens of contaminants released during the fifty years that the Brookhaven National Laboratory had been in existence were included in the study.

Some of the activists continued to go to the Long Island Breast Cancer Study Project meetings, but some began searching for other ways to contribute to the cause once it became clear that the study would not be all that they had hoped. Diane Sackett Nannery was one of the women who struck out on her own. The young post office worker from Manorville who had conceived of the very first breast cancer stamp decided she could improve on her idea, so she set her sights on creating a stamp that would raise not just awareness, but also money for breast cancer research.

Frustrated with what she saw as a lack of funds and the absence of relevant research projects, Nannery proposed that a second breast cancer awareness stamp be created, but this time the stamp would be sold at a premium over its postal value. Issued on July 29, 1998, the stamp features the phrases "Fund the Fight" and "Find a Cure" across an illustration of a mythical goddess of the hunt.

A year later, in 1999, Nannery's cancer returned. "I just remember sitting at the end of my bed, looking out the windows at the towers in the rain, thinking—I am going to die," Nannery said.

I spoke to Nannery, who was in her late forties at the time, over the phone in March 2003. She had been in bad shape recently, she explained in her gravelly voice, and never knew how she would feel from one day to the next. When I requested a face-to-face interview, Nannery explained that she preferred to just speak on the phone because this way if she wasn't up to talking she could just ask me to call back rather than having me run around and make new appointments.

And then she kept talking. For forty minutes.

"I've won so many awards—the Betty Ford Award, Lifetime TV, a Suffolk County award," Nannery said, listing them in a blasé tone. "It's not sour grapes, but all the recognition came when I was in remission. I would get resounding applause at my speaking engagements. They were applauding that I'd survived three, four, six years! When my cancer came back, the applause stopped."

By the time I spoke with her, Nannery had been on chemotherapy for metastatic breast cancer for over three years. This woman, described by so many with such terms as "tiger," "go-getter," and "unstoppable," told me how shopping with her husband for a washer and dryer the day before had tired her out. "When I was in remission, I could work at the post office during the day, speak, go to luncheons, and get six hours of sleep. But with active cancer, I don't have the energy."

"I was always the last person to leave the party. I loved to dance even into my forties and would usually be the one closing the bar," she was saying. I believed her. Recalling her fight for the breast cancer stamp, she said, "I thought we should have a stamp that raises awareness as a way to pay tribute to the women who didn't make it." Nannery had called herself a breast cancer survivor from the moment of her diagnosis, refusing to accept any other possibility, even as she studied the statistics of the disease and worked on her memorial stamp.

"My activism started immediately, but not consciously," Nannery says. She never went to a support group; instead, she found comfort in working on the breast cancer stamp project.

Nannery's cancer came back a year after her first malignant tumor was removed. She went into remission again, but realized that medicine and research was agonizingly slow for breast cancer. She wanted to do something that would ensure more money for breast cancer research, so she returned to her original mode of activism: the stamp. A percentage of every new breast cancer stamp is supposed to go toward research to fight the disease. When I asked Nannery about the results of this strategy, her voice tensed.

"We've raised hundreds of millions of dollars, but unfortunately, not much has changed." I asked her where all the money had gone.

"Some of the money goes to the Department of Defense," she said. "And at the time of the stamp, we hadn't deployed troops in this country in decades." The Department of Defense has a medical research division, and I asked if she knew how the money was spent, if there were reports available so she could keep track of the research being done as a result of the millions of dollars from the stamps. She had never seen one.

"The Department of Defense always seemed to work out well; the money is used for peer-reviewed study projects, which seem better to me than most of the research out there. Smaller groups get tons of money, but wind up producing fluff. Fluff isn't going to save me." Nannery did not know exactly what studies were coming out of the money from the stamp, though. At the time of our phone call, the United States was gearing up for the second Iraq war. How would this affect the Department of Defense's breast cancer fund?

"Good question. I have no idea. It would be interesting to see if there was a clause in the law that said the money could only be used for breast cancer research," she said, pausing. "I sure hope there is."

The next time I called Nannery was a week later, at the decided-upon time.

"I'm sorry, but it's not a good morning for me. I just took some pain medication and have to sleep in a while. Can you call me tomorrow?" Her voice sounded small and throaty, not the booming tones of the week before. I thought about the reality of her being on chemotherapy for three straight years, and of course I agreed to call back.

She was feeling better the next day, though obviously still not as well as the first time we talked. I asked her about the Long Island Breast Cancer Study Project, which I knew she had been active in sparking.

"I don't believe in the project," she said resignedly. I was surprised. I told her that I thought she had been very instrumental in the process.

"Oh, I was. I went the first year and a half—I went to all the meetings until I realized it was just an empty hope. Finally I said to my husband, 'I'm not wasting my time anymore. Nothing's going to come of it.'" The meetings she mentioned were a point of contention for many of the breast cancer activists. During the development of the project, it was established that the head researcher would meet with a team of activists every week to coordinate tests and ideas. But it was clear from the start that this was not exactly a group effort.

"Dr. Marilee Gannon, who ran the study, was a researcher, but not specifically of breast cancer. It was a daunting task and a lose-lose situation. The activists wanted an answer. They wanted someone to say: 'Yes, if you stop drinking the water and stop using this pesticide, you will stop dying.' But that's not what happened."

I asked her if she thought the six chemicals tested—the DDT and other pesticides and the diesel and cigarette smoke—made sense.

"This is where science gets scary. Science is very expensive and you only get funding for something that is already proven, for a test that already has a track record," Nannery explained. I was beginning to understand why the scientists had rejected the lists the activists had collected in their brainstorming sessions on Long Island's history and a typical Long Island woman's daily habits. But why test only a few items that were already known to cause cancer?

"To me it is common sense: If no one has ever looked at this particular thing, then it could be the answer. But you

have to know the outcome of the test before you do it because they don't want the tests to fail. What's the point?"
Nannery also brought up the idea of chemicals working
synergistically, something that Randy had mentioned as
well: What if it wasn't just one chemical, but chemical com-
binations that were unique to Long Island?

"I don't come from a cancer family," Nannery said. "I do
believe I was probably predisposed genetically, but something had to spark that mutation. But that something is
not necessarily one thing. It wasn't the one day I sprayed an
apple tree with pesticides in my yard or the one day I petted
a dog with a flea collar or the one time I inhaled car ex-
haust. But it could've been all three." The issue, Nannery
explained, was the sheer volume of women on the island
who were just like her; every breast cancer in the area could
not have been caused by three or four separate sparks—
there had to be some common ground that was unique to
Long Island. Or some common groundwater.

"All these women were on pins and needles when it
came close to the time the results were being released, but I
didn't even bother bringing the newspaper home. I knew it
was going to find nothing." And when the results did not
provide a definitive answer, such as "It's in the water," there
was a backlash against the activists. Nannery described the
feeling of defeat in the activist community. They had won
all of these battles, commissioned a multimillion-dollar
study, and still, a decade later, they had no answers.

"The women all got credit for getting the ball rolling,
but they also got the blame when the results showed noth-

ing. It was almost like admitting what you did was a fail-ure." Many of the activists took the stand that it was a giant first step, that ruling things out was as important as finding the cause of all of the breast cancer. But Nannery disagreed.

"At the beginning of the project, I thought I would be old in a nursing home and a young person like you would come to visit me, would say that you heard breast cancer used to actually kill women and that would be the past, an-cient history. But that is not how it happened." Nannery's voice wavered over the phone. After a minute of silence, she continued.

"That's not going to happen, because I am never going to make it to that nursing home. So I have changed my goal. Enough looking for the cause—that obviously is not going to work with the way science is set up in America today. We need to find a cure. That's the only thing that is going to save me now."

Diane Sackett Nannery was right. There would be no nursing home for her. Instead of a young person asking her about the old days when breast cancer was a killer, I was asking her about the disease that would kill her within the year. The few times I was able to speak with Diane, she seemed a different woman from the one described by her fellow activists and others who knew her, different from the newspaper stories that had her wisecracking with journal-ists and overpowering senators and representatives to get her way. Nannery was frustrated when she became too sick to attend speaking engagements, saying that it was actually in these last few years of her life that she felt she needed to be most visible. She had talked acidly about the media's love affair with success stories like Olivia Newton John and Kate Jackson. Just as the applause stopped when Nannery's cancer came back, so did the invitations to breast cancer events. Nannery, who never found comfort in support groups but did find solace in activism and public speaking, felt that she had been silenced. In her last months, she continued to write letters, trying to raise awareness about the dying side of breast cancer. She was concerned that so many women saw only the success stories, like her story in the beginning of her ten-year battle with breast cancer, and not the long-term trajectory of the disease.

"I called myself a breast cancer survivor from the first day I was diagnosed, but I didn't know what I was talking about," she said at the end of our last talk. "I wasn't a real breast cancer survivor until my cancer came back. I am a real breast cancer survivor right now because every minute of every day is survival for me."

Diane Sackett Nannery died Wednesday, November 19, 2003. She was just fifty-one years old and had lived with cancer for eleven years. I found out about her death the following Sunday, through a phone call with my mother, who had learned about it from a friend at hospice. I was surprised that I had not read about Diane's death earlier, and when I searched the Internet for mentions of her death, there were no notices—not on the postal service Web site, not on the Long Island Breast Cancer Study Project Web site, and not on any of the activist group Web sites. I finally found a small obituary in the back of *Newsday,* in which her husband, Ed Sackett, was quoted. "She called breast cancer a blessing. It was what she was born to do—help other people with breast cancer."

Although exposure to ionizing radiation is the only known cause of breast cancer, along with the established common risk factors such as heredity and high income, no part of the Long Island Breast Cancer Study Project looked at the Brookhaven National Laboratory, the largest source of nuclear waste and radiation on the island. Ionizing radiation is any radiation powerful enough to alter atoms by removing one or more electrons from their orbits, such as in gamma rays or x-rays. This type of radiation changes the molecular structures of cells, and it is these cellular changes that scientists believe cause cancer to develop. Before the dangers of ionizing radiation were discovered in the 1920s, radiologists who used x-rays without shielding developed leukemia at excessive rates. In the 1950s, studies were released that showed patients who had been treated with radiation therapy were more likely than those not treated to have leukemia and cancers of the lung, esophagus, bone, breast, and thyroid. We receive low doses of ionizing radiation everyday from background sources, such as the sun, but while these small amounts cause damage, our cells are able to repair that damage rapidly. At higher doses, or even minimally elevated doses over a long time, our cells just can't keep up with the repairs, and these cells either die or are damaged permanently, so that when they divide they split into abnormal cells. These abnormal cells are the ones that can often turn into cancer.

The Brookhaven National Laboratory is overseen by the Department of Energy, but it is funded primarily by the Department of Defense. The Department of Defense also funded the majority of the Long Island Breast Cancer Study Project. Diane Sackett Nannery suggested that the outcomes of most studies are assumed before they begin, basically because the aim of any scientific study is to test whether a hypothesis is true and most scientists can't get funding for oddball studies. But her statement also had a deeper meaning: Shoddy science is likely to be conducted when the agency paying for the study will benefit from whatever conclusions the study might make. In a case like that, the study can be tailored to produce favorable results, such as the studies funded by tobacco companies that claimed cigarettes don't cause cancer. And ultimately, those entities holding the money are the ones determining which studies will be undertaken at all. The largest source of chemical and nuclear waste—as well as ionizing radiation—on the island was not investigated in the Long Island Breast Cancer Study Project, which received a large part of its funding from the Department of Defense.

I had bought dozens of the semi-postal breast cancer stamp that Diane Sackett Nannery had helped create. So had most of America, it seemed; the stamp has raised $58 million. The National Institutes of Health gets 70 percent of the money. A congressional law determined that the Department of Defense gets the other 30 percent.

The U.S. Army Medical Research and Material Command division of the Department of Defense has so far received $15.1 million from the Breast Cancer Awareness semi-postal stamp. The division had spent only one-third of the money it received from the stamp by 2003. Federal government agencies such as the Department of Defense have not been subject to the same reporting requirements as other groups that benefit from semi-postal stamps, like the Heroes of 2001 or Stop Family Violence. Because of this discrepancy in spending, the Government Accountability Office—the same congressional audit group that demanded the Department of Energy take responsibility for the twelve-year tritium leak beneath the High Flux Beam Reactor—requested that the Department of Defense report where the money from this stamp was going just as the other agencies are required to do.

As the Department of Defense collects millions of dollars in research funds from the breast cancer semi-postal stamp, the Environmental Protection Agency—another arm of the federal government—collects taxes and federal money for the cleanup of over 1,243 Superfund sites polluted with toxic waste. Of these sites, 157 are federally owned, like the Brookhaven National Laboratory.

A portion of the sale of each breast cancer semi-postal stamp funds the Department of Defense, the organization that in turn pays the bills for the Brookhaven National Laboratory. It is hard to imagine that this cycle—money moving from the breast cancer stamp to the Department of Defense to the Brookhaven National Laboratory—is the one Diane

Sackett Nannery was hoping for when she petitioned for the stamp.

Over the years I had been away, the town had changed more than physically: The relationship between the Brookhaven National Laboratory and Shirley had been completely flipped on its head. Bill Richardson, then secretary of energy, had closed the High Flux Beam Reactor for good in 1999. He had also signed papers to allow a new nuclear particle accelerator, the Relativistic Heavy Ion Collider, to be built at the Brookhaven National Laboratory. The accelerator was built under the direction of the laboratory's new manager, Brookhaven Science Associates, a joint venture between Stony Brook University and Battelle Memorial Research Institute of Columbus, Ohio. John H. Marburger, president of Stony Brook University, became the new director of the federal facility. He had been widely credited for increasing the pace with which the laboratory cleaned up its chemical and nuclear wastes. In 2001, President George W. Bush nominated Marburger to become assistant to the president for science and technology policy. He was confirmed the same year and has been the president's top science adviser on nuclear weapons, the human genome project, and the space program, among other initiatives of the Bush administration.

Under the management of Brookhaven Science, 4,372 cubic yards of polluted soil—roughly eight and one-half basketball courts' worth—has been treated or removed, and 87,000 gallons of water have also been treated or removed.

The Peconic River, which flows east toward the Hamptons and had been receiving discharges of tritiated water, cesium 137, mercury, silver, copper, and PCBs from the laboratory's sewage plant, went through a stringent remediation process, which included scooping up polluted silt from the riverbank and replacing it with native vegetation. The Brookhaven Graphite Research Reactor, which emitted radiation through the air, soil, and groundwater, was also in the final stages of decommissioning.

Meanwhile, the nearby Indian Point nuclear reactors were running into trouble. During the 1980s, the Brookhaven National Laboratory had repeatedly held up in esteem Westchester County's Indian Point in contrast to the ill-fated Shoreham Nuclear Reactor, which, according to the lab, was shut down as a result of poorly-informed and hysterical activists. In 2005, however, tritium was found seeping out of the spent fuel pool at the Indian Point facility. Strontium had been found in an onsite well in concentrations three times above the drinking-water standard. Tritium and cesium 137 were both found in concentrations at ten times above the standard, and plumes were found pooling underground beneath the reactors. Throughout newspaper articles and Indian Point press releases, the fact that the contaminated water drains into the Hudson River—as opposed to a drinking-water aquifer in the Brookhaven National Laboratory's case—is meant to comfort. However, the Hudson River is used as a source of drinking water; Poughkeepsie, New York, where Vassar College is located, pulls its water from the Hudson, and during periods of drought, New York City also sources its water from the Hudson through the Chelsea pump station. In September 2007, four groups—Riverkeeper, Alliance for Nuclear Responsibility, Three Mile Island Alert, and Pilgrim Watch—sent a letter to Marburger, Bush's top science adviser and former director of the Brookhaven Laboratory, requesting that he pressure Bush to follow through on the Bioterrorism Act's Section 127, promising a stockpile of potassium iodide pills, which protect the thyroid gland in case of a radiation emergency, to communities within twenty miles of nuclear sites. These same groups have banded together in an effort to keep Indian Point from gaining an extended operating license for the next twenty years. The Nuclear Regulatory Commission (NRC) has acknowledged that—were it being considered today—Indian Point would never again be sited so close to New York City, and the groups want the plant to be shuttered for good.

Indian Point is in the middle of a public relations quagmire. The Brookhaven National Laboratory, however, has learned from its mistakes and adopted a more open approach to the public. Starting in 1998, a community advisory council, made up of non-laboratory citizens, has met every month to discuss the ongoing Superfund cleanup and other issues relating to the impact of the national laboratory on the community. They sponsor school science fairs and have started offering a program called Summer Sundays that allows families to visit the facility through a series of tours. A whole portion of the Brookhaven National Laboratory's Web site is devoted to "Environment, Safety, and Health," and its Office of Educational Programs has an impressive list of stewardship initiatives that involve local schools. Judging by appearances, Brookhaven had gone from being the town's proverbial haunted house on the hill to a model neighbor.

"Here for the show?" The guard's voice was full of gravel and boredom.

I stared at his worn braided-leather belt, the only part visible to me through Mark's window from my side of the car. I leaned in toward the steering wheel and was surprised to see a grandfatherly man with a puff of hair the same flinty silver as his booth. I had assumed he'd be in fatigues, a machine gun hanging from his shoulder, and at least young enough to put up a good fight. Instead, he looked paunchy and pale, his sunglasses crooked on his nose.

The guard handed a packet of papers through our window.

"The white one is for your dash, and the stickers are for your shirts. Keep the stickers on at all times," he said, waving us past. I looked down at the papers in my lap. I was still cupping our driver's licenses.

"He didn't ask to see our ID," I said, somewhat deflated.

"Nope," Mark said, smiling. "I guess we don't have to worry about being on a secret list."

The Brookhaven National Laboratory only runs tours on seven summer Sundays a year. The tours, which change each week across the seven-day season, are mostly aimed at school-age children, and have names like "Playing with Science" and "Watch Us Go and Grow Safely." I chose the only one that would focus on the Relativistic Heavy Ion Collider.

As we drove deeper into the lab's property, I saw that it was quite different than I had imagined for all those years. The campus beyond the gate was tucked deep into the woods, but after a few minutes of driving, the forest fell away and was replaced by long patches of dry lawn shaved close to bald, and it felt like we were entering some kind of airstrip. Low, barracks-like structures cropped up, and rows of olive-green jeeps and red-and-white emergency vehicles were parked like small armies, ready to go at a moment's notice. I did not see a single flower bed or ornamental bush. Dirt roads broke off the main drag and were named after the facility's founding universities (Johns Hopkins Road, Princeton Avenue). We followed the orange traffic cones until we found the main building and pulled in under an old oak tree to park—the lot was almost full.

Inside, I poked around the gift shop, deciding on a mouse pad and pen decorated with the lab's atomic swirl symbol. In the lobby, I stared at an exhibit dedicated to the hundredth anniversary of the publication of Einstein's relativity papers. We filed into a classroom and watched a presentation about fission given by a burly scientist eating an apple. His red laser pointer kept going dead. Afterward, we were told to line up for the tour; buses would take us to the two stops on this excursion.

I had forgotten how green and thick the seats on school buses were, like a layer of evergreen hide, tacky to the touch in the Long Island summer heat. Mark and I sat together near the back, thighs and elbows touching, knees grazing the green hide in front of us, not quite fitting into this space made for children. In the other seats, families bounced as the yellow bus rumbled along the dirt paths. We were deposited in front of our first stop, where we entered the wide mouth of a squarish, bunkerlike building with airplane-sized hangar doors thrown open. On one side of the doorway stood whirring silver machines connected to one another with clear-chambered walkways and a maze of steel steps. The wall of machines looked like the inside of a giant computer chip, with bright red, blue, and yellow tubes sticking out in spiny clumps, winding around each other and disappearing into the ceiling or down into the floor. On the other side of the doors, facing the giant computer chip, multiple stacks of concrete blocks were layered, like a wall of coffins. Between these was a short string of freestanding lockers. A few of the lockers had names scribbled on masking tape stuck to their vented faces. I wondered if these belonged to scientists working in the building or if they were filled with the belongings of a maintenance worker, like my old neighbor Jerry.

This colorful computer chip was the viewing deck for the experiments conducted using the Relativistic Heavy Ion Collider—"Nicknamed Rick for short!" the guide had chirped at the few children on the tour. The station itself was a solenoidal tracker, nicknamed, of course, STAR. After picking our way around the threads of colored cord on the floor and touring the frigid, computer-stocked rooms that splintered off from the giant computer chip, we were ushered back to the open hangar doors to wait for another bus to take us to a building just a few hundred feet away, where we could better view RHIC himself.

We stayed in the shadow of the open doors while waiting for the next bus. There was a watercooler nearby, and someone handed out Dixie cups of the lukewarm liquid. Off-duty tour guides with name tags were standing near the lockers while we waited. One man seemed more relaxed than the rest, with the air of being on a smoke break, though without the cigarette. A few of us nearby started asking him questions about the work he did, and whether it made him nervous to work with nuclear materials. He pointed to the wall of cement blocks.

"You see those? That's our protection. That beam crashes into those blocks. Each one of those is five feet thick," he said. I imagined standing behind one of the blocks as a beam of highly concentrated radiation crashed into it. "Of course, the block is then radiated." Unlike a nuclear reactor, I knew, an accelerator contains no nuclear inventory—there are no cooling pools with radioactive rods, for example—so an accelerator only produces radiation when in operation. "I wouldn't eat my breakfast off of it, but it's safe enough to walk by it," he continued. I looked again at the wall and imagined eggs cracking and frying against the cement coffins, yellow yolks spattering and running down the metal lockers. Just then, the bus pulled up, and our group was loaded into the yellow vehicle.

At the next stop, we all walked single file through two sets of double doors into a low, angular building. A female scientist was finishing up a presentation to some other group and told us to just go straight downstairs—we could look at her exhibits after we saw RHIC. At the base of the stairs and around a sharp corner we found another guide waiting for us. He was a visiting scientist from China and looked about twenty years old. He told us he was working on his Ph.D. and living at the Brookhaven National Laboratory for the summer. He seemed nervous and uncomfortable, and I wondered if they forced the visiting scientists to give these tours or if they signed up willingly. Hanging in midair behind our young guide was a thick painted pipe with the diameter of a hula hoop, with another dinner plate-sized silver pipe hugging close. These pipes were a small slice of a submerged ring two and one-half miles long—the same ring originally constructed for the failed Project Isabelle in the 1970s—with viewing stations like the one we were in perched along four points of the circle. This length of pipe was used to speed up and explode beams of gold particles, the guide explained. They would release one beam from one side of the ring and another beam from the other side of the ring and watch the two propel themselves around and around until they smashed into one another, creating a moment of nuclear fission on impact. A sort of atomic Nascar for geeks.

"Are there particles in there now?" asked a woman in a matching purple tank top and shorts. The young guide shook his head, smiling warmly. "No, no. We would not be allowed here if the machine was on. There are viewing stations made with layers of concrete five feet thick to protect from radiation produced by the impact."

The group nodded in response—he was talking about the STAR thing we had just seen.

"Well, where does the radiation that you produce go after you look at it?" asked a balding man in gym shorts holding his young son's hand.

The guide smiled patiently. "It disperses into the atmosphere," he said. "The beam hits a big block of marble and steel and the plasma dissipates."

The group nodded again, although we were a bit less convinced this time. The man in the gym shorts raised his hand again. The guide nodded in his direction.

"Well, what are you doing all this for? I mean, what are you trying to learn?"

The guide repeated what the guide on our bus had told us before dropping us off in front of the facility: They were trying to reproduce the first few moments of life—the Big Bang.

"Right, I get that," said the man impatiently. "But then what? I mean, why do you want to see that? What are you going to do with that information?"

The woman in purple whispered to her husband, "Make the biggest bomb in the world."

The guide ignored her and folded his hands in front of him, making a steeple with his index fingers. "Do you know the Internet?"

"Yeah," the man said cautiously.

"Well, scientists did not set out to discover the Internet. The Internet was actually a by-product of other experiments. That is what we are doing here."

The group nodded again. "Thank you for coming," the guide said quickly, officially ending our tour. We turned around and went back up the stairs, leaving him and his subterranean rings to wait for the next group.

Back on the bus, another guide, who had a black handlebar mustache and wore a short-sleeved button-up shirt, pointed to a cluster of white-tailed deer along the pitch pines outside the bus windows. "The Brookhaven National Lab sits on more than 5,000 acres, and we are surrounded by thousands of acres more of federally preserved sanctuary. These woods are full of nature," he said grandly, spreading his hands out like Vanna White.

I stared at the deer and recalled a study I had read that found an elevated rate of radioactive cesium 137, a waste product of the nuclear reactors, in the bodies of deer tested in the area. The governor had put out a warning against consuming any meat from deer killed on the East End of Long Island, adding to the warnings already in place against eating any of the local fish, which also register high levels of cesium 137, as well as plutonium 239, which functions as fuel for nuclear reactors. I listened as the guide continued to talk about staff picnics and volleyball games under the pine trees.

The man in gym shorts was sitting nearby with his son, and his hand suddenly shot up, interrupting the guide's lecture on the pastoral life of scientists at the lab. The guide pointed to him, smiling.

"Yeah, um, I just don't understand something about that Rick thing." The guide continued to smile, but without his eyes. "I know you guys are trying to recreate the first moments of life or whatever, but what I don't get is why? What good is that going to do us today? I mean, all this taxpayer money and you releasing all this radiation and—what for? What are you looking for?"

The guide squared his shoulders confidently at the front of the bus. He clearly had this one covered. "Are you familiar with the Internet, sir?"

After the tour ended, the bus deposited us where we had started. I looked around the antiseptic lobby at the visiting children twittering around happily, toting their new Brookhaven National Laboratory coloring books and candy-colored helium balloons printed with that Jetsonish atomic swirl symbol. Our group dispersed, and we walked out of the main building, which released us with the whispered whoosh of pneumatic doors. There was an ice cream truck parked next to the building, and an overweight bus driver on his break leaned against his yellow charge, a cigarette in one hand and a soft-serve cone in the other. A line of people stood in front of the ice cream truck, its off-key plinking echoing into the parking lot, and I shivered in the August heat. The blue of the sky was sharp against the scattering of ash-colored buildings. Above the tops of the trees, I could see the slender tips of the decommissioned reactors' smokestacks. They were sand-colored, and the bright red stripes that circled their tips looked like strings tied around someone's fingers, reminding them of something they otherwise would have forgotten.

# CHAPTER TWELVE

As Mark and I considered Shirley as a possible place to start a family, I was transported back into those years when I had called the place home. Smells often carried me back—the brine of the ocean mixed with the treacly scent of honeysuckle, a whiff of hot dogs crisping on a grill after an autumn thunderstorm. My car practically steered itself to the broken-down dock at the end of Cranberry Street, where I parked in the wet sand and walked toward the rickety, driftwood-colored structure poking out into the water. I ran my fingers along the initials carved into the wooden rails, the grooves and indentations beaten smooth by the salt and wind, and I expected to see names I knew, initials and messages from fifteen years ago, but I didn't recognize any of the names scratched there.

I crossed over the Smith Point Bridge and parked in the lot where my father had taught me how to drive. Walking toward the rhythmic sound of the waves through the underpass, I shouted the word *hello* into the tunnel to hear my echo, as I had so many times with the neighborhood girls before. On the other side of the dark passageway, a sign pointed toward the TWA Flight 800 Memorial, a well-manicured rock garden with a black slab of glossy rock rising from its center, listing the names of the dead beneath a giant wave carved in relief. I turned, pulling my long black coat closed at my throat as I continued down the path toward the water, surprised to find only a set of wooden steps in front of me—a decade of beach erosion had chewed up the rest of the old boardwalk. Smith Point Beach without its long strip of weathered boardwalk seemed alien. The sensation reminded me of the first time I stood in front of one of the roiling Great Lakes, trying to make sense of the familiar sound of crashing waves and the absence of salt in the air.

The effect of the town's new additions was just as disorienting as revisiting my old haunts. The section of land under the bridge where J. and I had parked in his blue Bonneville and where I used to go four-wheeling with my friend Dallas in his Jeep now had a large sign declaring it as the marina. But the small parking lot was empty, and only a single fishing boat sat overturned and tied up near the shore. I also learned that the golf course, which, along with the marina, had for years been heralded as the sign of a turnaround for Shirley, was about to close. The hundreds of acres—some of the last undeveloped land in town—were slated for an affordable townhouse development. No one in town seemed to care much about the change; the golf course had never delivered on its promise to transform Shirley into the pearl on the end of the string of glittering Hamptons.

In the time since I had left, however, the town *had* acquired its very first resident with Hamptons cachet. Anna Wintour, the British-born editor-in-chief of *Vogue* magazine and international arbiter of style, had bought a forty-two-acre spread along the Forge River. Wintour's property was an old colonial homestead once owned by the William Floyd family, and the farmhouse and six barns function as her family's summer home.

Not long after Wintour had purchased the estate, the only one of its kind in town, a dark bloom of algae seeped across the Forge River, and a stench of sewer gas and rotten eggs spread through the air. And every summer afterward, the dark stain appeared near the river's headwaters, close to the Brookhaven National Laboratory compound, in early May. By mid-July, the cloud would extend for most of the river's length and the stink would engulf Wintour's property, which is at the end of the river near the mouth of the bay.

When Wintour heard that a neighbor, a carpenter named Ron Lupski who was born and raised in the town, had started an organization to try to clean up the river, she offered her support. Ron started a group called Save the Forge River and petitioned local politicians for studies to figure out what was causing the destructive algae bloom, but no one seemed to take notice. Wintour gave a number of donations to Save the Forge River, which were logged as anonymous, and Ron updated her as he sent more and more letters to environmental groups and politicians, and was faced with more and more ambivalence.

In summer 2006, she showed up unannounced at a meeting that Ron had arranged to publicize the problems plaguing the Forge River. Preceded by bodyguards and wearing her signature black shades, she addressed the few local news-beat reporters covering the meeting, who were no doubt shocked by the appearance of a fashion icon. Until recently, Wintour had never publicly acknowledged that her house was in the Shirley area, and articles in magazines such as *World of Interiors* referred to it as her "Hamptons estate." A few snide articles had been published when she first made the move—with headlines including, "Shirley, You Jest"—but in general she had kept a low profile, her presence largely undetected.

Not this night. After her arrival was noticed, she leveled with the reporters and the crowd: "I think the problem really is that since this is not a chic community like the Hamptons, the local governments are not really doing everything they could to take care of it." After that meeting, Ron had Wintour's full and public support, and when he asked if she would march with him down the middle of town handing out flyers for the Forge River, she consented.

I had never walked in my hometown Christmas Parade before. But for as long as anyone I've spoken to can remember, on the first Sunday of December, the town's fire trucks, the ROTC unit, and the high school marching band—

along with local businesses, like South Shore Auto Works, John's Pizzeria, and Kreative Landscaping—line up at the Kohl's and Sears strip mall and walk east on Montauk Highway for a few miles, past the tattoo parlors in single-wide trailers, the aging bait-and-tackle spots, the discount beer depots, the decades-old family shoe stores, and Italian delis selling homemade rice balls and ravioli. At a corner shared by Davin's Funeral Home and Ice Cream Cottage, the parade makes a right turn down Mastic Road, ending just beyond the railroad tracks by the fire station and seafood store.

Most of Shirley's Christmas Parade floats are just cars or trucks decorated with holiday baubles and blaring Christmas music. Many groups don't even have a vehicle and are just made up of a collection of people walking together in matching hats or jackets.

At the parade staging area in the Kohl's parking lot, an hour and a half after everyone else had lined up and two minutes before we started walking the route, Wintour and her son, Charlie, materialized suddenly, as if they had been shopping in the nearby Sears all morning. Petite and tidy in ankle-length tapered jeans, a puffy cream-colored jacket, her jumbo dark sunglasses, and a wide smile, Anna moved laser-quick through the crowd until she reached Ron, who greeted her with a hug. Charlie, sweet-faced with dark hair and eyes, wore a tan oilskin jacket lined with silky brown fur, jeans, and knee-high green muck-boots. He held his mother's jacket in one hand and his cigarette in the other while Wintour pulled a Save the Forge River T-shirt over her blue sweater, and they walked a few steps with arms linked at their elbows. She chatted amiably with Ron and some of Ron's buddies, but after a few minutes of standing around, Wintour asked two or three times, "When are we going to start?" Mostly, the other parade-goers seemed oblivious to Wintour. A week later, when Ron's father saw her on Barbara Walter's special, "The Ten Most Fascinating People of 2006," he was surprised at how well she "cleaned up."

Ron and his carpenter buddies had decorated an old whitewashed school bus, covering it with rolls of thin plastic marine-themed tablecloth from the dollar store, blue tinsel, clumps of sea grass, and fishing nets. A Christmas wreath and mounted bluefish were stuck on the front grate of the bus, which was the official float of the Save the Forge River group. There was a cooler of beer on board, and while we waited for the parade to begin, the women took turns running into the nearby pizza and bagel shops for bathroom breaks. A stooped, dark-haired woman made rounds with a shopping cart full of pretzels and a small Sterno fire, selling the snacks for a buck a piece, and a homeless guy panhandled for change, holding out a torn coffee cup.

It was the first time an environmental group had asked to be in the parade. Ron usually walks with his carpenters' union, but he was able to convince a few of his work buddies to stretch white T-shirts with the words "Save the Forge

River" over their long-sleeve thermals and walk in front of the big white bus instead. He grew up on the Forge River and moved next door to his family's old house there five years ago. Since then, he had been noticing how different the river looked from the way he remembered it. He and his wife, Esther, cringe when they see kids playing in the water during the summer—they would never even let their two grandkids near the edge of the river, which borders their backyard.

"Esther swears the pollution killed our dog. He was just a puppy and he fell off the boat one afternoon. Three days later he was dead from a bacterial infection," says Ron, forty-three and fit, with a full head of thick black hair and a healthy tan even in the middle of winter. Over the past few years, Ron and his father, both avid fishermen, had noticed fewer and fewer grass shrimp, peanut bunker fish, and juvenile eels in the river water. The first summer after Ron and Esther moved into their house, they watched in horror as the dark cloud spread. The algae soon ate up all of the oxygen in the water, and Ron and his father saw dozens of crabs scuttled out of the water, limp and gasping for air. Dead ducks and fish lined the riverbeds, contributing to the rotten-egg smell.

After the same thing happened the following summer, Esther wrote a letter about the black slick of algae and stench emanating from the Forge River to Steve Levy, executive of Suffolk County. It was after Levy wrote back that Ron started Save the Forge River. "Levy wrote to my wife that she shouldn't worry—a good heavy rain would flush out the river and everything would be back to normal," says Ron. "Well, that pissed me off." Since then, he has involved the county Health Department, the Peconic Baykeeper, and the Department of Environmental Conservation, and together they have determined that a combination of unchecked development, decades of duck farming, and sludge from nearby industrial parks has irreparably damaged the river. He has petitioned for dredging, environmental restoration projects, and a work stoppage on two proposed senior developments going up nearby. "When I first started, I never knew nothing about the way politics works here. I couldn't get nothing done," Ron said. "I was almost ready to give up, when Anna called me out of the blue."

Once the parade started moving, Ron and I walked in front of the bus, which Esther was driving. Small and blonde and in control, she drove a school bus for a living and had driven this very 1990 bus for the past sixteen years, so she was used to the way it handled. But at one point she stopped the whole parade when she slammed on her brakes; two people from the day-care float behind us were dressed up as Goofy and Mickey, and kids along the parade route were lunging out into the street to hug the characters, coming too close to the back wheels of her bus. Ron ran back and told the characters that they needed to stay at least twenty feet behind the bus. When he gave her a wave,

Esther put the bus in gear and continued creeping along the road.

For most of the parade, Ron and I handed out mint-green flyers printed with information about legislation he was trying to get passed.

"Have you seen the movie about her?" I asked, nodding in Wintour's direction, nervous to say the words "Devil Wears Prada" in her vicinity.

Ron looked over his shoulder at the slim woman in giant dark sunglasses working the other side of the parade. Wintour and her son had been hoofing it down the center of Montauk Highway with the parade, handing out flyers and waving, but as far as I could tell, not a single person in town knew who she was.

"Naw," Ron said. "I haven't seen it yet, and I don't know if I want to see it. She's good to us, so that's all that matters."

On that parade day, Wintour certainly did not resemble the evil incarnate character from *The Devil Wears Prada*. Instead, she pulled on her Save the Forge River T-shirt and walked through my hometown alongside the big-bellied carpenters with neck tattoos and a bunch of local high school students Ron had managed to wrangle up. She stayed close to her son, running alongside Esther's big white marine-themed bus, first on one side and then the other, handing out her green flyers to the Shirley families that lined the streets. About an hour into the parade, halfway to the corner of Mastic Road, Wintour's son motioned to her with his cell phone and she came over to say good-bye to Ron.

"We have to peel off," she said, hugging him warmly.

Ron shook hands with her son and thanked Wintour for coming, making plans for the next time they would speak.

She turned to me and said good-bye, handing me what was left of her Forge River flyers. As we watched the two figures walk the opposite direction of the rest of the parade, Ron said to me, "She's such a nice lady."

I looked over at the slim woman again. The crowd lining the street parted, moving a plastic folding chair to make way for them. Wintour and her son cut through the ZZZ Radiator and Glassworks parking lot, and I watched her disappear into my hometown, her hair shining in the December sunlight.

When I spoke with Wintour a few weeks later, she talked about her respect for Ron. "He is so salt-of-the-earth," she said, still behind her dark glasses even in her own living room in her elegantly rustic farmhouse, bleached-out wide-plank wooden floors rambling unevenly throughout, a collection of tennis rackets sprouting from a container like a bouquet of flowers. "I'll do whatever I can to help him."

Wintour said that she likes her Mastic estate because it is close to the city—she can drive down the highway in a straight shot and jump off before the Hamptons traffic starts in full force. And she loves its compound-like solitude. "I just import the people I want," she said. "I don't mind the town. It's white trash, of course, but I don't care." If she had to leave her summer home, she wouldn't go to the Hamptons. "I'd probably go to Connecticut. But I don't want to. I want to stay here."

Since Wintour joined the fight in 2006, politicians have begun returning Ron's phone calls and letters; the county legislature has voted to put up signs along the river deeming it a health hazard and forbidding people to swim or eat shellfish; and after a personal phone call from Wintour, even the National Resources Defense Council has become involved, sending out press releases to its own media contacts and organizing experts for further testing on the river's pollutants. The Forge River was placed on the federal impaired waterways list, one of more than 600 in New York State alone. The combination of low voter turnout and low-income families historically placed Shirley at the bottom of the list of legislative priorities on Long Island. This response is unprecedented.

Over a delicious homemade dinner of pasta and shrimp at Ron and Esther's home, I stared beyond their modest backyard and into the river. It was still winter, and the river slowly churned by as the day lost its light. The water is only a few dozen feet from their deck, and I imagined that the smell and the black algae pooling across the river must be inescapable in summer.

"The way I see it," Ron said between bites, "we only had two choices: pack up and run, or fight it. So we fought it." After a few moments I realized he'd finished his thought.

"Well, but why didn't you leave?" I asked. I understood that, unlike Wintour who could choose to live anywhere, Ron's options are more limited—but still, he could move.

His utensils stopped moving on his plate and he looked at me. "Because it's my home, man," he said slowly. "Because it's my home."

On the night of the midsummer Save the Forge River fundraiser at the Wintour estate, Mark parked our red pickup truck alongside the dozens of other vehicles lining the road and we hopped onto the back of a golf cart driven by two boys who looked around twelve years old. They debated about the definition of a senator—how many each state had, which one was in the car that just pulled up—as we whizzed down the dirt path toward the house. The trees parted to a scene straight out of *The Great Gatsby*: a white cloth tent in the middle of an emerald green lawn, guests in khakis and summer dresses holding wine glasses in their hands as they strolled along, the water shimmering in the background. I recognized some faces from the Christmas parade and then realized that all of the burly men I had walked with were wearing matching white-collared golf shirts with "Save the Forge River" stitched across their chests.

The bartenders looked like male models, and a group of young women in flirty summer dresses—friends of Wintour's daughter—darted from guest to guest as they wrote down bids on their clipboards for auction items, everything from a golf trip to front-row seats at a fashion show. The former governor of Massachusetts and William Floyd descendant, William Floyd Weld, gave a speech about the area's history, and Eric Goldstein of the NRDC took the stage and told the guests about a woman named Lois Gibbs from another small blue-collar town.

"She was twenty-seven years old without a college education, lived in a modest three-bedroom home, and had a son with serious health problems who attended the nearby public school," Goldstein said. After giving some more details about this disenfranchised woman's uphill battle, Goldstein dramatically let the name of her town drop: Love Canal.

"The Forge River fight and Love Canal have three important factors in common," Goldstein said. "One: environmental harm. There is a threat to ecology and marine life, not to mention the nauseating smell. Two: government foot-dragging. The answer really isn't complicated—we need to dredge and replenish the river, and stop the pollution. And three: citizen activism. Ron could be the next Lois Gibbs." Goldstein pointed to Ron, who was standing off to the side, head bowed, and the crowd erupted.

Ron took the microphone from Goldstein and thanked everyone for coming. While he was there, Wintour's slim figure darted through the crowd and slid next to Ron, whispering in his ear with her back turned to the crowd. After an uncomfortable pause, during which they whispered back and forth, Wintour melted back into the audience.

"I'd also like to thank Anna Wintour, for the use of her home," Ron said, pausing for applause. "And I am happy to tell you that we've raised $150,000 tonight!"

As the food for the buffet dinner was brought out from the house, some people nearby began to grumble. "Well *I'm* not standing on line for dinner," declared one half of a tanned couple. Thunder broke in the distance, and some guests crowded under the tent for protection against the light rain that was starting to fall. Other guests headed in the opposite direction, flagging down the young golf cart drivers and heading back to the Hamptons only halfway through the party.

Shirley and the Hamptons have long relied upon one another to maintain their natural rhythms, and they must sustain this tricky embrace for survival. With Wintour's presence in town, however, the Forge River functioned as a great equalizer—rich or poor, everyone is downstream. Ultimately, however, the Forge River was not in the Hamptons. Another environmental fund-raiser for the Group for the East End held the same night out at the Wolffer estate in Sagaponack and winery pulled in $790,000.

A few days after the Forge River fundraiser, I stood in front of a clean white door, hesitating a moment before knocking. I hadn't seen Annemarie for more than ten years. We had lost touch since the years our families had lived only blocks away from one another. Her father had been the steamfitter that died of lung cancer when we were in seventh grade, two years after Jerry's death. It was Annemarie's living room that had reminded me of Jerry's as her father slowly wasted away.

After her husband's death, Annemarie's mother would drop Annemarie and me at the beach for late-night bonfires, or at the trailhead of a wilderness path, a break in the towering walls of green pine beckoning us into the night. Her taillights would flash red across the trail, and Annemarie and I would giggle and cling to each other as we stumbled through the darkness until we found our friends. None of the other parents would have let us disappear into that veiled dark, girls of fifteen wearing too much makeup. She must have felt that we could hold our own, that whatever lurked beyond the break in the trail couldn't be worse than what her daughter had already endured.

Even as Annemarie and I learned how to shotgun beer in the heat of a sparking campfire and accepted the alcohol-drowsy tongues of boys into our mouths, we never stepped completely off our track. We held on to one another as long as we could, until our own worlds splintered and we divided into different groups. By senior year we were distant, yet our sights were still solidly set on the same goal: leaving Shirley.

"I feel like I was just on autopilot, doing just enough to get out," Annemarie said. Both thirty now, we sat at her kitchen table, eating freshly-baked scones and talking about the past. Every few minutes she checked the baby monitor to see if her daughter was waking up from her nap yet.

When she greeted me at the door, I was struck by how little Annemarie had changed. Her eyes had turned down at the corners, but her face was unlined and fresh, even without makeup. She was wearing a pink top and a short heather-colored skirt, and at the end of her long thin legs her feet were bare. She still looked fifteen. Her hair was blonder, but other than that she was almost the same as I remembered her. We hugged in her doorway, quickly and a bit unsure, and I reeled a bit at the flood of memories that hit me—her smile, her halting laugh, the way her shoulders slouch just a touch when she walks.

We were in her condo, one of five small two-story homes clapped together in a neat and tidy batch. Driving up the William Floyd Parkway, I made a left into her development and tried not to look to my right. The Brookhaven National Laboratory hummed and whirred just on the other side of the highway from her house.

Annemarie went to SUNY Cortland, where she met her husband, Mike, who also grew up on Long Island, in Miller Place.

"What did you think about Shirley before you met me?" Annemarie teasingly asked Mike, who had come home after a day of teaching third grade in East Hampton.

"Well, it isn't really Shirley that changed," he finally said. "Shirley hasn't gotten any better. I just learned not to make any sweeping judgments about people."

Annemarie is also a teacher, and was near the end of her two-year maternity leave. She worked in the William Floyd School District when she first got out of college and said it still has a tough reputation among teachers, many of whom see it as a last resort. Everyone loved the principal, Mr. Feeney, who had been there for years, and the new school facilities were great, but the overcrowding and low budgets made teaching there difficult. Annemarie transferred to another school nearby as soon as she could and was hoping to take advantage of the perk that would allow her to take her daughter to school there when the time comes.

"Mike and I used to think that if the home life was good enough, the school shouldn't matter," Annemarie said. "But I think we'll do anything we can to keep Cali out of Shirley."

Annemarie calls Cali her miracle baby. I asked her to explain: I'd heard parts of the story—we ran into one another in a little shop in the Catskills by chance the past summer. My mother and father were there, and they were as excited to see her as I was. After introducing our husbands to one another and seeing Cali's baby pictures, my mom asked after her mother. Annemarie's face fell, and she said she had passed away. My mother told her she was sorry for her loss, and trying to quickly change the subject, asked about Jessie, Annemarie's little sister.

Annemarie's lip quivered just for a moment and her husband's grip around her waist tightened.

"She died a few months ago, too."

My mother and I stood still, trying to think of something to say as we watched the tears in Annemarie's eyes begin to spill over. She stubbornly tried to smile through them, apologizing as she wiped them away, and we awkwardly touched her arm and tried to comfort this woman we hadn't seen since she was just a girl. Tears continued to fall as she tried to carry on a conversation, asking us questions about what we were doing in town and what new things had happened. She was still crying when we said our good-byes. She told us she missed her new baby girl terribly, trying to explain why she couldn't stop crying. Her husband rubbed her back lightly as they walked out the door.

Now, almost a year later, we were finally getting together. She seemed vibrant and happy, in love with motherhood and her daughter, who had woken up and was now spilling liquid from the soap-bubbles bottle onto her toes and giggling madly while her mother and I talked on the backyard patio.

As Cali occupied herself with her sandbox and bubbles, Annemarie told me the rest of the story, how her sister had been feeling sick and bloated, and had gone for blood tests in early 2000. The two girls, Annemarie and Jessie, were out shopping with their mother when the doctor's office called them on their cell phone, telling them to get to a hospital immediately because Jessie needed treatment for kidney failure.

They diagnosed her with Goodpasture's syndrome, a rare autoimmune disease not unlike the ones listed in the EPA fact sheets on the dangers of 1,1-dichloroethylene, dichloroethane, benzene, and chlordane. Goodpasture's creates antibodies that attack body tissue and organs, typically the lungs and kidneys, mistaking them for foreign chemicals. Jessie's kidneys were badly damaged, and she was put on the donor list.

"They tried to clean her blood, taking it out of her and washing out the antibodies from her plasma and then pumping the clean blood back into her. There was only one plasmapheresis machine in the area and so they flew the machine to Cornell hospital and we took Jessie into the city," Annemarie explained. "It worked for a while, but then she started to feel sick again."

Annemarie was tested as a possible kidney donor for her sister and was a 50-percent match. "I knew it would take years for her to get a kidney from that list, and she didn't have years," she said. She had just gotten the job at Center Moriches, but they gave her a medical leave.

"They did it laparoscopically, so I only have three tiny scars. But it took me a few weeks to recover," Annemarie said. Five weeks later, it looked like the kidney had taken for Jessie, and Annemarie was back at school working, and even took a mountain-biking trip.

I wanted her story to stop there. I wanted to reach over and put my hand across her mouth, make her be still. The day was beautiful, the sky a blazing blue. We were just two old friends sitting under a patio umbrella, ice clinking in our glasses, talking about the past. I had the sensation of watching a flock of birds cross the horizon, their shadows dancing along the shushing reeds below them. If I could somehow freeze-frame the moment, the hunter's rifle wouldn't crack loudly across the silent landscape, and the bird, that small one to the left, wouldn't hang motionless in the sky for that agonizing moment, flying only by the unromantic physics of the wind keeping its wings afloat. I knew that in a moment that thing of hope and beauty, that small package of heart and bones, would fall from the sky and spiral without grace to the ground. And the other birds would fly on, pumping harder and trying frantically not to look back.

But, of course, I couldn't freeze-frame Annemarie's life. Her eyes were already marked with the sadness of the story she was about to tell me, and there was no way I could change that.

Annemarie and Mike were married in 2001. They bought the condo across from the Brookhaven Laboratory, making a conscious sacrifice, a bargain: They might get less of a house than they wanted, and it might be across from the Brookhaven National Laboratory, but their address would not be in Shirley.

"We only drink filtered water," Annemarie had explained when she poured my glass of water earlier. "We even fill our ice trays with it. There is no way I would drink the water from the tap, especially living so close," she said, nodding in the lab's direction.

They renovated the condo themselves, learning by reading books and watching home-improvement shows. Once the work was done, they set about making a family. It didn't take long—Annemarie became pregnant immediately. It was during her pregnancy that her mother started feeling tired, sometimes too tired to even get out of bed and go to work. Not long after, the doctors diagnosed throat cancer, saying that her chances of surviving were small. They suggested hospice, and Annemarie moved her mother into her newly renovated condo.

"And that's why I call Cali the miracle baby," she said, smiling. "I had this incredible amount of maternity leave, and I was able to spend all of my time with my mother. Meanwhile, my mother got to spend all of her time with her grandchild. It really was a gift." Annemarie's mother died in November, less than a year after her diagnosis. She knew her granddaughter for four months.

"Jessie had gotten married, and she and her husband moved into the Shirley house," Annemarie said. "Jessie desperately wanted to have a child, but the doctors weren't sure if it would be possible with her illness. They told her to stop trying, to just stick with the medication and get as healthy as possible and try again later." Annemarie stopped for a moment, refilling the bubble machine for Cali and admiring the rock she brought to her mother as a present. "I can't know for sure, but I think she may have been playing with her medicines and trying to get pregnant."

Annemarie's hand moved softly across her daughter's forehead, smoothing her chestnut-brown hair—the color I remember Annemarie having in high school—away from her face. Cali moved back toward her sandbox.

"She died of a heart attack. Apparently she'd had many of them, but we never knew that. They offered to do an autopsy, but I refused. Her body had been through enough." Jessie's final heart attack killed her quickly on a February night, three months after her own mother's funeral.

Annemarie shook her head, and the tears spilled down her cheeks again. I took her hand, but I knew there was nothing I could say. Even if I had been able to be there and comfort her in those difficult years, it wouldn't bring back any of the people she had lost. She forced a smile again, but didn't grip my hand back. I realized she had told this story a thousand times, that she was talking about deaths that had happened almost two years earlier. They were still painful, of course.

"I leave things out when I talk about it, so that I won't get so upset," she said. I thought of a way to distract her into dry eyes, like my mother would have, and I ask about the rest of her family. Does she have any cousins? Or aunts and uncles?

She sighed. "My one cousin died in a boating accident last summer. It was in the papers—maybe you read about it? He was in the Moriches inlet here and some drunk guy just crashed over him, sheared the top half of his boat clear off and then left him for dead. If the guy had gone for help right then, instead of running away, they think he might have lived. But he didn't." She took another deep breath. "My uncle died from a stroke a few months later. He was just heartbroken. But my aunt is Cali's godmother. I have some other family all spread out, but none that I really know."

I looked at her slender wrist, the sprinkle of delicate purple spider veins on her thigh. She continued.

"Jessie's husband is living in the Shirley house now. And that's fine. I don't ever want anything to do with the Shirley house again," she said. I thought of the quiet hush of her home, with her father stretched out on the couch in the living room, legs under a blanket. He would say hello in his robotic voice, but I think he knew the small metal voicebox at his throat scared us kids and mostly he kept quiet. I could see her small room, the posters on the wall. I think her favorite color was purple during that time. I remember her mother sitting quietly at their kitchen table, hands folded or flicking a cigarette, her husband dying in the next room. I thought of Jessie, her pudgy baby-doll face quick to break into a smile, wanting to come into Annemarie's bedroom, wanting to play with us, pouting when we told her she couldn't. Annemarie has been losing people since fourth grade.

I asked how she managed, how she was able to smile and tell me this story and call Cali her miracle baby. She set her jaw and looked past me at a spot just beyond my right shoulder.

"You just make a choice," she said, sighing. "You either lose it, or you keep going. I'm the lucky one. I'm still here. So I'll keep going."

She sat back in her chair and crossed her legs at the ankle. Cali took this as an invitation and dropped her sandy shovel to scramble up into her mother's lap. Annemarie gave her daughter a quick squeeze, closing her eyes, and released the hug before the child could begin to squirm. The dog sat at the screen door keeping watch, the scent of basil from a nearby pot mixing into the smell of cut grass, and Annemarie held the glass of water to her daughter's lips so she wouldn't spill.

Every time I go back to Shirley, I hear about some new tragedy: a record number of sex offenders were found living together in group homes tucked away throughout the town; a twelve-year-old girl was raped behind one of the Indian reservation's concrete-block homes after her grandmother offered her to her drug dealer as payment for some crack. Flipping through the newspaper, I recently read about a toddler in town who drowned in a neighbor's half-filled pool—he was named after his uncle and my friend Anthony, who had drowned in his own parents' half-filled pool just over ten years earlier.

Barbara Osarczuk from Carleton Drive moved to Florida. Randy Snell still lives in the same house—he says he would rather know the dangers he is facing than move to a new place and more unknowns. The class action lawsuit has been dragging on in court for more than ten years, but Richard J. Lippes, the Love Canal lawyer, is still holding out hope for the families he represents. The suit has been through three judges, and the nuclear side of the case has been thrown out. Although current law requires that the plaintiff prove only a 100-mill/rem (millirem) per year exposure rate to be considered for litigation, the judge held the Shirley lawyers to the pre-1992 Price Anderson Act exposure rate of 500 mill/rem per year because the time line of exposure occurred before the exposure rate was changed. Lippes could only prove a 300–400 mill/rem per year exposure rate, more than three times what he would need if the exposure occurred today. The chemical pollution and loss-of-home-value aspects of the lawsuit are still in play, however. Lippes maintains that the case will prevail, ultimately and substantially, citing the most damning evidence as a quote taken from a Department of Energy investigation into why the Brookhaven National Laboratory did not honor certain safety requests—such as the second liner beneath the spent-fuel pool. "They said they felt that every dollar spent on health and safety is a dollar taken away from scientific research," Lippes recently told me, the disgust hardly disguised in his voice. The next ruling will determine whether the case will continue, and whether it has a chance to ever see the inside of a courtroom.

Over the years, my mother has found two more benign lumps in her breasts. There is also another benign tumor growing on the half of her thyroid that the doctor was able to save all those years ago. None of my neighborhood girls have found any lumps yet, but we won't be surprised when we do.

And yet, so many of us are drawn back to Shirley, answering some siren call to The Town of Flowers. The high school principal, Mr. Feeney—who for years campaigned for a new structure for the students he cares about so much, understanding that the leaking, asbestos-filled portable classrooms that the district had been stuffing its children in was damaging their self-worth—always tells his students: There is life beyond Exit 68. Yet many of us never leave, and many others return.

My mother had to take a break from her hospice work. She found herself burning out, unable to handle the aching pressure of so many breaking hearts. Even though she no longer lives in town, she still returns regularly—some of her closest friends remain there, and we had an entire table set apart for the neighborhood at my wedding. In her new house, my mother no longer keeps a collection of cactus and aloe plants on the windowsill. A vintage bud vase hangs on the wall in her front hall now, and she always keeps it full of fresh-cut tulips.

My mother carries her scars on her skin, but my father's run deeper. Last summer we sat on the back porch of their small townhouse, the cicadas singing, the splash of wing against water ringing out from the lake behind their townhouse development as a heron flapped around. They had grilled fish for dinner, and my mother was inside washing up while I asked my father questions: How did you get to Shirley? Why did you stay? We talked late into the night, my mother refreshing our teacups and putting candles out on the glass tabletop.

He talked about his jobs, about the ones he lost and the ones he couldn't wait to get away from. He talked about clawing his way up, just to be pushed back down. He talked about what it meant to borrow the down payment for his family's first house from his best friend, what it meant to lose that best friend. My father shook his head at times, and when I began to think that he might not be able to go on, he took a deep breath, stared into the candle, and continued. He let loose a string of disappointments, of failures, of lost jobs, lost money, lost opportunities. When he finished, he looked up into a space beyond my shoulder and wondered aloud how he managed to keep going.

I looked at my father. I quietly reminded him of the things he has given his family and his friends. I reminded him of the education, the travel, the support, and the love that he has given me. I told him that I would never trade the home he made for my mother and me, and that I've never wanted for anything. I reminded him that we are sitting near a garden in bloom that he tends and makes grow, outside a house that is safe and warm and full of love. He nodded. He knows these things. But they cannot penetrate the hard coil of pain that has circled him. Later, lying awake in bed in my parents' guest room, I thought of other things I wanted to thank my father for teaching me: how to notice beauty in small things, like an acorn or a peach pit; how to grow potatoes in grass clippings; how to be quiet enough to hear the trees talking to one another; how to deadhead a flower so the nutrients can get to the newer blooms; how sometimes raw corn tastes better than cooked; how to read a map so you always have more than one route home.

Staring at the ceiling, I thought of my father's habit of collecting rocks. He is still a traveling salesman, and if he finds a rock he likes he will put it in the back of his car and bring it home and add it to his garden. He has hundreds of these rocks, from smooth black stones that fit into your palm to large gray boulders that require two hands to carry. He has formed these rocks into walls that protect his garden. I think back to the heavy stone walls I took comfort in from my dorm window perch at Vassar and wonder if he is trying to barricade himself in the same way I did. Unlike my mother, he truly believed in Shirley, and in the name change and the Woodlands development and the marina and the golf course and the new good-neighbor policy of the Brookhaven Lab. I picture my father with all of these rocks piled on his chest, and I worry that he will break.

showed me foxholes; left over from the Camp Upton days, they are some of the only remaining trenches still intact in the country today. I was taken on tours of the High-Field MRI facility, the Positron Emission Tomography facility, and the National Synchotron Light Source accelerator. I was told about incredible studies and unparalleled science, about heavy ion colliders and particle acceleration and nanomaterials. But I still hadn't found the information I was searching for.

So I tried another way. "I am still having a difficult time understanding the point of your questions," the Brookhaven National Laboratory's PR woman said to me over the cafeteria table. Over a turkey-and-cheese sandwich and a side of chips, compliments of my escort, I had listened to the U.S. Department of Energy's press manager speak with welcome candor about the lab's failings to communicate with local communities, particularly Shirley, over the past few decades. His open and relaxed manner and the small gold hoop in his left ear were as much a relief as his admission of imperfection on the Brookhaven National Laboratory's part—the first I'd heard following a string of very defensive interviews. Immediately after he left our small table in the Berkner Hall cafeteria, however, my hostess had made it clear that none of what he or anyone else had said that day was to be considered on the record. It was the first unfriendly moment between us, and I prepared myself for another as I asked her to explain what she meant.

"I don't understand why you want to rehash all of the pollution issues when they have already been the subject of newspaper articles. Why do you want to bring all of that up again?" Her eyes had narrowed.

"Well," I began. "I am interested in telling the story from Shirley's point of view. I am interested not just in the lab itself, but in the way the relationship between the lab and Shirley has impacted the town."

She smiled a small, tight smile. "But there is no relationship between Shirley and the lab."

I paused.

"But John just finished describing how one of his hardest days at the lab was the community meeting about the tritium that leaked into the groundwater," I reminded her. "He said more than 600 residents who learned about the contamination and water hookups over the radio showed up screaming and crying out of fear for their families."

"Many of those weren't even in Shirley," she said. "We really have no connection to the town at all."

In fact, 640 of the 800 affected homes were in Shirley.

"Well, I should get going if I want to make my next meeting," she said, rising abruptly from her chair. Like most of my tour guides that day, she struck me as a fundamentally decent person who'd probably like to do the right thing. I was frustrated that I was unable to make her understand that talking about the legacy of pollution at the Brookhaven National Laboratory was a way of protecting her own family, and all families living near polluted sites across the country, not just the people of Shirley. I thought of all the machines I had toured in the past few days, of all of the brilliant minds hard at work there—all of the brilliant minds whirring away just within the domed walls of the cafeteria itself! I looked past my host and spotted a table where some of the kitchen staff sat taking a break, slouching in their uniforms, eating lunch and drinking sodas, talking about their weekend. I wondered what they thought about all the experiments going on around them every day. I stared at my host and then again past her shoulder at the tired, smiling faces of the kitchen staff. Did they care how the universe might have looked in the first few moments of creation? Did they care about quantum chromodynamics and nanoscience?

Were their lives less valuable if they did not?

I walked out of Berkner Hall with my escort and into the chill of the January afternoon. We said our good-byes and I walked to the parking lot a few buildings down to my car, the slender tips of the reactor smokestacks visible above the tree line. I drove past the chestnut trees dropping their spiny clusters, past the gaggles of geese that clotted the lawns of the different buildings, past the hotel-style dormitories for visiting scientists, past the spider-legged water towers, past the blinking LED sign announcing "Safety Never Hurts!" and past the guard booth. I turned left, and within five minutes and two traffic lights, I was home again in Shirley.

# EPILOGUE

Tina and I sat on her wide wraparound porch overlooking the Susquehanna River in upstate New York. She peeled pictures out of an album and handed them to me.

"That's my fifth birthday party!" I laughed. I knew this photo—the old gang lined up along the edge of the street in front of my house, the rusted mailbox peeking through as if it too was one of the kids. Melissa had reproduced this image and sent a framed copy to Margaret and Andrea and me for Christmas a few years ago.

"I think this is your sixth," Tina said, handing me another picture, edges rounded like all photos from that time period. I had never seen this picture before. We were in Burger King, standing on the plastic seats, and Tina had her arm flung around my neck. We were wearing paper Burger

King hats and smiling so hard at the camera our eyes were squeezed shut.

Tina's face still had the same rounded cheeks. She had her father's deep brown eyes, and her mother's small, quick mouth. It was so strange to look into her face after all those years. A white stripe ran through the center of her short brown hair.

I found her just before she sold her house in Shirley, where she had been living, and we had been trying to get together for two years. She was recently married, and a few months after her wedding, her doctor found some lumps in her abdomen but told her not to worry about them. At her next checkup, they had tripled in size, and he immediately sent her for a radical hysterectomy—the lumps were tumors the size of softballs spread across the outside of her uterus.

She was still recovering from her surgery when we finally reunited at her new house upstate in the summer of 2007. She and her husband had rebuilt an old farmhouse along the river, doing most of the work themselves. My husband was off with hers on a tour of the construction— they would send us home with a set of vintage glass door panels that we would use on the house we had recently bought on the other side of the river in rural Pennsylvania. While the men exchanged stories and tips, dragging the doors across the lawn and loading them into our pickup truck, Tina and I lolled on her porch, drinking wine and watching a chipmunk hop through her garden.

"Did I tell you that they found my father's boat?" Tina asked. "The one that he used to drag me along fishing so that I could bail out the water with the pail?"

I was suddenly overwhelmed by the metallic salt smell of Jerry's old aluminum boat. I heard the whir of a line catching, the cold flop of a flounder on the wooden seat. The soft murmur of my father and Jerry laughing echoed against the fog.

"My cousin got a call from a fire department out east. Someone donated the boat to the department and the guy my mother sold the boat to never changed the registration, so it was still under my father's name," she said.

Listening to her voice, I relaxed deeper into my lawn chair on her porch, but in my mind Tina and I were sitting in the boat with my father and Jerry, the swell of the waves rocking us gently, the soggy orange life jacket cold against my neck.

"So I guess the old boat is still out there somewhere," Tina said, breaking into my thoughts. "Can you believe it still floats?"

I nodded, and Tina's face slowly opened into a smile, and she was that seven-year-old child again, bailing water for her father.

Back at our home later that night, after my husband and I unloaded the glass doors from our truck and crawled into bed, I tried to recall that feeling of being rocked back and forth by the waves like a lullaby, but I couldn't. Instead, all I could see was the empty boat, untethered and motor silent, waves slapping the silver sides as it drifted further away from the island, shining like a beacon under the morning light.

# ACKNOWLEDGMENTS

There are many people who were part of the life of this book. I have found an intensely supportive home in my publisher, and am grateful to every single person at PublicAffairs. In particular, I would like to thank Timm Bryson, Pete Garceau, Lindsay Goodman, Jaime Leifer, Peter Osnos, Dan Ozzi, Niki Papadopoulos, Whitney Peeling, Melissa Raymond, and Susan Weinberg. Special thanks to my sharply attentive copy editor, Michele Wynn, and my invariably patient and clever editor Clive Priddle, for his guidance, humor, and willingness to edit even in the wilds of Pennsylvania.

To the work and resources of the following people, I am indebted: On science, Dr. Helen Caldicott, Dr. Peter Bokuniewicz, Dr. Janet Gray, and Dr. Rubie Senai. On law, Richard Lippes, Craig Purcell, and Daniel Slifkin. On activism, Elsa

Ford and Lorraine Pace. On Lost Battalion history, Robert Laplander. Thank you to the Shirley, Mastic, Moriches Community Library, especially Linda Knell in the Local History Room, and to Philip Trypuc, for his father's incredible photographs. Thank you to the Riverkeeper, especially Basil Seggos and Lisa Rainwater. Billy Goldstein delivered impeccable research with industry and wit. Any failures are entirely my own.

Thank you to the many amazing teachers in my life, including Bob Brigham, Samuel Freedman, Lis Harris, Richard Locke, Honor Moore, Leslie Sharpe, and the one who started it all at William Floyd High School, Donna Gaspari.

Thank you to those who shared their stories with me: Ron and Esther Lupski, Annemarie McGee, Diane Sackett Nannery, Randy Snell, and Anna Wintour and Shelby Bryan.

Other friends who have helped at various stages in various ways: Daniel Ahearn of Ill Lit, Dr. Holly Anderson, Thomas Beller, Amy Benson, Tracy Chung, Teri Citterman, John Cochran, Selby Drummond, Patricia Heal, Allison Hoffman, Megana Hosein, Caroline Jackson, Brandy Keenan, Dorla McIntosh, Jenny Marone, Suzanne Menghraj, Leigh Newman, Patrick O'Connell, Justin Ravitz, and Carmen Scheidel.

Joan and George Hornig and Duncan and Maryann de Kergommeaux offered support, comfort, and places of solitude and beauty in which to write. I am honored to call you my friends.

I had a small team of angels circling me without fail during the five years it took to write this book. Thank you to Cris Beam, Carol Paik, and Jennie Yabroff for your brilliance, honesty, and friendship. Thank you to Patty O'Toole, my professor and friend, who offered soothing calm, infallible insight, fierce acumen, and the right combination of tea, wine, and dessert. You are the rarest kind of ally and I thank you for always being there.

Anna Stein's strength, intelligence, and wisdom have, when needed, acted as scaffolding for this book. I am indebted to Sam Lipsyte for introducing us. As a literary agent she is unparalleled; as a friend she is gracious and kind. Thank you for seeing what was there and helping to uncover it.

Thank you to the families in the neighborhood where I grew up and thank you especially to Margaret Parker, Andrea Como, and Melissa Gobrick, my Crazy Carnation Queens; you all have my love and deepest respect. Thank you to Tina Sherlock. I am so glad you are back in my life.

Thank you to my family, especially the late Kathleen McMasters and Richard Danzig, who both fostered a love of words early in my life. Thank you most of all to my parents, who are very private people by nature, for understanding and respecting my need and desire to tell this story. I hope you feel the love you've always given me within these pages.

And thank you to Mark Milroy, who pushes me when I need to be pushed, and walks ahead of me when I need a path to follow. You are my heart and my home.

**Kelly McMasters**' essays and articles have appeared in *The New York Times*, *The Washington Post
Magazine*, *Newsday*, *Elle Décor*, *Metropolis*, and *Time Out
New York*, among others. She teaches writing at
Columbia University and mediabistro.com, and
is the co-director of the KGB Nonfiction Reading
Series in the East Village. She lives in Manhattan
and northeast Pennsylvania with her husband,
the painter Mark Milroy.